KiDS in the Cockpit

A pilot book for safe and happy sailing with children

JILL SCHINAS

ADLARD COLES NAUTICAL
LONDON

Published by Adlard Coles Nautical
an imprint of A & C Black Publishers Ltd
37 Soho Square, London W1D 3QZ
www.adlardcoles.com

Copyright © Jill Schinas 2005

First edition published 2005

ISBN–10 0–7136–7229–3
ISBN–13 978–0–7136–7229–9

A CIP catalogue record for this book is available from the British Library.

A & C Black uses paper produced with elemental chlorine-free pulp,
harvested from managed sustainable forests

Typeset in Sabon
Printed and bound in Great Britain by
The Cromwell Press, Trowbridge, Wiltshire

Note: Whilst the advice and instruction contained in this book
are given in good faith, and with the intention only of helping other yachtsmen
and women, neither the author nor the publishers can accept any responsibility
for any loss, injury, illness or death which may result from following them.
Safety at sea is the responsibility of the captain of the vessel concerned.

Contents

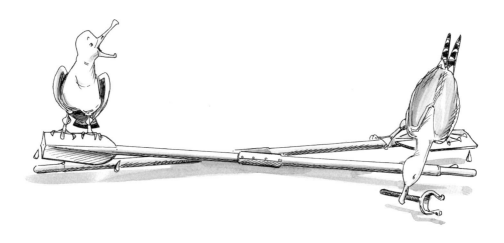

Acknowledgements and Dedication

I should like to express my gratitude to the many yachtswomen, men and children who, wittingly or otherwise, helped in the research and writing of this book. Where the contribution was unwitting, and where I have been unable to contact the people concerned, their names have generally been changed.

My own children need no pseudonyms, and to them my debt is greatest; Caesar, Xoë and Roxanne taught me everything I know about sailing with kids. The children also posed patiently in their lifejackets on innumerable occasions, and made their own lunch and their own amusements while Mummy wrote, read and scribbled *ad nauseam*. Caesar also helped to type up the manuscript and spent hours scanning photos, Xoë read and re-read the work looking for any errors, and it was Roxanne who came up with the title. This book is dedicated to the three of them.

Jill Schinas

Introduction

'**They're going to have a baby, you say!** My goodness! So that's the end of their adventures under sail.' This was the reaction that my parents received from friends and relations when they broke the news of our impending change in family status.

When the time came for us to start a family, Nick and I were not there to break the news ourselves. We were bumming around Venezuela in our 43ft ketch, *Maamari*. Our journey had taken us from England down to Africa and across the pond to Brazil, where we got married. Now we were in the Caribbean, looking for work with which to fund our future travels and building ourselves a crew at the same time. The end of our adventures? On the contrary, for us this was just the beginning. In a few months' time we would move on again, and the show would continue.

Oh, the baby was planned; of course he was planned! After all, what difference could an itsy-bitsy baby make to our life?

If you have picked up this book then plainly you are much more clued-up about babies than Nick and I were. The fact that you are studying a book about the subject goes to show that you have some inkling of the fact that taking a child to sea is not all plain sailing, whereas Nick and I had absolutely none.

How can it be that a woman – and a seawife at that – was able to reach the state of motherhood in complete ignorance of the awful ordeal that is involved in boating with babies? Who was responsible for this gaping chasm in my education? Who can I blame? None but my own dear mother. My mother and father were sailing long before I arrived on the scene, and after I was born Mum gave it up for all of three weeks. Then it was business as usual – with the baby aboard. What an example to set a child!

At that stage my parents sailed and raced a 12ft clinker dinghy. Later, when I was about two years old, they built themselves a Wayfarer in the living room of our half-completed home. The hard from which they used to launch their dinghies – the same from which my dad still launches his tender – is overlooked by a rustic quay, medieval in origin. Thus, the comings and goings of the racing fleet were always subject to the scrutiny of sightseers. When the race was over and the boats returned, an interested audience assembled to watch in wonder as we swooped down towards the hard.

At the last second, when it seemed inevitable that our craft must come grinding and crashing to a halt on the stones ahead, the helmsman would ram the tiller down, the boat would answer by rounding up into the wind, and the mate would hop over the side and grab hold of the forestay. On a breezy day the manoeuvre was quite dramatic to behold, and more than once, as I recall, Mum disappeared up to her armpits in the icy water.

After the sails were lowered, depriving the boat of her vital spirit and leaving her simply as a shapely box, then – behold – from under the tiny foredeck there would emerge a small boy, ensconced in a kapok lifejacket. After him appeared a toddler, similarly clad (that was me), and then my father would reach in and pull out a carrycot. By now the spectators on the quay would be standing mouths agape. More than once, I am told, we heard the cry, 'How many *more* have you got in there?'

Nick also grew up messing about in boats (in fact, in the same harbour) so we both know what it is like to be 'kids afloat'. People often imagine that sailing must be very tedious for a small child, but because we have 'been there' we know for a fact that, properly packaged, sailing is anything but boring for a youngster. Sailing was life itself for us when we were small; it was the pivot of all existence, and even when we were soaked to our skins and turning blue at the edges, we would never, *never* have swapped our boat-crazy existence for ordinary life. Born and bred to boating, Nick and I knew the scene from the inside, but what we did not know, before our son arrived on the scene, was just how hard it can be for the people doing the breeding.

My first Atlantic crossing was aboard a boat which had no self-steering, and because she was a lively creature – a fin-keeler – and could not be left for even a moment to fend for herself, her crew of three had a rather hard time. Still, it was fun and I simply could not wait to do it again.

My second crossing was aboard *Maamari*, and that was a honeymoon cruise. Actually, Nick and I did not get married until just after the crossing, but that sail was the blissful epitome of what a honeymoon should be. We idled along, watching the clouds and admiring the sea. We gazed at the stars, we read, we conversed... and when it pleased us we did nothing at all. The three weeks of that crossing were some of the happiest of my life.

By contrast, our first crossing *en famille* was a nightmare; I could not wait for it to end! With the kids aboard there was certainly no time for reading or relaxing. There was not a single moment when I could simply stand and stare. Indeed, there was scarcely time for the navigation and the watch-keeping. These activities, which we had once savoured, became nothing more than essential chores to be fitted in, as best we could, around the relentless, never-ending duty of attending to the needs of the children. Paul Heiney summed it up very neatly when he and his wife, Libby Purves, sailed around Britain with their kids. 'Two children, four months and only 30ft of boat. No nanny. Only Mummy and Daddy to turn to and *Grace O'Malley* wanting attention, too. I just don't think we can do it,' Paul told his wife. Well, Nick and I were in the same boat, metaphorically speaking, and similar words fell from my lips; we had bitten off more than we could chew. Let me make it perfectly clear: sailing with itsy-bitsy babes is *not* plain sailing.

But, wait a bit; isn't this the case whether we are afloat or ashore? Life with children is never what it was in the carefree days BC (Before Child). It is bound to be different, wherever we are and whatever we are doing. Take mealtimes, for example. Mealtimes among minors is such a fiasco that, in the good old days, those who could afford servants opted out of the feeding scenario – and most other infant scenarios, besides. Life with children is different, and we have to adapt. We give up candle-lit dinners, but must our sailing go the same way?

Not necessarily. The point, really, is that it does no good to whinge on about the way things were. We've made our beds, as the saying goes, and now we must find a way to get comfortable again. There are three solutions to the problem of sailing with small children. One is to give up. Sell the boat; console yourself with the idea that you can buy another when they are bigger. Curiously enough, almost nobody follows this option. Sailing is an addiction and you don't give it up just because the going suddenly gets tough.

The second option is the old-fashioned one: Mummy gives up sailing. According to this scheme, Daddy gets to go messing about in his boat, alone or with his mates, and Mummy and the kids carry on a separate existence. Hmm... Well, it wouldn't work for me, I can tell you!

The final alternative – the only viable one for a dyed-in-the-wool sailor – is to adjust your expectations. No more idling about; kids do not like idling: 'Why don't we *go* somewhere?' they moan. And now that our own skins are not the only ones to think of, we must try to avoid crossing the bar at low water with a three-foot swell running, or entering the Solent by way of the Needles with a westerly force six slamming into the outgoing tide. Avoid such delights and dangers until your children have developed a proper aesthetic sense and muscles which will enable them to swim like Olympic champions, and you can spend some happy days afloat with your kids but, when they are small, you will have to work at it.

When Caesar and Xoë were small, and we found that we had dived in at the deep end, I tried to find a book which would help us in our plight, but the only books on the subject of sailing with children seemed to have been penned by women whose youngsters were fast heading for their teens. The advice regarding the under-fives came from a hazy past and time had blurred the ordeal. Where was the instruction about changing a nappy at 45 degrees of heel or keeping watch with a toddler at your ankles? My babies did not fit the textbook model. They did not want to lie all day behind the lee cloths, gurgling happily. And so we were on our own. We had to learn the hard way. Well, we got down to it and learned.

My baby boy is now aged 13. His sisters are 11 and 6. Over the years we have enjoyed and endured many adventures afloat together. We have lived aboard and cruised in the tropics and also in the chilly Southern Ocean. We have sailed in the Solent, both in modern 'tupperware' yachts and in ancient old gaffers. We have travelled down through the French canals with a newborn baby. We have sailed in the Mediterranean and also in Southern Africa. We have capsized a yacht and gone through the drama of calling out the cavalry and being winched to safety, and we have also spent a couple of years living ashore and so had the experience of reintroducing the children to a lifestyle which they had more or less forgotten. All in all, we've had plenty of opportunity to learn about the art of sailing with children – and from this vantage point, it all looks pretty straightforward.

After 13 years of practice, sailing with kids is easy – but when I look back through my diaries and notebooks I see that it was not always so. I have a whole suitcase full of notebooks stuffed with thoughts and ideas, scrawled in the heat of the moment – in the cockpit or at the sink – on the subject of sailing with kids. Time has softened the memory and given it a rosy glow, but fortunately the notebooks tell it like it was: the fears, the failures, the good ideas and the bad. They recall the games we invented, the accidents we averted and the ones we survived. And how to fold a terry nappy at 45 degrees of heel. After 13 years of doing something, one inevitably tends to feel that there is nothing to it, but this book was not written *after* 13 years. It was written on the job.

So far, I have said a lot about sailing with tiny tots, but little about older children. How do they fit in on a passage down harbour or a voyage around the world? Well, on the whole, once they are old enough to fasten their own lifejackets and pump the loo for themselves, sailing with children becomes quite bearable again. In fact, with a small amount of imaginative input from Mum and Dad, a cargo of kids can become an enthusiastic crew. Family sailing at this level can even rival the magical days of drifting off into the sunset à deux. However, you do need to make the input; you do need to sell the thing properly.

When I set out to write this book I had it in mind merely to pass on a few tips which might help the reader to avoid the rocks and steer a safe course towards Happy Sailing, but as the project progressed I found that I was also presenting the reader with a glimpse of the cruising lifestyle.

Cruising begins as the idea of travelling under sail but gradually develops, quite subtly, into a whole new mindset. It would have been impossible for me to paint a true and accurate picture of sailing with children without lapsing into the cruising mentality. If some of it seems a little bit eccentric, be warned: if you decide to go you will soon be thinking this way too!

Pottering about in home waters and setting off for a six-year cruise around the world are very different things. For most would-be cruisers, their children's education is the major issue and so I have considered this in some depth. Safety is another major concern for all parents of would-be young sailors. Mothers, in particular, are apt to have fears about the safety of the vessel itself, and since sea-worthiness is, indeed, the foundation of safety at sea I have done my best to identify its characteristics. As a Worried Woman myself, I have also delved deeply into the subject of personal safety.

Many parents worry not only about their children's safety but also about their happiness. Putting aside feelings of compassion, unhappy children make for unhappy parents. Do children really like sailing? Well, I certainly did! And my kids certainly do. Since I have never known what it is like *not* to sail I find it immensely difficult to imagine a life away from the sea. I can vividly recall discovering, in my first term at school, that not everybody lived for sailing. I was supremely puzzled. What *did* they do then if they did not spend the weekends afloat? I asked my best friend Carol. 'Nothing,' she answered, and then, 'I watch telly.' What a way to live! Even at the tender age of five I was amazed.

I have scant memories of my homelife as a child. My childhood memories are of creeping up the edge of the channel against the ebb tide; of the smell of the saltmarsh; of the heel of the boat; of the solid feel of the water as it pressed against my hand while the boat rushed along. It is difficult to describe the feeling, but to me the sea is *marvellous*, in the true sense of the word.

A child can pick up on all this. Then again, he or she can also just enjoy sailing as a sport. If one's preference is for skiing or horse riding then, I suppose, one will be inclined to lead one's children in that direction. I have a love for sailing – and I have my parents to thank for that. Now I am handing the gift down to the next generation.

So here it is, then – the product of 13 years of intensive, gruelling research – the Pilot Book to Safe and Happy Sailing with Kids. In view of the erratic course that Nick and I have steered, I would certainly not wish to encourage anybody to follow in our wake but one thing I can say for myself: I may not have got everything right, but in all these years of sailing and cruising with children, none of them has ever asked that dreaded question, 'Are we nearly there?' So, I guess I must be on roughly the right heading.

⚓ **Note:** Throughout the book I have followed convention, referring to any unidentified child as 'he'. On the other hand, where the situation involves a parent who may be of either sex I have generally used the male pronoun only when referring to the skipper. Once again this is a matter of convention rather than of sexism; men tend to skipper and women tend to be more concerned with the well-being of their children. I trust that any couples for whom the roles are reversed, or altered, will understand my reasoning and not feel too offended.

1
For Safety's Sake

**Nets • Harnesses and lifelines
• How the 'professionals' cope • Lifejackets •
Being safety conscious**

Before my first child was born I had all sorts of ideas about how I would keep him safe; in fact safety became a mild paranoia. I would wake in the middle of the night, in a cold sweat, having just dreamt that the baby was about to fall overboard or tumble down a gaping hatchway. Responding to these 'premonitions', I laid elaborate plans for keeping my precious child cocooned. As soon as he could walk, I decided, we would fit intruder alarms to let us know if he was going on deck, and there would be a man-overboard alarm strapped to his ankle. There would be bars across every hatchway, he would wear a lifejacket at all times and, above all, I would never, *ever* let him out of my sight. So much for dreams and plans. Reality was rather different.

Before we study the safety question in any depth we ought first to identify precisely the dangers from which we are seeking to protect our kids. Aboard a sailing yacht there may be many potential threats to our children's safety, but most of these threats are also to be encountered in the home environment. Kitchens with unattended pans, bathroom cabinets containing medicine bottles, plastic bags that can suffocate – these and similar hazards are to be found universally. The main danger in the marine environment is, of course, the danger of drowning, and it is exclusively this issue which is the subject of this chapter.

There can be no denying that the sea is a potential killer. That much is indisputable. But, as we shall see, people see the risk in different lights and deal with it differently. At one extreme there are parents who insist that their children wear a lifejacket at all times, whether the boat is at sea or in harbour. At the other end of the scale there are folk who trust the child's instinct for self-preservation, and who seem to consider any kind of safety equipment an infringement on his liberty, or an insult to his intelligence.

Once Caesar was amongst us, I managed to get the safety issue into perspective – or, at least, *I* think I've got it in perspective. I walk the middle road and so receive horrified looks from either camp. Depending on the position from which you view me, I am either too lax or too stringent in my safety standards. There are no absolute rights and wrongs here, and readers must therefore judge for themselves the advice and opinions which follow.

● Harnesses, used with a network of jackstays, allow children the freedom to roam the decks in safety.

Nets: the first line of defence

Babies do not think much of lifejackets. If forced to wear a lifejacket, a baby is apt to howl. In the interests of preserving harmony as well as life, therefore, we need to find some other means of keeping our infants secure. The simplest solution is a net.

 ## The pros

I used to hate the idea of having a net all around the boat. I did not want our deck to look like a playpen. However, commonsense prevailed over vanity and we acquired a strong, nylon fishing net of appropriate mesh, and lashed it securely to the guard rails and stanchions. Netting is quite expensive, and 'knitting' your own is a mammoth undertaking – and you still have to buy the string. The net which we have aboard *Mollymawk* was an off-cut given to us by some trawlermen. The net that we had aboard *Maamari* was part of a large piece that we found buried in the sand.

Fishing net is bright green and if it is second-hand it whiffs a bit at first, but we found that we could put up with this. We also grew quickly accustomed to the new look of our vessel, and we discovered that a net is good for keeping all sorts of things, besides the kids, aboard. Buckets, the oars and yours truly would all have gone overboard, at various times, had it not been for the net. In fact, the only disadvantage that we have found is that it makes it harder for the flying fish to come aboard for breakfast. Having planned to do away with it as soon as the kids were steady on their feet, we find ourselves in

no hurry to take the net down and we now look on it as a sort of semi-invisible, low-windage, permeable bulwark; quite a seamanlike thing.

 ## The cons

Not everybody likes a guard rail net. Besides its appearance, some people believe that nets only confuse the child and disrupt his understanding of his environment. One school of thought says that young children are quite capable of identifying danger and developing a safe pattern of behaviour which avoids risks. This may be true, but none of us is very steady on our feet when the boat is lurching about (which it may do quite as easily in a rough and rolly anchorage as at sea) and a little child, if he happens to tumble in the wrong place, can easily roll overboard between the stanchions.

Some people cast doubt on the strength of the net and of the knots which secure it to the rail. It is true that netting rots and netting made of natural fibres, such as cotton, rots very quickly. Plastic netting degrades in the sun, but even in the tropics it is good for a couple of years.

No net at all is much safer than a rotten net, which provides a false sense of security. However, one could apply the same argument to almost any other item of safety gear: no lifejacket is better than one which floats the child with his feet uppermost; no flare is better than one which explodes in your hand and maims you for life. Just as you check the life-jackets each spring (you do, don't you?) and just as you replace any out-of-date

● A net is no aid to safety unless it encircles the entire boat, including the bow.

the pushpit or the pulpit. In this state, a net does indeed create a false sense of security, particularly in the parent.

I have never understood why people do not extend the safety net across the stern of the vessel. The reason for not extending the net across the bow is more justifiable as a net here makes it virtually impossible to drop anchor or weigh it again. The solution is to make this part of the fortification entirely separate from the rest. It should be in the form of a gate, permanently fastened to the pulpit on one side but on the other side laced with a line of a contrasting colour. While the boat is at sea, when the smaller members of the crew are not at liberty to wander about the deck, the gate is tied open, but once the anchor is down, or the boat is at her moorings, then the gate is closed. It takes only about 30 seconds to unlash such a gate, so it can hardly be considered a major inconvenience.

flares, so you must inspect the guard rail netting regularly. Test the integrity of the net itself, by attempting to break it, and check the lashings. Little children tend to fiddle with the lashings, and so you may find that you need to re-tie these quite frequently.

Another problem is that few people bother to extend the net around the whole boat. Some leave gaps for the genoa sheets to pass through, and hardly anybody nets

If the boat is to have a net at all, then it seems to me absolutely vital that the entire circumference be enclosed. If there are any gaps, your child will find them. I know of two youngsters who have gone overboard at the bow of boats which were netted everywhere else. Both lived to tell the tale, but only because, in each case, Mother was on hand.

Harnesses and lifelines

The function of the guard rail net is to keep the child from falling over the side while the yacht is in harbour and, except on a very small boat, where the child might actually be able to topple over the

rail, it is a sufficient safety aid. I have never required my children to wear life-jackets or harnesses while our yacht is moored. On those rare occasions when the motion is so radical that they might be flipped over the rail, they are obliged to amuse themselves below decks, but under most circumstances, if the hook is down they are free to play where they will.

You will learn to keep a listening watch when your kids are playing on deck. A boat is quite an effective sound-box, and the patter of even the tiniest feet is usually quite noticeable if you are under them. Naturally you cannot expect to be able to listen to the radio at the same time, and you will want to pop your head up every now and then, but the net takes the worry out of the situation. However, once the anchor is aweigh everything changes.

As long as the boat is stationary, and provided that she is not moored in a strong current, rescuing a child who has slipped over the side is fairly straight-forward. A bit of forward planning helps; rescue is simpler and quicker if there is a boarding ladder already set up, and an inflatable tender is also useful. A wise parent ensures that both facilities are at the ready as soon as the boat is moored.

With the boat under way, rescue becomes vastly more difficult, to the extent that it is absolutely crucial to prevent anybody – and a small child in particular – from going overboard. The guard rail and its net are no longer a suf-ficient aid to safety when the boat is under way, and the child must be attached to the boat with a lifeline.

A cautionary tale

Before we go any further I must emphasise the fact that I am talking here specifically about yachts, and not about dinghies or open boats. Nobody should ever be tied onto an open boat, which is very much more likely to capsize or sink. Many years ago, I stood on the beach at Hayling Island, on a very windy day, and watched a lug-rigged open boat of the Drascombe type sail herself under. It took less than two seconds. One moment the boat was there, surging along the deep-water channel which leads to the sea, and the next she had been swamped. Her crew of eight adults and children did not even get the chance to move from their seats. One moment they were in a boat, and the next they were in the water, and all in exactly the same positions. Bits of boat were popping up all around them.

Because this accident took place during a big regatta, with dinghies flying about all over the place, a rescue boat was instantly on hand. Within a few seconds, the shipwrecked mariners had been plucked from their embarrassing predicament – but I leave it to the reader to imagine what could have happened to any of the crew who had been tethered to the boat.

I must admit that my views on the subject of harnesses are by no means universal. If you stand and look at the traffic leaving an English marina on a sunny, summer's day, you will notice that – almost without exception – the children are wearing some kind of buoyancy aid, but that very few of them are attached to the boat. Conduct the same census at a French marina and you will find that few of the children are even wearing buoyancy aids, still less any kind of harness. I am told that French law requires that a lifejacket be carried for each member of a yacht's crew but, according to my observations, carrying them is about as far as it goes.

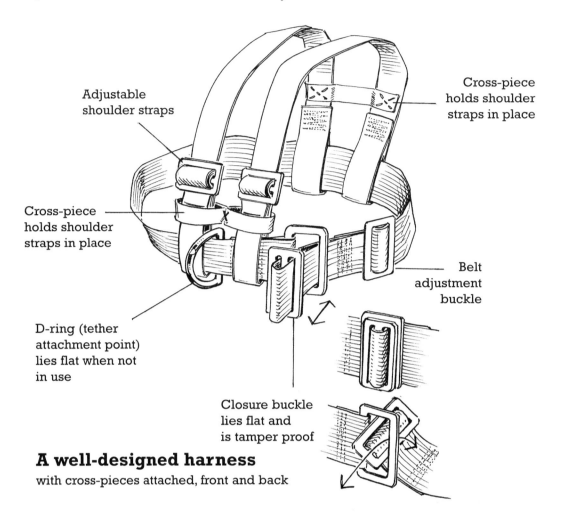

Adjustable
shoulder straps

Cross-piece
holds shoulder
straps in place

Cross-piece
holds shoulder
straps in place

Belt
adjustment
buckle

D-ring (tether
attachment point)
lies flat when not
in use

Closure buckle
lies flat and
is tamper proof

A well-designed harness

with cross-pieces attached, front and back

In South Africa, Canada, Australia and the United States there are also stringent regulations concerning the safety of a boat and her crew but, so far as I am aware, there is no nation which insists that its sailors wear, or are equipped with, harnesses. I would be the very last person to suggest that there *should* be legislation of this kind – the sea is the only remaining place on earth where we are truly free to do as we please, and any kind of law which seeks to control our behaviour at sea threatens that freedom. I am merely observing that the emphasis everywhere in

● Harnesses worn with the tether attached to the back (on the left) and to the front.

the world is on staying afloat, and not on remaining attached to the boat. To me this seems short-sighted.

 Aboard a very small boat, or one with a small cockpit, harnessed children are a liability to the whole crew, but if space allows then any children who lack the stamina to swim for an hour should, in my view, be hooked onto the boat. To me this seems to be a matter of elementary commonsense. Not fitting your child with a harness, to keep him from the possibility of falling overboard, is like not latching the garden gate and thereby exposing him to the danger of the road beyond. But as I say, not everybody sees it this way.

Amongst cruising folk, attitudes to personal safety are varied. There is nobody watching us when we are 'out there' and, likewise, there is nobody for us to watch. People therefore develop their own safety procedures. Some of these are described below, but before I allow anybody else to put in a word, I will describe my own way in more detail.

Safety rules aboard
Maamari

When my children were small we had one golden rule aboard *Maamari*. Regardless of conditions, and regardless of whether we were sailing across the Atlantic or just motoring around the harbour, if they came up from the cabin the kids must be wearing their harnesses and they must be hooked on. There was no scope for argument here. This was an immutable law.

I did not think that the children could be stupid enough to fall overboard while we were motoring around a flat harbour,

but I wanted to keep things simple. I wanted no discussion about whether the sea state was good, average or poor. Under-fives are not capable of recognising the transition between fair weather and foul, and are not mentally equipped to discuss things objectively or to accept esoteric explanations. They like to know where they stand. The Harness Law left them in no doubt.

When we sailed with friends aboard other yachts, the Regulations Concerning the Wearing of the Safety Harness often had to be relaxed – four pairs of adult legs, two infants and two tethers is not a feasible proposition in the cockpit of a Folkboat, for example, but aboard our own ship we had a standard procedure. The far end of each child's tether was clipped, semi-permanently, to a stout eye-bolt at the bottom of the compass pedestal, and the leash was allowed to trail along the cockpit floor and dangle down into the cabin. The children were not allowed to emerge from the cabin without being hooked on.

When the children were very small they required adult assistance with their harness lines, because the attachment point was on their backs. If we turned the harness around so that the ring and the hook were on the front, then the kids could release themselves, and we did not consider this to be an advantage. We wanted to know for sure that if we hooked them on, they would stay hooked on. The lines themselves are also less of an inconvenience when they are attached to the child's back. A line trailing down the front tends to tangle around the child's legs.

At the end of his tether

Properly used, a harness line should be attached in a position which makes it impossible for the wearer to end up trailing in the water. This rules out use of the guard rail – which is, in any case, not a very adequate strong point; plenty of people have gone over the side and pulled the guard rail after them.

Adult safety lines are nearly always supplied with a hook at either end, but children's tethers are generally not. They are intended to be fastened semi-permanently to the harness, by way of a loop. This practice is a potentially dangerous one. You simply cannot anticipate every emergency at sea. To cite an extreme example, a survivor of the *Marques* shipwreck told me that most of the crew who went down with the square-rigger, when she was suddenly overwhelmed, were wearing harnesses whose lines were secured by means of a loop. He himself only got free by cutting his tether with his knife.

In the event that some ghastly accident suddenly overtakes our ship, I want to be able to release my children instantly, without going hunting for my penknife. You also do not want to be forever helping your child in and out of his harness every time he wants to go below, or put up with the tether trailing behind him, which is a respectably mundane reason for requiring a hook at both ends.

At the far end, the tether should be fastened to the boat with a double-action hook, because these are difficult for a small child to work and are therefore fairly tamper-proof. For the end which fastens to the back of the harness something much lighter is needed. We used small, simple Wichard hooks. They are not as

People often tell me that they have tried using a harness ...

strong as the big, high-tensile Gibb and Wichard hooks, but those are quite a burden for a toddler to wear all day.

For the lines themselves we used half-inch diameter, three-strand nylon rope. With a breaking strain of 7,500lb, this stuff is as strong as really tough webbing and easily meets the standard required by the Ocean Racing Council. I prefer to trust a good, 6in eyesplice rather than put too much faith in salt-soaked, sun-drenched stitching.

In harness

Caesar and Xoë wore harnesses from the moment that they could first walk. There is nothing much to be gained by putting a harness on a crawling baby. Some people use 'reins' on their small fry, but I have never seen the point; you cannot turn your back on a crawling baby, even if he is tethered.

I cannot recall that I ever had much trouble persuading Caesar to wear his harness – but my diaries and notes give a contrary impression. Discomfort seemed at first to be the source of the irritation. Good, tough webbing of the appropriate breaking strain is fairly stiff and impliable, and a toddler's soft skin chafes easily.

I padded the shoulder straps of the harness with pieces of terry towelling. Problem solved? No.

Although Caesar soon got used to the harness itself, he absolutely hated the tether. At times he would even insist on remaining below decks rather than submit to the indignity of being kept on a lead. He received our explanation of its function as a criticism of his skills of balance and self-preservation. The tether was an insult.

People often tell me that they have tried using a harness on their child, but that he just gets into a tangle. We had a few tangles, of course, but unwinding himself from the compass pedestal was never Caesar's problem; he simply resented being tied up like a dog. I considered demonstrating my empathy by wearing my own harness at all times, but the idea of being perpetually constrained was such a drag that I baulked – which says it all, really.

I wish that I could be as relaxed about my children's welfare as some of my French cruising friends – but I am what I am, and Caesar just had to learn to live with it/me. In time he came to regard his harness as an ally, and whenever he heard the anchor chain going up he would run to fetch it and clamour to have it put on. Wearing the harness and tether had become a habit, and little children thrive on habits.

When we were on passage, Caesar and Xoë used to wear their harnesses day in, day out, above decks and below, without a complaint. They would even fall asleep in them – which reminds me: it is important that the buckles and fastenings on a child's harness are flat. Avoid the sort of design which features a right-angled key, serving as a combined fastener and D-ring. A child cannot lean back comfortably or lie down with this sort of ironmongery digging him in the spine.

It is also important that the shoulder straps are secure. Roxanne once did a Houdini with her harness; I turned around to find it lying in a heap on the cockpit sole whilst she was scampering off to break bounds. Tapes, or bands of cloth, joining the straps to each other at both front and back render this stunt impossible. Crewsaver's junior harness is one make which is fitted with such bands.

If you are making your own harness, be sure to use the proper materials: pukka marine webbing with a 2-ton breaking strain, not the stuff you find in the haberdashery shop, and sailmaker's thread, which besides being tough is also said to be UV resistant.

Emancipation

When the children were small (under seven) I was completely immovable on the harness issue. The kids wore their harnesses or else they stayed below, and that was that. Roxanne (six) still wears her harness at all times when the boat is under way. So long as she is tethered I need not worry on her account. I can help to raise the anchor, grapple with the sails or check on the dinner or the chart without giving a moment's thought to her welfare or her whereabouts. If she is clipped on, I know that she is safe.

Now that they are older, I am more flexible over Caesar and Xoë's use of the harness. It would be idiotic to insist that they remain hooked on when the yacht is sliding along over an oily sea. In such conditions the kids are nowadays free to roam. They are sufficiently aware and sufficiently experienced to know that they need to keep clear of the sheets and booms. They know that the foredeck is a dangerous place to be during a gybe or while we are tacking, and they obey, on the instant, the order to come aft or to duck. They have earned the right to be treated as Able Seamen.

Because they are allowed more freedom when the wind is light and the sea low, Caesar and Xoë enjoy such conditions quite as much as a wild, wet romp. When the wind is up, they are still required to wear their full regalia and to remain in the cockpit. In moderate conditions I moderate the ruling. The children are now old enough to appreciate the difference between a force three and a force six, and to notice when the swell is up. Xoë has just about reached the stage where she can accept that in some conditions she may roam, in some she must wear a harness on deck or else stay in the cockpit, and in some she must wear a harness and stay in the cockpit. I feel I must emphasize the fact that she has only just reached this happy place! For a child who still moans every time he is told to don his harness the blanket ruling (harness at all times) is, in the long run, more conducive to harmonious sailing.

When the crew includes children of differing ages and abilities, flexibility in the matter of the safety rules can become something of a problem. If one child is allowed to go on deck without a harness, younger members of the family are likely to feel hard done by. Age has its privilege. The main thing is for the parent to make her decision, based on individual circumstances, and then to stick to her guns. There should be no wavering where safety is concerned.

● Roxanne emerges from the cabin already wearing her harness, and waits for someone to attach her tether.

How the 'professionals' cope

It was only when I began researching this book that I realised how few ocean-cruising sailors regularly use harnesses on their children. Many prefer to rely on other means, and a good few do not bother about safety at all. To give the reader some idea of how 'full time' cruisers deal with this I would like to introduce a representative cross-section of live-aboards.

The laid-back approach

At one extreme we have Jean-Paul and Shelagh, a French-Irish duo who sailed aboard a big ketch called *Papillon*. Theirs was a supremely relaxed style of parenting and, indeed, of living in general. Their finances were precarious, and contrary to the typical yotty-islander interaction, they used to beg food from the natives.

Nick and his parents first met the couple in the Indian port of Cochin, where Shelagh was just about to give birth to a daughter. Her first child, Finbar, was about 15 months old at this time. When he sailed aboard *Papillon* from Mauritius to Madagascar, Nick noticed that Finbar had the free run of the ship. He was often to be found playing on deck by himself. He wore no harness or lifejacket and the only concession to safety was a net on the guard rail. This was punctuated by large holes for the genoa sheets and the anchor.

Wilful neglect

Jean-Paul and Shelagh's laid-back approach to life is far from unique in the cruising world. Aboard the Wharram cat, *Maui*, safety seems to be a dirty word. Swiss citizen Helmut Koch and his South African wife Carla apparently fear nothing from the ocean, or else simply view the future, and the welfare of their three small boys, with fatalistic detachment. The children never wear harnesses or life-jackets. In fact, there are no lifejackets carried. Nor is there a liferaft, or any other kind of safety equipment. When asked what would happen if the boat sank, Helmut shrugged and said, 'We'll all go down together.' Cosy.

Some people admire the Kochs, in a slightly shocked sort of a way. Others consider this style of parenting to be outrageous; they accuse Helmut and Carla of gross parental negligence, they pity the kids, and they declare that to put to sea in such fashion is illegal. On the last count, the detractors are wrong; you may do as you please on the high seas. You can dance naked, operate a still and let the kids run about unfettered, all without infringing any laws. And long may this remain the case. As to the other accusations, these are subjective issues. Even the people who are horrified by the careless manner of their upbringing would have to agree that Helmut's three sons of the sea are only to be pitied if they drown. While they live, they are having a whale of a time. And as Helmut himself was raised in a similar manner, bumming around the world on a cruising yacht, no one can pretend that the man does not know what he is about.

Utter folly

Now I think it is only fair to say that mothers are almost invariably more concerned over their children's safety than fathers are. Maybe it has to do with the effort we put into getting them safely aboard the planet. It is Mum, generally speaking, who sets the boundaries. Dads are often just as strict in reinforcing the matriarchal whim – but sometimes they let us down.

In the Caribbean island of... well, perhaps it would be best not to mention the island by name. At any event, in this sun-soaked, sand-encircled isle, a boy whom we shall call Tyson lived with his parents aboard a beautiful, old, wooden yacht. Tyson was the child of a Franco-American relationship and, as such, enjoyed and suffered parenting from opposite poles. On the one hand, his American mother Karen was excessively concerned with safety and, to use her words, she 'sat on him'. Tyson was never allowed to wander more than two yards from her side. By this I do not mean that the child was restricted in any way. He was not; he wandered completely at will and Karen dogged his every footstep.

Tyson's father Yves, being a Frenchman of the Tabarly type, went to the opposite extreme. He appeared to take very little interest in the boy and, more to the point, would not hear of spoiling the looks of his classic yacht with a guard rail, still less a net. Mummy therefore had to be vigilant.

Intensive parenting places a tremendous strain on an individual and after a while Karen could take no more. She decided that it was Papa's turn to do his bit. Yves had just won a contract to deliver another, near-identical yacht across the Pacific from New Zealand to San Francisco, and between the two of them the couple decided that little Tyson

should go along for the ride. I am not sure how much experience Karen had of sailing, but I am quite certain that she had no idea of what lay in store for her toddler on this trip. One other thing I know: a promise was made concerning the use of a safety harness. But promises are easier made than kept.

The skipper of a yacht, even with the best will in the world, does not have time to keep tabs on a small active child. When the yacht in question is short-handed and ill-equipped, with no self-steering, then the crew are already stretched to the limit. Stick a toddler into the equation and he is on his own. According to one of the two men who helped Yves to sail the boat across the ocean, Tyson lived as he pleased during that passage. He would appear on deck, day or night, in all weathers, and he was *never* dressed in his harness. The child had not been raised to obey – no discipline had ever been exerted on him – and so he ignored all pleas from the helmsman to go below. As often as not the helmsman was the only other person awake, and it was generally not possible for him to leave the wheel and go chasing after the boy. To have abandoned the boat to her own devices in rough weather would have jeopardised the rig. This two-year-old would go roaming along the side deck, in the dark, in the gale, while the water ran hungry fingers of foam over his feet.

That Tyson survived his first ocean crossing is testimony to a child's ability to take care of himself. The fact that the boy was accustomed to being on a near-identical boat was clearly a major advantage, but one cannot help believing that his guardian angel must have been keeping a very close watch. By the end of the trip she was probably as close to a nervous breakdown as Karen had previously been.

Discipline

For every anarchist hippy bobbing about on the ocean waves there are at least two liberals, and there are even some people out here whose home policy tends towards right-wing extremism. Perhaps my harness policy sounds a bit extreme to some. Other families have managed to run a safe ship without the use of such props – but in their place these people have often needed to use equally vigorous laws.

For the Weiss children aboard *Blue Water Gipsy*, sailing was a way of life. Their parents started cruising before they were born and so Steven, Nigel, Chloe, and Neil had always lived aboard a yacht. Like many long-distance cruisers, the family were really travellers and live-aboard escapees first and foremost. They did not particularly like sailing and they dreaded long passages. They liked to spend several months in one port before moving on.

While the boat was in harbour, the Weiss family's days followed a steady routine. Günter Weiss was a German and although he had married an English woman and claimed to be an Anglophile, something of his upbringing still clung to him and he believed in an ordered lifestyle for the whole family. Mealtimes, school, bedtimes and bathing routines were all rigidly enforced, a tendency which is unusual, to say the least, with this get-away-from-it lifestyle.

While the boat was at sea, things aboard *Blue Water Gipsy* were less structured – at least from the children's point of view – but in one matter their parents did impose a strict discipline. While they were under 12 years of age, none of the children was allowed to come up from the cabin without first calling out to ask for permission. If the weather was considered rough, then the kids were not allowed outside at all. They were permitted to go out of the cockpit only if the weather was calm.

The Weiss children did not wear life-jackets, and until they were in their teens and began to help with the handling of the

● If her doll is provided with a harness, the child can impose the rules on him, and may then be more willing to accept this discipline herself!

boat, none of them wore harnesses. During 19 years of cruising none of the kids ever went over the side while the boat was under way, and so it would seem that rules alone were adequate for this particular family.

Nervous discipline

Other families with a more relaxed attitude to life have also found rules to be a sufficient aid to safety. Some, however, are evidently less confident about their shipboard standard of discipline.

Michael and Pam, an English couple with a centre-cockpit Nicholson, adopted a similar procedure to the Weiss family but reinforced it with lifejackets. Five-year-old Tom and his little sister Shannon were not allowed on deck at sea unless they were togged-up, and they had orders to stay in the cockpit. When I asked whether orders were really enough for such young children, Michael admitted that the rule sometimes had to be reinforced with discipline.

Orders seem to me to be an unfair means of controlling a very young child who, even if he understands, may be insufficiently mature to resist his urges. Engrossed in his play, he may also forget the fact that what is perfectly permissible in harbour is outlawed at sea. At the tender age of 15 months, Caesar would obey instructions to remain in a certain well-defined area; 'don't step over that line' worked very well in his case. But I would not have trusted his life to such obedience, and nor did I want to have to watch him like a hawk. Although it may seem like a contradiction in terms, a harness gives a child freedom, the freedom to play outside without constant vigilant

supervision, and without the threat of punishment for disobedience.

As to the use of lifejackets on the ocean, this also seems to me to be totally inappropriate, largely because a buoyancy-aid type lifejacket (the type which is invariably used) is insufficient for the purpose of saving a life on the high seas. We shall look more closely at that in a moment.

I also feel that it is unfair to expect a child to remain wrapped in a 1in thickness of foam when the temperatures are in the eighties, as they generally are in the tropics. But *Rosalind* was not in the tropics when we met Michael and Pam. She had scarcely left England. Nine years down the road, she and her four crew are still girdling the world.

A careful approach

A few parents employ a belt and braces attitude towards safety at sea, using both harnesses and lifejackets. One child raised according to this creed was Luke, nine years of age when we met him and an only child. He and his parents lived aboard a 45ft Hartley called *Moogooloo*.

According to his parents, Peter and Maggie, Luke always wore a harness while *Moogooloo* was at sea, and if he wanted to go out of the cockpit he had to wear a lifejacket over the top. Not a regime of which the boy approved, one gathered, but as Peter said, 'He just had to lump it'.

When he was small, Luke had even been required to wear a harness while the boat was at anchor or on the slip. It is definitely possible to go overboard on safety (pardon the pun) but the idea of using harnesses when the boat is high and dry is a sound one. The risk of falling off a boat may be lower when she is ashore than when she is pitching and rolling, but the consequences are equally dire. I once came across a French couple whose little boy had fallen from the deck of their boat while it was still under construction. Because the boat was a centre-boarder and therefore drew very little, the child's fall was not even six feet, but he was still concussed and suffered temporary vision problems. The 12ft fall from the deck of a Hartley could easily have been terminal, and Luke's parents were wise to keep him safely tethered.

Trust misplaced

The cruising lifestyle seems to be a breeding ground for cross-cultural alliance, or perhaps it is just that international couples are peculiarly attracted to travel. Already in this chapter we have seen a Franco-Irish union, an Anglo-German one, a Swiss-South African alliance, and a Franco-American one. Now we are going to meet an English-Polish duo, John and Maria, aboard their steel sloop *Orion*.

Unlike most ocean cruising yotties, John had already been sailing for many years before he decided to cast off from the shore life, but for his wife Maria and their small son Damien the passage from England down to the Algarve was a first. Being three months pregnant at the time, Maria did not think much of the experience – pregnancy is a sure-fire recipe for seasickness – but two-year-old Damien evidently took the matter in his stride. He seemed perfectly happy with his new life and lot.

John and Maria did not seem to have thought of trying Damien in a harness and relied for his safety on a lifejacket of the foam buoyancy-aid type. The child was obliged to wear this at all times, whether *Orion* was in harbour or at sea, and he also wore it in the dinghy. Having lived with the encumbrance for several months, young Damien was pretty much resigned to the situation by the time we met. While his mother dressed him he would invariably murmur, 'No jacket. No.' But he never made a scene or offered any actual resistance.

Maria evidently had implicit faith in her son's lifejacket, and although it would most certainly *not* have been adequate had he gone overboard in a rough sea, it appeared to fit him well enough. So it came as something of a shock to hear, a few months later, that when the jacket was tested it floated the boy with his feet in the air! More on that subject in a moment.

Likeminded – and at odds

Of course, there are cruising families whose shipboard safety protocol is similar to the one which I advocate. South African live-aboards, Dylan (seven) and Nathan (five) always wear harnesses when their big, red, steel sloop *Enigma* puts to sea. Likewise, nine-year-old Remington, six-year-old Ashton and their little sister Sierra all wore harnesses all of the time when sailing aboard *Brittany*, a 35ft Nonsuch. In each case the children were required to wear their lifejackets only while playing in the dinghy.

Neither of these families had been cruising for any great length of time when we met them. One couple who have had rather longer to test their methods are Cathy and Donald Reeves, an Anglo-American team whose lovely yacht

Symphony will have completed her circumnavigation before this book is in print. When her baby boy began to get mobile, Cathy made him a safety harness – but for the Reeveses a harness is something to be used only in rough weather or out on the foredeck. In fact, Cathy's children are only required to wear their safety harnesses when Mum and Dad are wearing theirs. There was, Cathy told me, only one rule aboard *Symphony*: the children were not allowed to set foot outside the cockpit while the boat was under way. Once Finlay and Ellen had been told about the danger of falling over the side, they always respected this rule – or so their mother said. This would certainly not have worked for my kids.

Notwithstanding her children's respect for the golden rule, Cathy said that she always watched them – and this is something which would not have worked for *me*. But there I go again, laying down my own law. The fact of the matter is that safety at sea is a very individual, rather complex issue – and we are not through with it yet.

Lifejackets

As we have seen, few live-aboard cruisers dress their children in lifejackets while they are sailing; but most people sailing in home waters do. Home-cruising yachts tend to be smaller than blue-water yachts, with less room for a web of harness lines, and a lifejacket is the obvious next option. The majority of parents also require that their children wear lifejackets whilst playing in the dinghy, and all but the most eccentric carry lifejackets for use in an emergency. Essentially this means that there are three separate requirements for a lifejacket. Can we expect one jacket to meet them all? Well, that depends... and to answer the question we need to look at what is available.

Spoilt for choice

In the days of my infancy, when a mother wanted to buy a lifejacket for her child she went along to the chandlers and bought it. And it was an anonymous, plastic-covered, foam waistcoat with brass eyelets up the front and a string with which to lace the gap. In those days there was no question of whether the lifejacket was the right one for the job; it was the only one.

Widespread increases in disposable income have not only enabled more families to take up sailing but have also encouraged us to become a lot more fussy about safety – and, for that matter, about comfort and appearance. With a greatly expanded market and a more discerning, demanding consumer, the marine safety industry has had the opportunity to expand and improve, the outcome being a super-abundance of efficient, reliable, attractive lifejackets for all sizes and ages. And Britain has something to be proud of here, for it is the designs of the British company, Crewsaver, which lead the field, and by several lengths, most other current manufacturers being mere imitators.

So, in Britain at any rate, the parents of the boating baby are nowadays spoilt for choice. Spoilt – but also confused. If you take the time to ponder the range of lifejackets now on offer it is actually rather bewildering. Many parents, faced with a rail of assorted lifejackets, plump for the nearest, or the cutest, or the one which their offspring selects on the basis of comfort and colour. And bearing in mind that these things are not cheap, most mothers instinctively reach for a jacket with plenty of growing room. Most dads are also affected more by price than design. Some of these kiddies' lifejackets cost over £100, but you can get one for under £30. No point in spending a fortune, hey? Not on something which, in the case of the weekend sailor, might only see the light of day a dozen times before the season is over. After all, colour and styling apart, a lifejacket is a lifejacket, right? Wrong.

When is a lifejacket not a lifejacket?

First things first. Before we go rummaging along the rail, trying out lifejackets for size and style, we need to sort out the difference between a lifejacket and a buoyancy aid, and we need to understand the various categories of lifejacket available.

Under European law, a manufacturer can only sell lifejackets and buoyancy aids which meet certain specifications and conditions and which carry the CE mark of approval. There are four CE categories, and they define each 'lifejacket' according to the amount of buoyancy that it provides.

Buoyancy is measured in newtons. According to the dictionary, a newton is a unit of force which imparts an acceleration of one metre per second per second to a mass of one kilogram. As such, it may not appear to have very much to do with lifejackets, but we are further told that ten

newtons are approximately equal to one kilo (2.2 lb) of buoyancy. The amount of buoyancy needed to keep a person afloat will obviously depend on his weight and bulk.

Buoyancy aid is not a euphemism for lifejacket. The difference has now been legally defined – in newtons, of course. A buoyancy aid must provide a minimum of 50 newtons of buoyancy. The minimum for definition as a lifejacket has been set at 100 newtons (100N). These standards replace the former, to my mind more logical definition, whereby a lifejacket was a lifejacket only if it could be expected to turn the unconscious wearer onto his back.

Virtually all children's lifejackets are classified as 100N lifejackets. According to the legal definition, lifejackets in this category are 'suitable for swimmers and non-swimmers' and give 'a reasonable assurance of safety from drowning in relatively calm waters' – whatever *they* might be! 100N lifejackets are 'not guaranteed to self-right an unconscious user wearing waterproof clothing and should not be expected to protect the airway of an unconscious person in rough water'. As a matter of fact, no lifejacket will protect the airway of its user in rough water – for that kind of protection you need a sprayhood – and no lifejacket is absolutely guaranteed to roll its wearer onto their back. However, some manufacturers manage to give the impression that their children's lifejackets will perform this stunt by stating that they are 'designed' to do so. The proof is in the pool; when testing 100N lifejackets on my children I have found that they consistently *fail* to right the wearer.

One cannot help but wonder whether the parents who invest in the Crewsaver

Supersafe 100N or the Baltic Easyfit 100N are aware that, under the old definition, these items would only have qualified as buoyancy aids. Well, at least we have established one thing: if a 100N lifejacket might, under some circumstances, be insuffcient for a child, a 50N buoyancy aid would be of no use to him whatsoever. Accordingly, the law defines this category as being 'only suitable for competent swimmers'.

Newton's Law

100N lifejackets are generally considered to be adequate for use in relatively calm, coastal waters (eg the English Channel or the Chesapeake in fair weather). Those venturing offshore with their children should, however, be looking for something with a bit more buoyancy. Ideally, anyone heading out onto the open sea should be equipped with a 150N lifejacket, which provides a performance equivalent to the old-style BSI-rated lifejackets. In other words, they should right an unconscious wearer. (The matter of righting an unconscious wearer is something of a red herring, in my opinion, but it does give a good indication of the level of buoyancy available and suggests that it might be about right.)

150N lifejackets are deemed suitable for use in all but the most severe conditions. For 'severe conditions' you need a 275N lifejacket and, so far as I am aware, nobody makes these in children's sizes. I guess cruising with your kids in the Southern Ocean has yet to become sufficiently popular to create a demand!

For our purposes, then, there are two different categories of lifejacket, the 100N and the 150N. Within these legal defini-tions there is a wide range, in terms of design appearance and construction; but before we get carried away with thoughts of maximum safety and minimum cost, let us just consider what it is that *your* child actually needs from his lifejacket.

A lifejacket is the sailor's very last chance when all else has gone dreadfully wrong and, as such, it must be adequate for the purpose. The trouble is, as I have already hinted, the same piece of kit is generally expected to serve at least two other functions: that of safety aid on a rough ride ashore in the dinghy, and of protecting the child while he plays, either under oars or on the jetty. It may also be in regular use while the yacht is at sea.

On the face of it, this is not a problem. If you are in the oggin, you are in the oggin, and whether you fell off the boat or it sank beneath your feet might be thought to be of little relevance; water is water. This is the view that most people take. Upon reflection, however, you will see that falling off the jetty into the marina is *not* the same thing as finding yourself awash in the middle of the ocean. If you have ever tried swimming in waves, you will know what I mean. If you have swum at the beach, you will know that it is 'wetter' than cruising up and down the municipal pool. Now imagine the waves magnified 20 times, picture 30ft of water beneath you – picture two miles beneath you, if you mean to cross the Atlantic – and ask yourself if you would be happy to drift around, awaiting rescue, with nothing better than a plastic foam waistcoat for support.

'Okay,' you say. 'Let's make it buoyant: the most buoyant lifejacket on the market.' Ah, but wait a bit; we are not through yet.

50N

Lifejacket definitions

275N

100N

150N

Turning the matter on its head, what parent wants to force his child to wear a Mae West while he plays in the dinghy?

The lifejacket issue is a complicated one. Many parents, ocean cruising parents in particular, decide to ignore it. Following Ostrich Policy they buy their child the cheapest second-hand buoyancy aid they can find and then stow it away in a locker, under the warps and fenders: 'After all, it's only for an emergency, and we won't be having one of those.' (Oddly enough, these are also the sort of people who enter the lottery each week.) Ostriching is one way around the lifejacket problem, but it is not the intelligent way. The sensible thing is to consider the different requirements, each in turn, and to identify the gear most suited to your own particular purpose.

Child-proof

The lifejacket that a child wears at play takes a real beating. It must be more rugged than a pair of jeans. It will get wet, muddy, covered in food, and if the cover is not very durable it will also get torn. Plainly the jacket should also be as

● Solid foam 100N lifejackets are the most appropriate for playtime use.

compact as possible. If it hinders his movement the youngster will quickly come to view it as an enemy.

I think most parents would agree that a 100N lifejacket, or old-style buoyancy aid, is perfectly sufficient for unsupervised play on the jetty or in the dinghy. Although it is not inconceivable that a child might knock himself unconscious in the course of his activities, the chances are so incredibly remote that the roll-me-over type 150N jacket looks like considerable overkill. To be capable of taking the rough and tumble of kindergarten treatment a lifejacket needs to be made of solid foam, and a 150N solid foam lifejacket is a seriously bulky piece of kit, not at all suited to playtime use.

Playing safe

Whenever we return to England I am always struck by the way in which live-aboard attitudes differ so greatly from weekend-sailing ways, and this difference is particularly obvious when considering children's lifejackets. Whereas cruising kids play on or by the water every day of their lives and yet seldom wear any buoyancy, weekend-sailing children are dressed up in their lifejackets from the minute they bundle out of the car.

It has to be admitted that there is considerable justification for wanting a child to wear a lifejacket when the boat is in harbour and alongside. Children do not tend to fall off boats that are at anchor if there is an adequate net on the guard rail, and they seldom go over while under sail, but children *do* go overboard from yachts which are alongside. Tales of children being dredged from the bottom of the marina abound. A very close friend

lost his son in this cruel way. The three-year-old boy simply disappeared from the boat while his father was ashore and his mother below decks, attending to her new baby. Dad thought that the child had stayed with Mum. Mum, when she realised that the child was absent, assumed that he had gone off with Dad. A diver later found his body under the boat. The child had presumably set out to follow his father but slipped between the boat and the jetty.

This is the absolutely classic sailing-related tragedy. The times when the boat is alongside are the times of greatest danger for your non-swimming child. In this sort of situation a lifejacket buys peace of mind.

While we are on the subject of children playing, I have observed an interesting variation on the rule which says that two is company but three is a crowd. One child playing on his own can fall in without anybody seeing him go. Two children are a safer proposition because if one falls in the other will surely notice and raise the alarm. With three children, however, you are almost back where you started, for if one falls in while the other two are engrossed in some other business, they may absent-mindedly assume that he has simply wandered away. In one horror story told to me by some cruising friends, the youngest of four children disappeared from a jetty while his brothers and sister played on. Once again, the body was found under the boat.

Evidently, the task of getting from the deck to the jetty should be made either very easy for the child, or else utterly impossible, the choice depending on his swimming ability and upon whether or not he wears a lifejacket as a matter of course. As further insurance against tragedy, a parent should cultivate the habit of looking for quayside ladders, or any other means of getting from the water. Do this in every new port, and encourage your children to do the same; ask them, if they are old enough to understand, 'Have you decided where will you climb out, if you slip?'

Most children are unaware of the difficulty that they would have in climbing even onto a floating pontoon. If circumstances permit, have them jump in and find out. Even the relatively simple matter of getting onto a boarding ladder may be beyond a small child. The longer/deeper the ladder, the easier the task. If you keep your boat in a marina and do not have a ladder permanently mounted on the boat, consider the possibility of nailing one onto the jetty.

For what it is worth, none of my children has fallen off the jetty or slipped between the boat and the shore (yet) but Xoë did once manage to fall out of the rubber dinghy while she was rowing around the marina with a whole gang of kids. Because she was wearing a buoyancy aid the incident was no big deal, but it is worth observing that she could not get back into the boat and her friends could not lift her, although the eldest was 13. (And Xoë was only three, and small for her age.) The other kids got her ashore by towing her along behind the dinghy by an arm. Having reached terra firma the wayward creature got straight back into the boat, and off they all rowed again very merrily – but what a different story it would have been had she not been wearing an adequate buoyancy aid.

Ship to shore

Once again, the matter of whether a child should wear a lifejacket for the journey from the ship to the shore is debatable. Most home-waters sailors favour the idea, and most live-aboards mock it. By now you may be of the opinion that blue-water cruisers are a rash, foolhardy breed, but in this case there is a little bit more to the business than first meets the eye.

In 12 years of cruising and sailing with my kids I have seldom had cause to fear for their safety while we were aboard the mother ship. In all the miles that we have covered and the hours we have spent at sea, there has been only one occasion when their lives were in danger. By contrast, there have been many, many times when adventures involved in getting to and from the shore have given me considerable cause for alarm.

Excepting the one occasion when Caesar slipped off the deck of a friend's sloop, my children have never fallen overboard from a yacht. Their tumbles have all been from the dinghy. Roughly half of these falls have been through the child's own fault. When a top-heavy toddler leans over the side of a dinghy the laws of physics insist that he must topple in. Most live-aboard kids have done this, or else been caught in the act, at least twice before they are two. Watch out for it.

Of course, it goes without saying that the little darlings tend to perform this acrobatic flip while you are *not* watching, and mine always did it when the water was so flat that it had never even occurred to me to put them in lifejackets. I did once catch Caesar by the ankle as his head hit the water, and I have done much the same for Xoë, who dozed off, hypnotised by the bubbles in our wake, and suddenly lurched over the transom in a wholly unexpected manner.

Xoë chose the exact moment of our coming alongside for her stunt, and this is definitely the favourite one. You have just battled against wind and tide to arrive, the oars are unshipped or the motor stopped, and you are standing up with the painter in one hand and the other on the guard rail. At the moment when you are about to flick the line around the stanchion and make fast, you hear a splash – quite a little splash. Drat! What has he thrown over the side, now? Some item from the shopping bag, no doubt. You turn your head quickly to investigate, and – WHERE HAS HE GONE?

Contrary to popular belief, toddlers do not immediately sink – or, at any rate, none of mine ever did, nor have I ever come across anyone else whose child went down like a stone. In my experience, toddlers float, but they float with their belly uppermost and their head hanging down. Their arms and legs wave wildly as they struggle to right themselves.

But if your child was in the stern of the boat and you are standing in the bow then, right now, you will not be able to see whether he is afloat or on the bottom. The shock of his sudden disappearance sends a hot flush through your veins. You abandon your grasp on the rail, and there is a moment of horror and confusion when it occurs to you that the dinghy will drift back, over the child, but in less than a second you are there; you have him in your hands; you are lifting him out of the water. And while you hug and comfort him and your pulse slows down, the dinghy gradually drifts away – which is

why you must never put the oars on deck until you have first made fast the painter.

Accidents of this sort come out of the blue, and the quaking and trembling follow afterwards. More nerve-wracking, and far more dangerous, are the heart-in-mouth beach landings and the anxious journeys back to the boat through nearly-breaking waves. They are not so much a feature of home-waters cruising, but if you are going to go kicking about in less sheltered parts of the world then you will find that you often need to get ashore on beaches which are exposed to the ocean swell. I swear these dramas take years off my life. I suppose they are the marine equivalent of watching the stock market collapse; too much adrenaline and nowhere to spend it.

Naturally, if we can see from the anchorage that the getting ashore will be grim, then either we do not go or else, if we decide to risk it, the kids wear their lifejackets. I must confess that this does not calm my nerves greatly, and when faced with actual, closed-cell foam proof of my concern the children are apt to become fearful and tearful. Small children are not capable of recognising a rough landing place, but they soon learn to associate a lifejacket with the possibility of an unscheduled swim.

Dinghy dramas

Some of our more exciting beach landings have been made in the Cape Verde archipelago. These islands lie in the path of the trade winds, which whistle tirelessly through the valleys. One might expect that the leeward side of the more massive islands would be sheltered. So it is, but somehow, however calm the anchorage, the swell still manages to creep in unseen. Unseen, that is, until it finds the beach.

After you have spent the whole day intent upon making the haven of your choice, to arrive and yet be denied the opportunity of getting ashore is too frustrating. Did we come all this way for nothing? Surely we are not going to be defeated by a few little waves lolloping onto the beach?

We had hardly dropped anchor off the little village of Tarafal before a crowd gathered. We were so close to the shore, it being steep-to, that we could have conversed – except that the sound of the waves dumping on the stones would have drowned the attempt. They were not particularly big waves, and there was no surf; just the one line of short, steep waves which kept rearing up and then dumping.

While we watched and considered the matter nervously, a small open fishing boat appeared on the scene. Without the least hesitation her crew headed her for the shore, and a moment later they were hauling the boat up the beach with the help of their friends. Nothing to it. Now it was our turn.

We dressed the kids in their lifejackets. The full works; 100N aids inflated to become pukka 150N lifejackets (see pg 27). We boarded the dinghy and half a dozen strokes carried her to the shore. Nick swung the stern onto the pebbles – the safest way of landing if you have passengers in the stern – and as the transom touched the stones, the boat stood up in the air and turned a somersault.

I cannot recall whether I was thrown out or managed to jump clear. It all happened so quickly that I hardly knew, even at the time. Nick was somehow

An upsetting moment

catapulted into the water and there were two fishermen standing with him, hanging onto our upturned dinghy. But what about the kids? Where were they? I glanced around in panic, to find that Caesar and Xoë were both safe and dry in the arms of another pair of fishermen. Without the quick intervention of these local guys, the whole thing would have been much messier. The pebbles of which the beach was made, and onto which the children might have been flung, were about the size of my head.

Crash helmets would have served a better purpose, at Tarafal, than lifejackets. There have been other times when lifejackets would have served our needs very well, but we did not have them aboard. Arriving off the tiny Turks and Caicos island known simply as Salt, we anchored in waters as still as the proverbial millpond. The shore was only about half a cable (100m, 300ft) distant, and our landing place lay tucked away behind a little off-lying wall, or mole. There was not a wave, or even a ripple in sight. The idea of dressing the kids in their lifejackets... well, it would have been absurd.

Salt, as the name suggests, was once a salterns. We spent a happy afternoon ambling around the ruined pans and then, as evening drew nigh, we noticed that the wind was getting up. If the wind gets up while you are aboard, you notice it straight away, but it can easily rise unnoticed while you are ashore and distracted. We headed for the harbour and home, but by the time we reached the anchorage *Maamari* was bucking up and down like a bronco, and we were horrified to see that there were waves *breaking* in the gap between the detached mole and the shore!

There was no question but that the yacht had to be moved. The once calm anchorage was now the open sea. The anchor could not be expected to hold on for long while the bow plunged in and out of the water. If we could not get out to her, we were going to lose the boat – but how could we manage the journey in safety?

● If the children's lifejackets had been left aboard, and were therefore not available for the ride from shore back to ship, the kids sometimes wore swimming aids such as this solid foam 'egg'.

One possible option was for Nick to row back out to the boat and fetch the children's lifejackets, but the wind was still rising and in the interval the seas would have become bigger. Worse, it was getting dark, and in the dark we would be unable to see the waves and time our passage amongst them. There were really only two choices; either we went for it, or else Nick went out alone and sailed the boat clear of danger. This would have left me to kip with the kids beside the salt-pans and await his return, who knew when? Rightly or (more probably) wrongly, we decided to go for it.

Suffice it to say that the ride out to the yacht was traumatic. I was actually shaking with fear (not something I have ever done before or since, so you can picture the scale of the drama). I was well aware of the near impossibility of supporting two non-swimmers in a rough sea. We arrived very wet and shaken, but otherwise intact. And the funny thing is that the kids were perfectly calm and relaxed throughout the whole ordeal. No lifejackets, you see.

Unwanted baggage

Until you have tried it, you can have no idea how tiresome it is to spend the whole day lugging around a couple of chunky foam lifejackets. In fact, tiresome is a gross understatement; impossible comes much closer to the truth. Picture the scene. We have just arrived in a new harbour. There is a good breeze blowing against the tide, and so the anchorage is rather choppy. We have half a mile to row and at the end of it there is a beach landing, but we are too far off to be able to see whether there is any surf.

When we get ashore, we will tie the dinghy to something good and solid. Depending on the circumstances, we might also lock it with a padlock and a piece of rigging wire. (These days, you cannot be too careful; certainly you cannot afford to leave anything lying around in the dinghy.) Finally, having thrown a last look at the yacht and assured ourselves that everything will still be here on our return, we will set out to explore.

As I say, you have to have been there to understand. You have to have spent all day encumbered by those accursed lifejackets. You have to have seen the sights with them tucked under your arm and lunched with them on the seat beside you. ('We mustn't forget them.') You have to have tried buying a week's groceries with the lifejackets already filling your rucksack and a tired, fractious child already on your hip or dragging at your heels. I am sure we all know what fun it is to go trailing round the supermarket with a pair of small children in tow. Now picture yourself in a strange town, herding your youngsters across a busy street with two bags of shopping in either hand *and* a lifejacket under each arm.

Get the kids to wear the lifejackets? If the climate permits, this is a first-rate solution to the problem, but if the weather is hot, it is out of the question.

After you have spent a day sightseeing with a lifejacket under each arm, you will want to give up cruising with kids. You begin the adventure feeling bright and enthusiastic, but an hour later you feel like an overloaded mule. Perhaps you think I am laying it on a bit thick, but my most vivid and enduring memory of some of the places we have visited is of lugging around the lifejackets.

There are three solutions to the problem of lifejackets for the ride ashore. The first is to buy cheap, second-hand 100N lifejackets or old buoyancy aids at a boat jumble and leave them in the dinghy, hoping for the best. If they disappear you will not have lost a lot financially, and you will (if you are wise) still have other lifejackets available for use in an emergency.

The second solution is to buy juniorsized auto-inflating lifejackets (see pg 27) and remove the bottles and capsules, depending instead upon oral inflation. These jackets are comparatively light and compact, but even the ill-made, rubbishy brands are relatively expensive.

For the budget sailor the third method is best. It consists of a block of polystyrene measuring roughly 8in x 4in x 4in and having a webbing strap passed through the centre, from one side to the other. This foam 'egg' is strapped to the child's back. For a child over 18 months the egg makes a first class swimming aid, but it is NOT a lifejacket, not by any stretch of the imagination, and it cannot be guaranteed to float a baby in an upright position, with his head above water. It is, however, a great deal better than nothing. Since it is valueless, it can be left unattended in the dinghy. Following the same philosophy of 'needs must', one could also use armbands or other inflatable aids as easily portable emergency buoyancy. I just wish that I had thought of this when my own kids were small. It would have saved me a great deal of anxiety.

Lifejackets in extremis

Lifejackets aboard ship, lifejackets for play and for the ride ashore and, finally, we need also to prepare for the worst; we have to equip our young crew with the sort of lifejacket which can be depended upon to serve their needs in the event of the ultimate disaster. If you ever find yourself in a position where you really need this piece of kit, you will certainly wish that you had bought for your child the very best, most reliable lifejacket on the market. Certainly you will wish that he was wearing a well-designed 150N jacket, rather than a foam waistcoat. Ideally, it should be possible for the child to wear his emergency lifejacket over the top of a safety harness, or vice versa.

So, can one lifejacket fulfil all of these widely differing functions? It would seem that what is really needed here is two pieces of kit, the ultimate and the daily-use, buoyancy aid type. However, good quality lifejackets are not cheap, and space aboard a yacht is always at a premium. Fortunately there is a solution.

Air-foam lifejackets

The solution to the problem is an air-foam lifejacket; a lifejacket which gets its buoyancy from a combination of an air-bladder and chunks of closed-cell foam. With the bladder deflated the device is a 100N lifejacket, the item which I have been referring to, colloquially, as a buoyancy aid. In this state it is the ideal thing for a child playing in the dinghy. When the going gets tough, however, three or four puffs of air turn the buoyancy aid into a fully paid up 150N lifejacket. Hey presto! Two lifejackets for the price of one.

So far as I am aware, Crewsaver are the only people making air-foam life-jackets at the moment. They used to make quite a range of air-foam jackets but have now withdrawn all but two designs from production. These are the Seababy/Seatoddler/Seachild, and the BSI.

The Seababy and its siblings are waist-coat-style lifejackets which come complete with their own integral harness. This might seem to be the cure-all; with this one lifejacket we can equip the child with the full wardrobe of safety gear. This was obviously the manufacturer's intention, and to a large extent they have fulfilled their brief. The only trouble is that, in my experience, the child seldom needs to wear both the harness and the lifejacket at once. Therefore, he still needs a separate harness. (It is possible to remove the harness from the Seababy, indeed removing it is the work of a moment. However, it takes a good ten minutes of head scratching and *sotto voce* cursing to put the thing back together again.) Nevertheless, and regardless of whether or not one means to use the in-built harness on a regular basis, Crewsaver's Seababy is the state of the art buoyancy aid-cum-emergency-lifejacket for smaller children.

The Crewsaver BSI also plays the dual role of 100N/150N lifejacket. Being of the over-the-head type, it fulfils the need for a lifejacket which can be worn over a harness, but only if the harness is worn with the tether attachment on the back.

Unfortunately, even the child's size Crewsaver BSI is too big for people of less than 20kg (44lb). Crewsaver used to make a smaller model, known as the Seasafe, and other companies have in the past produced similar air-foam lifejackets for kiddies. Alas, there seems to be none in production at the moment. The fact is that once a child has reached a body weight of 44lb, he is likely to be

● The ultimate: the Crewsaver SeaBaby converts from a 100N to a 150N Lifejacket and also incorporates a harness with an aft attachment point.

approaching the age where he should be trusted to mind his own harness line. Henceforth he will need to wear his harness with the D-ring on the front – something which is not possible with an over-the-head lifejacket.

Sad to say, there is, at present, no part-permanent-buoyancy 150N lifejacket which permits the use of a harness with the tether worn on the front. There used to be a waistcoat-style air-foam lifejacket (the Crewsaver Sport) which was designed expressly for the purpose of allowing access to a forward-facing safety harness. Why is it no longer made? It is no longer made because Crewsaver have bowed to public pressure; the latest thing in children's safety gear is the auto-inflating lifejacket.

Auto-inflating lifejackets

Now there's an appealing idea; a neat, slim waistcoat which, in time of need, bursts into life as an authentic 150N lifejacket. While they are fooling around in the dinghy, the auto-inflating life-

jacket, it might be thought, offers our children the minimum of intrusion, but should they suddenly find themselves swimming for their lives, whether in the marina or in the middle of the stormy ocean, they will be magically provided, in an instant, with maximum protection. As they hit the water, the automatic inflation mechanism will fire the trigger, the gas will be discharged and the life-jacket will appear from nowhere. Marvellous, that is the way the thing appears on first acquaintance.

Auto-inflating lifejackets have been around for a long time, but children's auto-inflating lifejackets are a novel idea. In the space of the six or seven years since they were first introduced they have become immensely popular, but I wonder if the people who buy them for their kids have really thought the matter through.

When you think about it properly, an auto-inflating lifejacket is obviously completely *unsuitable* for dinghy play. A lifejacket intended for playtime wear must be durable and child-proof. It should not be dependent on bits and pieces with which the child might easily tamper. Clearly, it is also less than ideal that the sole source of buoyancy is a somewhat flimsy air-bladder, which might get punc-tured. As if these reasons were not enough, there is also a pecuniary one. Unless his parents have money to burn, the child's playtime lifejacket should not be dependent on CO_2 cartridges and a high-tech trigger mechanism. If your children are anything like mine, they can be almost guaranteed to give themselves a good soaking while messing about in the dinghy, and at somewhere around £12 a

● From the sublime to the ridiculous. When it is placed alongside a solid foam lifejacket providing equivalent buoyancy, the attractions of the 150N auto-inflating jacket are quite obvious.

shot for the recharge kit, this makes the affair of maintaining the jacket in working order a rather costly one.

These facts rather rule out the use of an automatic in the dinghy, but perhaps this type of lifejacket might prove convenient at sea. Perhaps... but there are a few more hidden drawbacks.

Drawbacks to auto-inflation

The first, most obvious problem with an auto-inflating aid is that it might not inflate. If your child has pulled on the toggle, which manually activates the inflation trigger, and has neglected to own up (perhaps not even being aware that the CO_2 cartridge is a once-only device) then the lifejacket will certainly not inflate when it is next called upon to do so. To be fair, deflating the jacket and putting it back inside its protective cover is a task which would defeat a very small child, but it is well within the scope of a seven-year-old.

➤ Another interesting little detail: it is possible to burst the inflatable bladder in an automatic lifejacket. To do this you simply blow up the lifejacket orally and then either pull on the cord, or dunk the jacket. In theory at least, a well-made lifejacket will not burst – the better ones are now designed to withstand 'double inflation' – but the jacket will obviously be placed under excessive strain and is likely to be damaged. ➤

Crewsaver advise that the buyer of an auto-inflating lifejacket should get his child to try it out in the water and see how it works. Sound advice. Rather costly advice too, of course, but in the case of a child I would say that familiarisation is absolutely essential. *Practical Boat Owner* tested 11 different lifejackets on nine children, and whilst the older kids, aged seven and eleven, seemed happy with automatic gas inflation, the younger ones, from six years down, were quite frightened by the sudden, loud hiss and the instant appearance of a rigid, constricting collar: 'Despite a very careful briefing from her dad about what was going to happen, Chloe (two and a half) was clearly unimpressed by what happened next.' (*PBO* March 2001.) And she was only splashing about in the swimming pool, with her dad and her big sister at her side. A child who actually fell in from a moving yacht and found herself abandoned and alone in its wake would be even less inclined to be of good cheer when her lifejacket suddenly exploded and tried to throttle her.

A word of warning for blue-water sailors

Possibly the only thing to be said in favour of automatic lifejackets is that children certainly do like them. Caesar and Xoë definitely prefer their automatics over conventional foam buoyancy aids. However, junior-sized gas-inflation lifejackets are not ideal for blue-water cruising, and for a very simple reason: the small size 22 or 23g bottles which they require for their operation are just about impossible to find overseas. CO_2 bottles are banned from air freight, so that one cannot even get them sent out.

Auto or manual inflation?

Whilst I consider gas-inflation lifejackets to be wholly inappropriate and possibly even dangerous for the use of small children, I do believe that they are ideal from the age of 10 or 12 upwards. A child of this age is ready to take an active part in the sailing of the boat, ready to get involved in sail changes and other foredeck dramas, and he therefore needs the

same sort of protection as an adult; plus a bit more.

My gas-inflation lifejacket is manually operated, because I want to have the opportunity of making my own choice, if I go over the side, about whether a huge airbag will help or hinder me in my situation. I am willing to gamble on being conscious and *compos mentis*. However, I would not want to count on a 12-year-old's ability to remember to find and operate the toggle if he ended up in the drink. Adult wearers have been known to forget and have been found, drowned, in gas lifejackets which were perfectly serviceable but which they neglected to activate. On this basis, I feel that an automatic jacket is more suitable for a youngster.

Automatic inflation is available through two different systems. The standard system involves a capsule containing a little coil of paper and a powerful, spiked spring. When the capsule gets wet,

● An auto-inflating jacket with integral harness is ideal for a teenager who is ready to become involved in the working of the yacht.

the paper dissolves and releases the spring, which punctures the gas bottle. The alternative Hammar inflation system relies on water pressure for its operation. A Crewfit Hammar inflation lifejacket will not burst into life in your damp hanging locker or while you are shipping it green – in fact, it may not even operate while the wearer is floating on his back in the sea; it will not operate until the mechanism has been immersed to a depth of 10cm (4in). Bear this in mind – and see that your child, if he has a Hammar inflation jacket, understands how it works. Plenty of people have been rescued complaining angrily about lifejackets which fail to inflate, only to discover afterwards that the mechanism in their jacket was faultless. In theory, a person could even drown or die of hypothermia in a Hammar inflation jacket if the jacket failed to roll him onto his back, and the mechanism is obviously completely unsuitable for a lifejacket intended for a small child.

Which to choose?

There are now several manufacturers producing junior automatic lifejackets. Not all of them are good quality reliable products. Although they were not the first to introduce a junior model, it is Crewsaver who designed and pioneered the modern, split-front, gas-inflation lifejacket. The Crewfit is the original; all other similar lifejackets are imitations.

Crewsaver lifejackets are not cheap – on the contrary – but before you decide that a budget-priced copy will fit the bill equally well, you should consider the possible consequences of going for the cheapest. It is the life and death of a child

that we are talking about here. If your child needs a lifejacket – actually *needs it*, to save him from drowning – then he needs one which will work. What point is there in dressing him up each weekend in something cute/cheap/convenient if, when it comes to the crunch, the lifejacket turns out to be deficient?

But surely, all these lifejackets have CE Approval; can we not put our trust in the legal standard? CE Approval merely demonstrates that the merchandise meets certain criteria. In the case of a lifejacket, it tells us that the particular design has been shown to provide a certain amount of buoyancy. It does not prove that the buoyancy is in the right place, or that the product will function appropriately. It does not prove that the product went through any kind of quality control.

Although similar in design, automatic lifejackets are not completely identical and they function with varying degrees of efficacy. I have even come across a junior automatic of a 'chandlery' brand which, according to the packaging, needed to be fitted with a 22g bottle but which was supplied with a 20g bottle. When the bottle was fired, the lifejacket was flaccid. In defence of his merchandise, the agent informed me that a lifejacket should never be fully inflated, as this would damage it!

The only way to be sure of any product is to test it, but you cannot try-before-you-buy a lifejacket. Lacking the opportunity to see with our own eyes, we are obliged to act in faith. I prefer to place my trust in the equipment that is used by the professionals. If merchant seamen, the armed forces, the police, and the RNLI all trust the Crewsaver Crewfit, then it ought to be good enough for me and mine.

Having made my choice, I tested the children's automatic jackets, as indeed I also test their foam jackets. I was very sceptical about the auto-inflating aids but I have to admit that whatever intrinsic drawbacks this style of jacket may possess, when it came down to getting them wet, the Crewsaver Crewfit Junior and the Crewfit Hammar scored ten out of ten. The performance of these jackets was absolutely faultless.

Caesar, who was wearing the Hammar inflation jacket, was gratified to find that it inflated itself far more quickly than he had anticipated. Inflation appeared to commence almost instantly, and the jacket was fully inflated and supporting him within the space of three seconds.

Being determined to give the jackets the hardest possible test, I decided to let Roxanne try the Crewfit Junior. Roxanne could not swim, and so we would get a brutally honest picture of the way in which delayed inflation might affect a casualty wholly unable to support herself. Having watched her big brother demonstrate the adult jacket, the child leapt off the side of the boat, in accordance with instructions – and disappeared in a cloud of bubbles. ('It all went white,' she said afterwards, 'and I didn't know where I was.') Roxanne had been absent for about one and a half seconds and we were just getting ready to panic, when suddenly she popped back up to the surface with the lifejacket already springing into life. The shock of her immersion and the coldness of the water were what worried her. Based on what I had read, I expected the inflated jacket to be constricting around the child's neck, but it was not; it did not press against her neck at all. She was,

however, quite frightened by the way in which the device held her on her back. More on that subject in a moment.

There is just one more point which I should like to make about inflatable lifejackets, before we move on. In order to qualify for the CE rating, lifejacket designs are tested, but only in a swimming pool. We were testing the jackets in a relatively sheltered bay in a force three. If we are thinking in terms of an aid suitable for a mid-ocean or stormy sea disaster, we need to have an idea of how it will perform in the waves.

Finding himself in the drink, a man overboard who is still on the ball will presumably be inclined to face downwind, away from the waves and weather. Such an action requires a deliberate effort, however, for an unresisting body supported by a lifejacket will inevitably be turned so that it faces into the wind. Turned so, the man or child overboard will be exposed to whatever the waves throw at him, and if his jacket has a 'split front', as have all modern gas-inflation lifejackets, then the waves may be able to 'channel' up between the two lobes of the inflated bladder and throw themselves right into his face. The two lobes of a well-designed air-only jacket are cut in such a way that when inflated they are forced together – the lobes on a Crewfit actually overlap slightly – and this makes channelling less likely. Cheaper jackets, cut in a more economical manner, do not offer this protection.

How can a parent find out about this before parting with his cash? He cannot; the inefficiency of a lifejacket only becomes truly apparent in the water. One can either take a chance, therefore, or else go for a tried and trusted brand.

Permanent buoyancy lifejackets

Like a lot of other modern marvels, auto-inflating lifejackets bring with them complications. For an easy life and complete peace of mind, good, old-fashioned foam is the answer. You know where you are with foam! Even if you decide to equip your youngster with an automatic lifejacket for use at sea, you would certainly be wise to dress him in foam while he plays.

Two different types of foam are used by the leading manufacturers in their CE Approved lifejackets. The better quality products are made from chunks of PVC foam, and the budget-priced models contain thin layers of polyethylene. One can easily deduce which type of foam has been used by feeling the edge of the lifejacket.

Jackets made using polyethylene foam take a long time to dry because the water remains trapped between the layers. This may seem trivial, but in fact it is very important that a lifejacket be kept dry. Believe it or not, there are bacteria which eat damp plastic foam!

Things which get salty are never dry thereafter. Because salt is hydroscopic, it absorbs moisture from the air, and so it is very important that a lifejacket which has got wet is thoroughly rinsed in fresh water. Naturally, it should be rinsed by hand and not in a washing machine – an obvious point, you might think, but Crewsaver have found it necessary to print this warning in block letters in their catalogue. Nor should the jacket be placed to dry on top of a radiator, or – perish the thought – in a tumble drier.

Compression also causes shrinkage of the foam and loss of buoyancy, so a lifejacket should never be used as a cushion, or buried beneath a pile of warps or sails. Both types of foam can be compressed, but polyethylene much more easily than PVA.

If you have only one child and want to buy a 100N lifejacket, then you might consider a polyethylene one, but if you want something that can be handed down, a PVC lifejacket is a better investment. Our only polyethylene aid is battered and bent, whereas the PVC equivalents, despite having been subjected to many more years of abuse from the children, are still in good shape.

Foam lifejackets come in two different styles, over-the-head or waistcoat. Children sailing in cooler climes generally seem to prefer a waistcoat, which is also easier for them to put on unaided.

Waistcoat-style lifejackets fasten with a zip, and from the parent's point of view this is a double-edged sword. On the one hand, the jacket is so easy to fasten that children as young as three can manage the business for themselves. On the other hand, they can also take the jacket off again by themselves. And some of them do. One sweet little three-year-old of our acquaintance used to slip out of her nice new lifejacket every time her mother's back was turned.

Most (but by no means all) waistcoat-style lifejackets are equipped with a pair of laces at the collar. People generally seem to regard these as surplus to requirements and neglect to tie them, but if your child is an escape artiste you can make things a little harder for him by threading one of the laces through the hole in the zipper and tying a bow. A double bow, if necessary.

Try it out!

Crewsaver and Baltic both recommend that children are encouraged to try out their lifejackets in the water. This surely makes sense; in the event of a crisis, a person who is accustomed to swimming in his lifejacket will stand a much better chance of survival than one for whom the experience comes as a shock. Furthermore, if there are any deficiencies in the design of the product it is obviously best to know about them in advance. Obvious or not, of the several dozen parents with whom I discussed children's lifejackets only one had actually tested the gear in this way – although *every single one of the others was 'meaning to' but had not yet got round to it!* And the mother who had tested her son's jacket found that it floated him upside down, with his feet in the air.

It is very important that a lifejacket fits the wearer properly. Baltic make a point of emphasising the fact that lifejackets 'are not designed for the child to grow into'. But lifejackets are expensive and so parents do, inevitably, try to buy something that will fit for several years, and put a younger child into the older one's cast-off. If the crotch straps are used there is a reasonable chance that a jacket which is oversize will still perform correctly. If the straps are not used then the lifejacket will ride up in the water; I suppose it might even be possible for a child to fall out of the bottom of an oversized waistcoat-style lifejacket, if he were not wearing crotch straps.

More cautionary tales

Roxanne, at three years of age, looked sweet in her Seababy lifejacket. It fitted her nicely and, according to the label, was well able to support her 15kg (33lb). However, when Roxanne jumped into the pool the lifejacket (in its uninflated 100N state) was clearly shown to be inadequate. It floated her, but with her mouth below the surface of the water. Either the foam had shrunk considerably – a distinct possibility as the lifejacket was now nine years old – or else the manufacturer's claim was optimistic. Had we not tested it, Roxanne would have continued to wear the jacket, perhaps with dire consequences.

I think it is also worth noting that the lifejacket which supports a seven-year-old may not support a toddler. Yes, you read me correctly there, and this time I am not talking about the distribution of the buoyancy. Caesar, when he was 18 months old, did not think much of being dunked in the sea, and yet I was determined to test his lifejacket. Fortunately help was at hand in the form of seven-year-old Chloe Weiss, of *Blue Water Gipsy*. Chloe loved swimming and was only too pleased to help. She slipped into the baby-sized lifejacket – it was very short, but we had no problem in fastening the zip – and she jumped into the sea. And there she lay, on her back, amply supported by the jacket. The manufacturers evidently allowed a considerable safety margin, or so we concluded.

ERROR! We had missed the point. Chloe could swim. Chloe could float on her back just as easily without the lifejacket. The fact that it supported her, or seemed to, was no indication of whether it would support Caesar. The only way to be sure of the value of a particular lifejacket is to test it on the particular person for whom it is intended.

Crotch straps

Once you've started to try them out in the water, you quickly realise the value of using crotch straps with a lifejacket. Crotch straps keep the jacket from riding up, and so maintain the buoyancy in the right place. They are part of the equipment's design, not just a tack-on 'extra' for paranoid parents.

Crotch straps are a pain, but not in the literal sense. Fastening them up is a nuisance. Unfastening and fastening them again when the child decides (immediately) that she wants a pee is trying on a parent's patience, but the kids themselves are not the least bit bothered by their straps. Nick's new Crewfit comes complete with a set of crotch straps, but I cannot see that they will get much use. By contrast Caesar (who is very safety conscious) and Xoë (who is not) both *insist* upon wearing their crotch straps.

● Over-the-head style, part-foam, part-air (100N/150N) lifejacket with crotch straps.

Where did I go *right*? Perhaps it comes of encouraging the kids to use the kit in the water. Having experimented, they know exactly what will happen when/if they wind up using the lifejackets in earnest.

Roll-me-over

In the course of their experiments in the pool Caesar and Xoë particularly like testing the gear to see if it will roll them onto their backs.

When the names were changed, and the thing which we knew as a buoyancy aid suddenly became a 100N lifejacket, manufacturers started trying to give their 100N jackets the self-righting capabilities of the more efficient 150N aids. In an effort to achieve this, the modern 100N is unevenly built, with buoyancy on the chest-side not at the back. Some manufacturers seek to give the impression that their 100N jackets will, indeed, do the trick, but I have yet to come across a 100N Lifejacket which will self-right my kids.

All this presupposes we actually *want* a lifejacket that will roll the child onto his back. Is it likely that he will be unconscious when he goes overboard? How great is the risk of his being smacked on the head by the boom, and will a lifejacket save him anyway in this event? Plenty of people have been killed outright by the boom. Better that both the boom and the child are kept under proper control.

Concussion is probably not the commonest cause of drowning amongst seafarers – it is estimated that fewer than ten per cent of MOBs are unconcious when they hit the water – but it is a fact that a person who remains in cold water will eventually lose consciousness. Even so, there are other things to be considered.

● Pinned on her back by a 150N auto-inflating jacket, Roxanne is clearly on the verge of panic; this despite the fact that her dad and her brother are only just out of the shot.

● Same child, same chilly sea – but with her air-foam jacket in its uninflated state, Roxanne has control of her body and is perfectly content.

Xoë's Crewsaver Seasafe, in its uninflated 100N state, would not roll her onto her back, but a couple of puffs of air brought it into its 150N mode. In this condition the lifejacket rolled the child onto her back in the space of one second, and she then proceeded to roll her way around the pool. She had no difficulty remaining on her front when she wanted to but she was enjoying the game. Yes, a roll-me-over lifejacket is fun for the child – *but only if he can swim.*

Watching Xoë at play I remembered a test which we performed with this same lifejacket when Caesar was small. Since the lad was unwilling to test it himself, we roped in his good friend Neil Weiss, who was of the same size and weight. Uninflated, the Seasafe supported Neil in an upright position, rather as a swimming aid does. He was as contented as could be, but the merest wavelet would have slapped him in the face and a succession of waves would probably have drowned him.

With the addition of a couple of puffs of air we converted the Seasafe from a buoyancy aid (100N) to a lifejacket (150N) and then we sent Neil back into the sea. This time the jacket kept his mouth well clear of the water, but the poor little fellow was far from content. He was terrified! The jacket had him pinned on his back, and he was completely unable to resist its force.

On a purely practical level, the child's discomfort may not seem to matter. After all, a lifejacket is for emergency use; better that the child should suffer a bit of trauma in a super-duper 150N aid than be swamped in a comfortable 100N aid. This logic is fine, but it takes no account of the immediate effect of trauma. Neil's eyes and mouth were wide open with fright; lying on his back with his mouth agape, he would still have fallen victim to the first wave. In his struggles to get upright he was also wasting energy which, in a genuine overboard situation, would have been better conserved in the form of body heat. Hypothermia is a considerable risk for the MOB even in the tropics, and in temperate zones it is the major factor in many drownings. A childhood friend of mine died of hypothermia while safely supported by a bulky lifejacket.

There is no satisfactory answer here. Having considered the situation I find myself concluding that a small, non-swimming child would stand a poor chance of surviving in the open sea *whatever* type of lifejacket he wore. One more reason for preferring a safety harness and tether.

Sea babies

What about the safety needs of a babe in arms? Since a tiny baby is not mobile it could be argued that he does not need a lifejacket; after all, he is not capable of falling overboard. If the ship gets into trouble, however, the smallest member of the crew needs at least as much protection as the more able. So, what have we got that is suitable for him? Not a lot, actually.

When Caesar was a baby, I rather fancied the idea of one of those inflatable yellow cots that are carried on certain transatlantic flights. The plane in the passenger instruction video has evidently crashed on an untypically calm day, and the cot is shown bobbing about in a gentle, rock-a-bye sort of a way. It occurred to me that, in the event of an Abandon Ship situation, conditions might be a little less ideal, and the cot a bit less stable; the merest puff of wind would send it sailing off faster than I could swim.

For those still attracted to the principle of a floating cot, Crewsaver have now come up with a more seaworthy design. They call it the Cosalt Crib, Cosalt now being the parent company. Intended mainly for cruise ships and ferry companies rather than yotties, the Crib is really

neither a cot nor a lifejacket, but a kind of aquatic sleeping bag. A large foam pillow supports the infant's head and further buoyancy in the chest area keeps his body afloat.

Instead we kitted Caesar out with a Helly Hansen Mini-Aid, but it only ever had one outing from the bag, when Caesar was about nine months and I decided to take him sailing in the dinghy. He howled non-stop from the moment I put it on, until we returned and I released him. Among my collection of references, I have a photo of another small child looking most unhappy in an identical aid, and one of my little niece crying miserably when she found herself in the embrace of some other small 100N device. Babies do not like lifejackets. But that is not the only problem.

The fact is that babies are awkward little people when it comes to keeping them afloat. Dressed in a swimming aid of the lifejacket type, or with flotation attached to his front or back, a baby of under one year is a highly unstable craft. His head is so heavy in proportion to his body that he tends to topple over. In fact, the only swimming aid that works well with a small baby is the Floaties ring, an inflatable double ring with a seat suspended from the hole in the middle.

Helly Hansen have now come up with a new 100N lifejacket of which the smallest size is intended for babies from 5kg (11lb). Babies as tiny as this are sometimes not even old enough to hold up their heads, so the task of providing them with suitable buoyancy is a major challenge! The new aid is shorter than the old one, which was too long and hindered the infant when he was sitting. On the debit side, the collar is necessarily large, and therefore unpopular with mobile babies.

Being safety conscious

A large slice of the statute books is taken up with safety nowadays, and so we have seat-belt laws, speed limits, fire regulations, laws pertaining to the transport of passengers, and so on and so forth. In most countries there are also laws which insist on seafarers protecting themselves with lifejackets, flares, etc. We Brits feel a burden of concern over safety and accordingly we equip ourselves in any case. In fact, we are actually more safety conscious than the citizens of more over-regulated nations.

Being safety conscious is all very well, but it is possible for our concerns and precautions to overshadow all the fun; I would like to set the matter in perspective. The risk of a child drowning as a result of a boating accident is very slight. The risk of his drowning at the beach or in fresh water is considerably higher, and the statistics relating to traffic accidents and accidents in the home are quite upsetting. In this chapter I have been obliged to go looking for trouble, but taken by and large sailing is really very safe. Does this information make you want to relax your guard? No, I didn't think it would...

Some cruising philosophy

It seems to me that something may have gone slightly awry with Western thinking. We have reached a state where if something goes wrong, if somebody drowns, somebody *must* be to blame; there is no such thing anymore as simple bad luck, or the hand of fate.

I am hardly in a position to criticise, caught up as I am in the same ideology, but I wonder whether we might not be carrying this thing too far. By way of contrast I have given the examples of Helmut and Carla Koch, aboard their Wharram cat, and Jean-Paul and Shelagh who are (hopefully) still bumming around the world in *Papillon*, but there is another French live-aboard to whom I have made only passing reference. This man lost his son overboard, yet continues to cruise. He was, like Helmut Koch, a true son of the sea: a fisherman on the Grand Banks at the age of 13, and after that the captain of a trawler and then an oil tanker. He could not give up the sea just because it had stolen his child, but, more to the point, the accident did not consume him with guilt or cause him to become suddenly safety conscious. He carried on cruising – he is still cruising 25 years on – and his eldest surviving son is as gung-ho and carefree as any French sailor could be; there were no safety nets or harnesses for him in his youth, and nor are any such precautions taken on behalf of his little brother. This utterly charming, ever-smiling, completely fearless eight-year-old has sailed some of the roughest seas in the world, rounded Cape Horn twice and crossed the Atlantic via Tristan da Cunha, and all without the merest whiff of a safety precaution. Despite the fact that he cannot swim, his father sees no reason to encumber the child with a lifejacket, either at sea or while he plays in the dinghy.

'Some people never learn,' you may say. Perhaps. Or perhaps this French *matelot* knows the value of a life lived without fetters, as well as the possible price to be paid. From what I have seen, I am firmly convinced that children raised without 'safety nets' grow up fitter, in psychological terms. Those who do grow up...

But those of us who lack the courage and confidence to raise our kids with enough rope to hang themselves must play by the rules. Most sailors, and surely anyone who has taken the trouble to read this far, will agree that each member of the crew needs a lifejacket for emergency use. Whether your child actually wears a lifejacket in the normal course of events will depend on your own personal ideas about safety. As you will have gathered, I do not consider a lifejacket to be an adequate safety device for a non-swimming child.

Without wishing to be too much of a killjoy, I should also like to point out that while the seafaring child should be taught to swim at the earliest possible age, the ability to doggy-paddle across the width of a swimming pool is almost irrelevant in a seaway. Indeed, a child's increasing competence and confidence in the pool or at the beach can promote a false sense of security. Only this morning I received new evidence of this fact when Roxanne (six), on being told not to climb on the pulpit, said 'I don't care if I fall in. I can swim, now.' She can swim about 50ft.

Even a proficient swimmer may be at risk. At the age of nine, Caesar was completely water-safe – or so I thought, until the day that he jumped into the marina, not realising quite how cold the water was. He broke the surface with his face the very picture of panic; he could only gasp, slapping his hands on the water and generally behaving in the manner of someone who is drowning. Shock had paralysed his swimming ability. Fortunately I had

only to lean over and haul the child out – but after this lesson the kids were back to wearing their buoyancy aids in the dinghy.

Child overboard

If you intend to rely on a lifejacket for your child's safety while you are at sea then, for goodness sake, please practise your man-overboard drill. Children *do* fall overboard. It does not happen often, but it does happen.

Sailing in company with two other vessels, the South African yacht *Assylum* left Sao Vicente (Cape Verde) for the Caribbean. Her crew consisted of a young couple with a little girl of about two, and the child's parents had very sensibly taken the precaution of putting a net around the deck. While the yacht was in mid-ocean, however, in spite of the net, the little girl somehow ended up in the sea.

Two-year-olds do not bob about, waving their arms and yelling for help, but fortunately the little girl's mother was on deck and saw her child go over. She jumped straight after her. Well, what else could she have done? The father was down below, but by an incredible stroke of luck happened to be awake. He heard his wife's shouts, affected a successful rescue, and everybody lived to tell the tale.

I do not know whether the girl in this story was wearing a lifejacket. A child wearing a lifejacket would be at a considerable advantage, that much is certainly true, but even a lifejacket is no guarantee of survival. When your child goes overboard, whether in his 100N aid or in a magically inflating 150N jacket, will you really feel able to leave him lying in your wake, alone and terrified? Perhaps you should. Together, you and the skipper can

● South Atlantic Ocean: force 6–7, swells 3m, water temperature 10°C, boat speed 8 knots. Of what use would a lifejacket be to a child who went overboard in these condition? Safety lies in remaining secured to the vessel.

seen again. In fact, I know a story about a nine year old... but you don't want to hear it.

Watching the waves roll by our boat as she surges along on the back of the trades, I am always acutely aware that anybody who goes over the side has probably left us for good. Even if we manage to find them again, they will surely have been smothered in spray and choked by the tumbling waves; I believe that a life-jacket sprayhood is at least as important in this sort of situation as the lifejacket itself. So far as I am aware, nobody makes sprayhoods to fit children's lifejackets.

Even if you manage to get back to your child overboard before he is swamped, you still have to get him on deck. Many yachtsmen close their mind to this part of the problem yet, reading accounts of both real and simulated MOB drills, it would seem that this is where your troubles *really* begin. Adults who have been in the water for only a few minutes might be able to help themselves in this way (depending on their level of fitness), but a small, shocked child must be considered wholly unable. You *have to have* some means of getting him back aboard.

An American symposium exploring different methods of MOB recovery by conducting 20 rescues of 'unconscious victims' made the discovery that it was pretty much impossible to rescue the victim without putting another able-bodied person into the water.

One of the best ways of helping a child who has gone overboard might be with a rubber dinghy. Ocean-cruising yotties generally carry the dinghy inflated, or half-inflated, on deck. I do not know of

probably spin the boat around more quickly. But can you abandon your child, knowing that the next wave might swamp him, lifejacket or no lifejacket?

For the sake of people intending to sail offshore, it should also be pointed out that rescuing a person or object from sheltered waters is an absolute doddle when compared to the challenge of recovering someone lost overboard at sea. Retrieving a fender from the Solent aboard a nippy 24ft fin-keeler, is a very different matter from recovering someone who has fallen into 3m swells and white-caps from the deck of a high-sided, semi-long-keeled 40-footer. In these average trade-wind conditions, a person can go overboard, disappear behind a wave and never be any specific instance where an MOB was rescued through the use of a half-inflated dinghy, but I believe the method would work if the sea were not impossibly rough. It would surely be safer to do this than to place a second person at risk in the water, and that would seem to be the only other option.

With a wet-suited, lifejacket-wearing assistant in the water, the American symposium found that recoveries could be completed in a matter of ten minutes using a lifting device. The researchers did not think much of triangular mesh lifting devices, with one side attached to the guard rail and the apex tied to a halyard but Lifesling-type devices came in for plenty of praise.

The Lifesling is essentially a cross between a lifebuoy and a padded halter, but unlike other lifebuoys it is not deployed in the immediate event of a man overboard. It is thrown only after the victim has been found, and it remains attached to the boat on a 150ft length of floating line. It can be difficult to get your casualty right alongside the boat, but with a Lifesling aboard the skipper has only to get within 20 or 30ft. He then tosses out the sling and tows it in a circle around his man. Once the victim has got hold of the sling, the boat's way is stopped, he is pulled alongside, and a halyard or (better still) a dedicated hoisting tackle is attached to the halter.

The American testers rated Lifesling-type devices 'the best single piece of gear for crew overboard rescues', but plainly the odds of a small, panic-stricken, half-drowned, chilled-to-the-bone child catching onto the idea and onto the sling itself are not good. ONE MORE REASON FOR KEEPING HIM FASTENED TO THE BOAT!

A matter of style

Most children, having reached a certain age and discovered the difficulty of walking on water, accept the need for a lifejacket of some sort. Unfortunately, this does not necessarily mean that they will accept *your* choice. Once they were old enough, I never had any trouble persuading my lot to wear the gear I thrust at them, but I can remember my nephew objecting strongly to his perfectly nice, well-fitting, waistcoat-style jacket. He much preferred to borrow his cousin's tatty old over-the-head job. A little madam of our acquaintance objected strongly to having to wear her snazzy pink jacket but was, apparently, quite happy to drown in an over-sized red and yellow stripey number of an identical style.

Pandering to this trait, certain manufacturers produce lifejackets covered in fish or cavorting teddy bears. There is nothing wrong with this, provided that the predominant colour of the jacket is still bright and highly visible, but be careful not to allow infant whim to dictate the *type* of jacket. To select for your child a polyethylene 100N lifejacket purely on the basis that it was covered in cute purple penguins would be daft, to say the least, if what he really needed in order to be safe was an air-foam 150N jacket.

A child cannot possibly comprehend what is at stake here, and it is therefore irresponsible to allow him a say in the matter. The choice of equipment on which his life may one day depend lies properly with the child's parents.

2
Ship Shape

**Seaworthiness ● Safety and comfort
● Below decks ● Toddler proofing ● Sailing with friends ●**

Keeping our children aboard or, at the very least, afloat is only one aspect of providing for their wellbeing while we sail. Fundamental to safety at sea is the design and condition of the boat itself.

In my reckless youth I used to sail happily aboard any craft which offered a free berth, seldom questioning the competence of the skipper and never giving so much as a thought to the seaworthiness of the vessel to which I entrusted my life. Aside from my father's boats, I do not believe that any of the boats that I sailed in those days carried much in the way of safety gear.

Caught in rolling combers one time, in the western entrance to the Solent, I realised, for the first time, that the boat in which I sailed did not have a self-draining cockpit. The white-fanged waves which leapt aboard drained directly into the bilge. There were no flares and there was no radio; my companion was a staunch traditionalist and until this moment had regarded such things with scorn. Our little ship was being carried relentlessly towards the shoals and when she struck the end would be swift; she would be pounded to pieces.

This was possibly the first time that it occurred to me that you could get yourself into serious difficulty messing about in boats; however, we survived – the combers were soon passed – and within a fortnight I was out there again, negotiating the Chenal du Four in fog, in a mouldering, prehistoric gaffer whose skipper had already twice before been rescued by the RNLI. The young seldom give much thought to their mortality. Life is for living, and to the maximum.

In view of the unconventional way in which my kids have been raised, my friends and family are to be forgiven for imagining that such is still my philosophy – but it is not. Motherhood changes us; it slows us down and it ties our hands. All of a sudden, I am responsible for other skins besides my own, am entrusted with the care and keeping of others too feeble to help themselves. The days of pumping our way across the channel are over, for nothing but the best will do for my children.

Throughout our adventures, safety and seaworthiness have been a primary consideration. Were it not for that fact, there are certain dramas which we might not have survived.

Seaworthiness

When your home is a floating one and your stomping ground is an ocean there is plenty of scope for fluster. Aboard a yacht whose crew have no desire to venture beyond the sight of land the level of safety required will be lower, but still its foundation will be the same: seaworthiness.

Seaworthiness is a boat's fitness for the sea conditions she must face, or might *conceivably face*, and it is upon this criterion that the sailor's ultimate safety depends. No amount of flares and life-jackets will take the place of a seaworthy design and construction, and so it is with this consideration that we must begin our discussion of safe sailing with kids.

Children can affect the structural integrity of a vessel.

All sorts of things may contribute to or detract from a vessel's seaworthiness. Boats can be built of many different materials, and in terms of safety there is little to be said for one material over another. Fibreglass, wood, aluminium, and steel all have their pros and cons. (Ferro-cement yachts tend to be rather fragile and their only merit is their relatively low cost.)

When assessing the seaworthiness of a yacht you need to consider not only the type of materials used in her construction but, more importantly, their present state and the quality of workmanship employed in the building. A boat, like anything else, can be badly or well built. The fact of its having been professionally built is not, in my experience, a firm indication of quality.

Few new parents are aware of it but the presence of young children can also affect the structural integrity of your boat. This health warning ought really to be stamped on the main beam and published by the RYA in their newsletter. Well, admittedly children do not tend to make a direct assault on the vessel – although I have heard of a toddler who, acting on his older brother's instructions, got his hands on a brace and bit and tried scuppering the yacht on which his family were guests. What I had in mind, however, was the less direct effect which children can have on the health of a boat. Because the satisfaction of their needs fills almost every moment of the day, the parents of young children will find little time in which to meet the maintenance needs of their yacht, and its seaworthiness can easily be compromised as a result. Never is this truer than in the case of a wooden boat.

I love wooden boats. There is nothing to equal the mellow friendly feel of an old cabin whose varnished mahogany bulkheads glow as richly as velvet in the light spread by an oil lamp. But wooden boats require a tremendous amount of tender love and care. My parents used to own a wooden yacht – but not when I was tiny. Nick's family owned a wooden yacht – but they owned it in partnership with another family, so that there were several pairs of hands to share the annual chore of varnishing and painting.

Wooden boats need even more attention in the tropics. Varnish degrades very quickly in strong sunlight and wood shrinks in hot dry weather. Erling Tambs owned a wooden boat and perhaps, were it not for his little boy, he might have found the time to caulk her seams. As it was he nearly lost the boat, and the boy, on a day sail between two Polynesian islands. Her seams opened up and the water came in faster than he could pump it out.

Steel also requires regular maintenance. Fibreglass takes care of itself to a much greater degree and is therefore the ideal material for a family bogged down by nappies and nap times.

As the children get older they spend less time under your feet and are also far more amenable to spending winter weekends in the damp, chill often somewhat smelly cabin of a boat up on the hard, so that ownership of a wooden antique becomes possible again. In fact, once they are in their teens the kids can help; Nick and I both have vivid memories of being put to good use with a scraper.

The forgotten factor

Read this before you cross Biscay with your kids. If you mean to venture offshore there is another aspect to seaworthiness, one which is very often overlooked. In storm conditions, the design of a yacht's hull and the shape of her keel are absolutely crucial to her ability to survive.

Seaworthiness: The Forgotten Factor is a remarkable book by Tony Marchaj, a naval architect, one-time Finn national champion and an aerodynamic research scientist. In the course of more than 300 pages of complex theory, explanatory diagrams and case histories, Marchaj seeks to draw the attention of the yachting world to a fact which ought to be startling: modern yacht designs are not seaworthy. That at any rate, is the learned gentleman's finding, and looking at the facts which he presents, and bearing in mind certain well-publicised yachting disasters, you are obliged to admit that he has a point.

Design seaworthiness is not, essentially, a matter of opinion. Seaworthiness is defined by the way a boat copes in unfavourable conditions. A boat which can be pushed over to an angle which her crew find alarming is not necessarily an unseaworthy one. On the contrary, I know of one old girl, *Voortrekker*, who goes over on her ear and drags her rail in the water in the merest breeze, but it would take more than wind alone to heel the boat any further. *Voortrekker* was built in the 1950s as a racing yacht and she has sailed in the BOC singlehanded race around the world. In contrast to this old lady, modern racing yachts built to run the same route are far less inclined to heel, but when they do go over they are much more likely to go all the way.

The point at which a yacht over-balances and topples upside down is the foremost criterion of her stormy-seaworthiness; coupled with this is her tendency either to spring back up again or else to remain inverted.

Until recent years the idea that a yacht might actually stay sitting on her back was unthinkable; yachts either bobbed back up or else, if their ballast fell out, they sank. Then, in 1996, Tony Bullimore capsized his yacht in the Southern Ocean and all over the world people saw his vessel's upturned hull on their televisions. Tony's keel fell off; that is why his boat stayed upside down. More remarkable, to sailors who watched the news coverage, were the pictures of another similar yacht which was also floating up-tails-all, *but with its keel still attached*. This boat capsized – and stayed capsized!

But none of this was at all surprising to my husband, Nick. Nick had already cap-sized a 43ft Beneteau whilst crossing Biscay. Although less radical in its design than the high-powered machines which turned turtle in the Southern Ocean, this boat shared with them certain design char-acteristics, and it too remained inverted for some time.

Just a few years after Nick's mis-adventure, another Beneteau capsized very close to the spot where he had come to grief, and on this occasion there was loss of life. In the inquest that followed, it was found that the yacht in question was, by its design, 'not fit to cross Biscay'. And 'Amen to that,' said Nick.

Maamari also capsized. We capsized her in the South Atlantic. Did it twice, in fact, and with Caesar and Xoë aboard. It was not a fun experience and I hope that I never have to go through anything of the sort again, but if I do, may it be aboard a boat whose ballast ratio and stability curves are the same as *Maamari*'s; she did not remain upside down for even one sec-ond but she *sprang* back up to the surface.

Spot the difference: racers v cruisers

What, then, is the fundamental difference between a 43ft ketch designed by Bruce Robert's and a 43ft Beneteau? If you already know the answer, if you know about keel configurations and can tell the difference between a cruiser-racer and a genuine cruising yacht, please skip what follows. Equally, if you intend sailing only in relatively sheltered coastal waters, a knowledge of the features which contribute to ultimate stability will be largely academ-ic. This little diversion from the main theme is for the benefit of worried mums who need to know a sure, steady, staid sailing boat from a fast, flighty, fun machine.

Back to basics: form stability

Boats handle in different ways according to their different underwater shapes, for example, deep, narrow hulls tend to heel very readily, beamy ones less so. To phrase the matter in the proper technical terms, different hull shapes engender different degrees of *form stability*.

Catamarans depend exclusively on form stability, but this alone is not enough to keep a monohulled sailing yacht upright. When the wind pushes on her sails, a monohull heels. Waves may also threaten to tip her over. In order to counteract these forces a monohull needs ballast.

Ballast can take many forms. When the crew of a dinghy sit her out, they are serving as ballast. Racing yachtsmen sometimes perch in a row on the weather rail in an effort to limit their vessel's angle of heel, but a yacht cannot be considered seaworthy unless she is able to cope with and counteract heeling forces through her own design merits and her own structure.

Modern racing yachtsmen sometimes use water for ballast, pumping it to and fro across the boat according to their point of sailing. Iron and lead are the materials more commonly used. Loose ballast is generally considered to be a safety risk – if it gets loose, stability can be seriously compromised – and the modern cruising yacht carries her ballast hanging beneath the boat in the form of a keel. Ideally, the keel should be integral with the hull (ie in the case of a GRP yacht, inside the same moulding) but it often consists of a shaped lump of metal which is through-bolted to the keelson.

Keels

A keel actually serves two purposes. Like the centreboard in a sailing dinghy, it is an underwater wing, providing lift and helping the boat to go to windward. Without a keel of some sort, a sailing boat cannot go to windward.

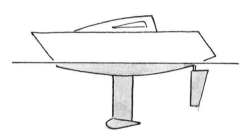

FIN KEEL
Speed and weatherliness but at a cost
of ocean-worthiness.

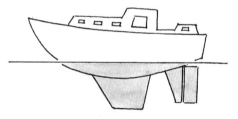

SEMI-LONG KEEL
Cruising choice. A compromise
between fin and long keels.

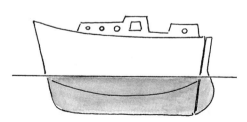

TRADITIONAL LONG KEEL
Ultimate ocean-worthiness but at a cost
of speed and weatherliness.

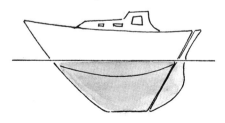

CLASSIC
Traditional compromise between
speed and seaworthiness.

The most efficient sort of keel is aero-foil shaped, exactly like an aircraft's wing. Most aircraft are motor driven; for the best analogy with a sailing boat we need to look at gliders. Whereas motor-driven aeroplanes have dumpy wings, a glider's wings are long and thin (they have a *high aspect ratio*, to use the technical jargon) because this provides more lift. By the same token, a sailing boat will be lifted to windward more readily if her keel is deep (the equivalent of a long wing) and short (the equivalent of a narrow wing).

As we have seen, the keel also functions as a counterweight, opposing heeling forces. The deeper the keel and the further the ballast can be placed from the hull, the less weight will be needed to keep the boat upright. This is a simple matter of leverage.

From this it might be inferred that a deep (draught) keel, short in terms of its fore and aft length, is best. It is certainly the most efficient in terms of getting the boat to go to windward. Having a lesser area, it entails less drag than a bigger keel, and it therefore also results in a faster boat. However, weatherliness and speed are only secondary considerations in the matter of seaworthiness.

A deep short keel is called a *fin keel*, and racing yachts are invariably fin-keelers. But traditional yachts have big, heavy, long keels – because experience has shown that a *long keel* works best in a big, dangerous sea.

Ultimate stability

Are you still hanging in there? Perhaps we seem to have wandered rather far from our theme of sailing safety, but bear with me for a little longer, please. One day

when you are caught out with your kids in a stormy sea you may be glad to have the reassurance of these words – provided that you have followed their logic.

The modern fin-keeler and the traditional long-keeled yacht each relies for its stability on a different ratio between form stability (derived from hull shape) and stability from ballasting. The fin-keeler tends to rely principally on form stability. Because the weight of its ballast is relatively small, the vessel is light enough to sit on, rather than in, the water. Fin-keeled yachts tend to be beamy and comparatively flat-bottomed. They are designed to plane: to climb up onto their own bow-wave and so exceed their hull speed. The hull speed of a 50ft boat is around seven knots, but a 50ft racing yacht will do 15 knots and more.

A flat-bottomed hull is not easily tipped, but once it has begun to tip, it tips with increasing readiness. Ultimately a fin-keeler, once its form stability has been overcome, will have to rely on the dollop of lead at the end of its keel. In the case of the Beneteau that Nick overturned in Biscay, the lump of lead was evidently insufficient. The boat went over, rolled by a huge wave – and it stayed over. Being beamy and having wide, flat decks, the boat had even greater form stability when it was on its back! The mast balanced the leverage effect of the keel, and it was only after the mast snapped that the weight of ballast was sufficient to roll the boat upright again. By this time the hull was half full of water – the foredeck was actually awash – and Nick reckons that if it had remained upside down for one minute longer the boat would have gone to the bottom.

At the other end of the scale, the traditional long-keeled yacht relies for its stability on a considerable weight of ballast. This boat is heavy and sits well down in the water. Surfing and planing being remote possibilities, there is no reason to give her a flat bottom. A rounded bottom makes the boat more sea-kindly; she still pitches and yaws, but in a gentle, less jerky way and she does not slam. Narrow hulls and rounded ones heel readily, but the weight carried in their keels, combined with their low centre of gravity, discourages these boats from falling further.

Taking into account all the various measurements, a naval architect can chart the stability of a given vessel in graph form, and a study of these *stability curves* makes plain the dynamic difference between the fin-keeler and a long-keeled yacht. A traditional classic such as the Folkboat, with a full, long keel, will be fighting to stay upright until the waves have turned her perhaps 170 degrees from the vertical. Even a Contessa, which has only a semi-long keel, will be trying to get back on her feet until she is almost 160 degrees from the vertical. A half-tonner, on the other hand, will be falling after the seas have pushed her to 115 degrees. For her, a knock-down (with the masthead touching the water) could very easily become a full-blown capsize and a full-scale disaster.

There are plenty of traditional long-keeled yachts cruising the world but the majority of modern cruising yachts are hybrids which aim to find a healthy compromise between storm-handling and weatherliness. There is more to seaworthiness than the ability to bounce back up from a capsize. Being able to beat off a lee shore is important too, and here a fin-keeler stands a far better chance than a classic Colin Archer. The hybrid – the *semi-long-keeled* yacht – can claw her way offshore in a gale and, as we have seen, will handle heavy weather almost as well as her thoroughbred ancestors.

Personally, I welcome the opportunity to sail in all manner of craft, and would jump at the chance to do the Fastnet in something seriously radical – with flared sides, and a spike for a keel, and with an admittedly slender hope of surviving a force ten. But when it comes to crossing the Irish Sea or the Atlantic with my children, then nothing but the most *oceanworthy* vessel will do. I know, from experience, that to be caught in a position of extreme danger, and to realise that one has jeopardised the lives of one's nearest and smallest is gut wrenching. An oceanworthy yacht minimises the likelihood of ever finding yourself in this position.

Sea-kindliness

To anyone not planning to head offshore, a vessel's storm-handling ability and her chances of surviving a knock-down probably seem rather irrelevant, but keel configuration and hull shape also encourage certain other characteristics.

The formula-one fin-keeler gives her crew a wild, wet, exciting ride, and the family saloon version provides the same sort of experience, albeit to a much milder degree. Is this what you and your children want? A long-keeled yacht will track; she will grip the water well and will be inclined to steer a steady course. A fin-keeled yacht is like a primitive aeroplane; she has no directional stability and is forever trying either to head up into wind or to bear off towards the gybe. In order to keep her on course, her helmsman is required constantly to intervene.

The difference between a fin-keeler and a long-keeled or semi-long-keeled yacht is similar to that between downhill skiing and building a snowman. Children can and do learn to hurtle downhill on skis but not, generally speaking, when they are tiny; tiny tots are happier making snowballs. Teenagers, on the other hand, often actively seek thrills and spills, so that rocking and rolling and whooshing along in a fin-keeler may be quite appropriate for this age group.

Capsize? Don't panic!

Having seemingly written off the fin-keeler and written at length about the possibility of capsizing, I feel that I should now put the matter in perspective and settle the nerves of anyone new to adventuring under sail. For a start, astonishingly few yachts do come to grief, either on the high seas or in inshore waters – and I use the word 'astonishing' with reason, for we encounter plenty of completely unseaworthy craft on our travels and I know that many more ply home waters. Statistically, sailing is really remarkably safe. Fin-keelers may be a little bit less safe and a lot less sea-kindly than a long-keeled boat, but the vast majority of fin-keelers which set out to circumnavigate the world return home in one piece.

One other thing needs pointing out: although we tend to rate the weather according to the strength of wind, *it is waves and not wind which can overturn a yacht*. I concede that a full-blown hurricane could lay a boat on its beam ends – a hurricane can hurl a 40ft cruising yacht

a hundred yards inland – but we do not get that sort of wind in the British Isles. Even the famous hurricane-force wind which hit the English south coast in 1987 and wreaked so much damage could not have turned a yacht upside down. It takes a wave to capsize a yacht, and it takes a seriously big wave at that.

Small children often quail and wail when the yacht heels, but I have found that their fears are based on what appears to them to be logic. Once it has been explained to the child that the wind *cannot* push the boat over, then he is generally perfectly happy to see the lee rail awash. In the case of a very timid child, the helmsman can demonstrate his control by luffing, or letting the sheets fly.

Just for the record (in case anybody is still feeling nervous), the wave which capsized Nick's Beneteau was so big that he could hardly find words to describe it. 'It was so wide,' he said, 'that I could not see the edges, and it was taller than a house. It was breaking all the time, all along its length, and I could see, when it was still a mile away, that it was going to wipe us out. I must have watched it for at least a minute before it hit.' Genuine *Boy's Own* stuff, and decidedly not the sort of thing ever to be encountered in the English Channel.

The bigger, the better

Size is another factor which has a strong bearing on seaworthiness and comfort. That, in any event, is my opinion, although plenty of small craft have crossed oceans and even circumnavigated the globe. Larry and Lin Pardey place their confidence in a small boat and reckon her as fit, if not fitter, than a larger vessel when it comes to riding out storms. The Pardeys are very experienced – so experienced that I hesitate to contradict their opinion – but I venture to suggest that although their 28-footer survived some atrocious weather, the famous duo would have survived in even *better* style in a bigger boat of similar design.

A small boat is flotsam in a big sea, and is far more likely to be rolled, swamped, pitch-poled and flung about than a bigger one. Commonsense insists that this is so, and modern science agrees. For example, tank tests have apparently shown that the height of a breaking wave needs to be twice the beam of the yacht to roll her over. This is an oversimplification of the situation, but if we assume that we are dealing with boats of a similar design, the smaller one can be expected to make heavier going of a rough sea and succumb to a smaller wave.

Anecdotal evidence also supports the logic of this argument. While we were cruising in the Cape Verde islands we met an Israeli family who lived aboard a 28ft GRP sloop of classic design. Youval and Iris and their two little girls had sailed from the Mediterranean all the way down to Gambia in their little boat and had adjusted reasonably well to the cramped conditions which were inevitably their lot. In fact, they had only one big problem: whenever they put to sea they got caught out in a storm.

The story of this family's journey down from the Canaries was really quite harrowing. Conditions were so bad that they had been obliged to put into port, not once but twice! By contrast, our own

journey down from the Canary Islands had been perfect. *Maamari* had romped along, borne on the trade wind. Storm conditions, and even gales, are so unusual on this stretch of coast that we were prompted to ask Youval to check in his logbook and tell us the date of his excursion. When he did – you've guessed it – we found that we had been travelling south at the same time.

There was no storm. Conditions were average for the time of year (January) – a good, steady force five to six – but the little leaping waves which had chased us along evidently looked vastly different when seen from a boat with only 18 inches of freeboard.

Youval's boat was ideally suited for the purpose for which she was built: coastal sailing. She was very seaworthy but because of her small size could not, in my view, have been considered genuinely oceanworthy.

Choose the right boat

By now it should be apparent that, while ultimate stability ought to be the concern of anyone intending to wander off into the wide blue yonder, oceanworthiness need not be the number one consideration for the family who mean to sail in home waters.

A blue-water cruising yacht is ideal for that purpose and not for many others. Certainly, if I lived and sailed on the south coast of England, I would not want to own a big, cumbersome, semi-long-keeled yacht. Between the two extremes of the racing thoroughbred and the staid, plodding, ocean carthorse there is a multitude of different breeds of boat. Even amongst fin-keelers there are radical and moderate designs, to the extent that one cannot really draw the line between moderate fin keels and shorter semi-long keels. Then there are yachts which have bilge keels, two stubby little keels which protrude from the hull, one on either side. Other yachts have a centreboard – a steel plate which can be raised or lowered with a tackle – and some have an aerofoil-shaped lifting fin keel.

The bilge-keeler and the centre-boarder are both considerably less safe than a well-designed fin-keeler in terms of their ultimate stability, but provided you do not intend crossing an ocean, and provided that the crew are content to travel at a leisurely pace and to rely on an engine to get the boat away from a lee shore, then there is nothing to be said against either. My father's yachts have all been bilge-keelers and centreboarders, and he has enjoyed hundreds of safe and happy sails on either side of the English Channel without ever finding himself compromised by their lack of ultimate stability. Sailing in home waters, you can listen to the forecast and choose whether or not to test your ship in a gale, but the ocean sailor must take whatever life throws at him, whether he likes it or not, and his boat should therefore be able to endure the very worst.

Safety and comfort

An understanding of seaworthiness is crucial to safe sailing, and safe sailing is what we are after when we are all at sea with our children, but there are other criteria which are also important when choosing a yacht which will be a suitable home from home for a youngster.

Size matters

Oceanworthiness apart, there are other rather obvious reasons for choosing a decent-sized boat for sailing with kids. The 26ft SCOD or Contessa, which makes such a cosy nest for a pair of newly-weds, will be little better than a hen-coop with the addition of love's fruit. A small baby takes up a surprisingly large amount of space, even if you are committed to keeping his paraphernalia to a minimum. Six months down the road, he needs space to move about beneath your feet, and by the time he is 18 months old he will be running and climbing.

A largish 26-footer, such as a Dauntless or a Centaur, will accommodate a toddler perfectly well for a daysail and reasonably well for a weekend cruise. The Woodbridges, a family of seven, even managed to squeeze themselves into a 24-footer. Together with my own small hoodlums and their dad, I have spent many happy weekends gunk-holing in the Solent aboard all manner of small craft, from GRP 'caravans' to slim and sleek, cramped and crowded old gaffers, but there is, as I have said, a very big difference between spending a weekend on the water and living aboard. Youval and Iris, for instance, had adapted to grovelling about in a boat which lacked standing headroom and the four of them coped remarkably well with living in each other's pockets, but it was evident, nonetheless, that their living conditions placed them under strain.

Many ocean-cruising couples have been defeated by the arrival into their lives and ships of a walking, climbing, inexhaustibly active fiend in nappied form. Russian sailor, Vitali, embarked with his wife on a leisurely turn around the world but, like so many others, the couple added to their crew along the way. Ivan, the first addition, was born while they were in America and his little brother signed on in Australia. As far as their father was concerned, one child was more than enough aboard a 26ft boat and two were 'impossible'. The family were throwing in the towel and heading for home – 'Unless,' said Vitali wistfully, 'Unless I can persuade somebody to take my boat in exchange for a much bigger one.'

Capacious cockpits and the mainsheet menace

Moving on from our scrupulous consideration of the hull itself, let's look at the features, both above and below decks, which are desirable in a boat intended for sailing with children.

Since the crew will spend most of their time afloat sitting in the cockpit, and since kids need space not just to sit but to move about, the ideal cockpit from our point of view is a big one. Big cockpits are a bad thing in terms of seaworthiness. In a rough sea, the cockpit which will hold two tons of water is a liability; the one-man pit is far safer. Regardless of this fact, *Mollymawk*'s is a two-ton cockpit. There are five of us in the crew and we consider adequate living space a major priority.

Although it is big, *Molly*'s cockpit

does not pose an undue risk for it is equipped with four large cockpit drains, one in each corner, and it empties itself in under one minute. A self-draining cockpit is absolutely essential when sailing offshore. (It is of far less importance in coastal waters, where the seas are seldom big enough to come aboard.)

A centre cockpit is a considerable boon when sailing with children, particularly if you mean to sail offshore. I used to regard centre cockpits with scorn; command-capsules, I called them; they isolate the sailor from the sea. I grew up sailing in sheltered waters and knew no fear of waves; I liked to have the water boiling past right beside me.

I have since discovered the advantage of being in some part 'isolated' from waves that sweep up from astern and would swamp an aft cockpit. A centre cockpit is also safer for the children in more direct terms. Because it is further for'ard, at a point where the vessel is wider, the centre cockpit generally has wide, protective coamings and deck space on either side, and brings with it the added advantage of an aft cabin, something which we will consider in a moment.

A yacht with an aft cockpit can be made more secure and comfortable by fitting cloth spray dodgers onto the guard rail on either side.

It is worth taking a good look at the cockpit and identifying any features which could be a liability to a small child. The most common problem is the position of the mainsheet. For maximum effectiveness, a mainsheet should lead from the after end of the boom. This position gives the greatest mechanical advantage. However, unless the boom is very long, as in the case of a gaffer, a mainsheet fastened to its outer end will dangle menacingly over the after end of the cockpit. Dangling mainsheets always look menacing to me because I have been grabbed under the chin by one, when I was innocently minding my own business, and very nearly flung overboard. And I was 18 at the time, and had 18 years' experience of booms and mainsheets. If I was fool enough to sit where I sat, within the ambit of the menace, how could a small child be expected to remember that this snug-seeming corner was a dangerous one?

Maamari's mainsheet led from the after end of her boom. When we sailed alone, Nick and I lived with the danger that this entailed, as it gave the most efficient, seamanlike means of hauling in the sail, but as soon as Caesar could toddle we (or rather I) decided that the hazard was unacceptable. The mainsheet was moved to a point midway along the boom and sheeted to a track on the cabin top, just for'ard of the companionway. Sheeting the sail from this position places strain on the boom and it is therefore important to spread the load; it should not take off from one single point. The

Children cannot be relied upon to duck instantly when somebody shouts.

● A track sited immediately in front of the companionway is a particular hazard.

amount of effort needed to bring in the sail was now very much greater, we also found it necessary to fit a winch.

There is nothing new about the idea of running the mainsheet from midway along the boom, but in many cases the mainsheet track is laid across the cockpit itself. Although not actually a threat to life, a mainsheet car crashing across the cockpit on a track is still dangerous. A track sited immediately in front of the companionway is particularly hazardous to small children. You cannot supervise the child's every coming and going from cabin to cockpit. In the midst of a gybe your attention is bound to be elsewhere, and if the youngster should happen to appear and rest his hand on the track at the very moment that the car slammed across... Well, the result would be messy, to say the least.

More important even than the position of the mainsheet is the manner in which the crew allow the boom to cross

the boat. If the boom is allowed to go flying across, the way that a racing dinghy is gybed or put about, then eventually one will lose either the mast or the kids. Or both. Whether tacking or gybing, the boom must be brought towards the centreline in a controlled manner, with the mainsheet, and then released in the same controlled, careful way when the helm has been adjusted.

When the boat is going downwind the boom should always be held back with a preventer – a system of lines or a simple rope lashing – so that, however careless the helmsman, the boat cannot gybe all standing (that is to say, of its own accord, in an uncontrolled manner). This is basic good seamanship, but many a sailor has been lost overboard or had his brains spilled when his yacht gybed all standing, and the precaution is especially important when sailing with children. Children cannot be relied upon to recognise an impending gybe or to duck instantly when someone shouts.

More strings and things

Besides the mainsheet there are other lines which can pose a threat to the safety of small children. Any flailing rope is a whip, waiting to flog the unwary. Children sitting on the foredeck should always be called aft before the boat tacks, otherwise they are likely to be struck by the jib sheets as the boat luffs. The working jib sheet, as it snatches and judders under the shifting weight of the headsail, can be dangerous to a child sitting on the leeward sidedeck.

Mooring lines under load can also pose a threat. If the weight of a biggish boat is borne by too light a line, the line will break. I have seen a heaving line break when the person to whom it was thrown, misunderstanding its purpose, made it fast. The boat was blown away from the quay, so that its weight all fell on the one piece of 'string'. This line broke with explosive force, right in the face of a six-year-old boy.

One of the greatest shipboard dangers, so far as small children are concerned, is the genoa sheet winches. Small children are mimics and having seen their parents playing with the winches they invariably want to do likewise, but every small child who goes to sea must be told, in tones clear and comprehensible, that the winches are not to be touched. Little imagination is needed to picture the result, to a small child, of uncleating the genoa sheet while it is under strain.

Self-tailing winches are a particular liability in this respect as there is no real uncleating to be done. We always take an extra turn around our self-tailing winches, for safety's sake.

Copycat under-fives indulging in pretend play are also capable of endangering other lives if they start to fiddle with the cleats on the mast. Little children tend to be restricted to the cockpit while the boat is under way, but it is not while the boat is sailing that this risk is greatest. If a child, in the course of play, accidentally uncleats the mainsail while the boat is sailing, all that happens is that the sail suddenly falls down. Embarrassing, and likely to provoke the skipper to strong language, but not a major drama. But the same little darling playing with the cleats while the boat is at anchor might very easily release the topping lift, the line

● Children love to join in and help but can do themselves a lot of harm if their play involves the running gear.

which supports the boom when the sail is lowered, and the result of this could be a nasty headache, a broken compass, concussion, or worse (depending on the size of your boom and the thing it happens to hit). The topping lift, for safety's sake, is best secured back onto the outboard end of the boom. If this is not practical, it can be rove through a strong point – a chain plate, for example – and then tied back on itself, at a point well above the child's reach.

Cleats and lines are quite irresistible to the small sailor. I have watched a four-year-old absentmindedly untie a bowline and cast the dinghy adrift. Good seamanship demands that the crew be able to cast off the jib sheets and halyards in a hurry, and so we cannot afford to secure such lines in a complicated, foolproof way, but lines whose quick and easy release are not so critical should be made off with a locking turn or extra hitches, as appropriate.

Gates and fences

A tall, stout guard rail has obvious merits. A low fence is, in my view, a liability. Others may disagree (Nick does, for one) but I find that a guard rail lower than knee-height acts only as a tripwire. And no fence at all is decidedly safer than one which is so flimsy that it threatens to collapse when the crew fall against it.

Erling Tambs sailed halfway around the world without a guard rail. He preferred to depend on a home made harness and tether for the safety of his little boy. Tony Tambs' favourite pastimes were trailing his tin bucket in the sea and pretending to fish, yet he survived. A well-designed harness with a secure tether is more reliable, as a means of keeping the child aboard, than a fence – but, as we have seen, a tall, stout fence covered in netting is a great comfort in port.

I am not in favour of guard rail gates. They may be useful if the boat is alongside, but the sudden appearance of a hole where once there was none is a real liability where small children are concerned.

Sugar scoops are another feature which many families find useful. Sugar scoops are actually a rating rule anomaly. (A boat is measured by her waterline length, whilst she is in harbour. While the boat is at anchor the sugar scoop rests just above the water, but when the boat is under way it sits on the stern wave and so adds to waterline length and to speed.) Some people find that getting the pushchair, the shopping and the kids from the dinghy to the ship is easier via a sugar scoop. Those in favour of the scoop also maintain that it will serve in time of need as a boarding platform for a man overboard, but in reality it would only be suitable for this purpose in calm or sheltered waters. Boarding at the stern is an alarming exercise in even the most moderate ocean swell, requiring careful co-ordination on the part of the casualty.

Down the hatch

So far as kids are concerned, falls aboard the boat are far more common than falls overboard. One thing which all yachts have in common is a couple of gaping 'manholes' in the deck. Some boats have more than two. Our new boat has five; five opportunities for falling 6ft.

Maamari's three hatchways used to bother me greatly when Caesar was small, and with good reason as it transpired. First he fell down the forehatch and then he fell down the aft hatch, but it is worth noting that neither occasion was his fault. The forehatch had a broken hinge at the time but was propped open so as to admit the draught, appearing safe while being anything but. As I left the child in his father's care and went below my parting words were, 'Mind he doesn't climb on the hatch.' After 12 years of training, Nick is now adept at caring for infants, but this was in the early days. Caesar had only just become mobile, and his dad had not yet got the hang of things. The baby came plummeting down into the cabin. Fortunately, he landed feet first. He was shocked rather than injured, and a cuddle soon put things to right.

I was to blame for Caesar falling down the aft hatch. The hole was covered only by a mosquito screen (which was usually removed by day) and again a child of six months could not have realised that it would not take his weight. This time he landed awkwardly and bruised his leg.

Neither Xoë nor Roxanne has ever fallen down a hatch – yet – and nor have any of my kids ever taken a tumble down the companionway, although they have sometimes come perilously close as they scamper right across the corner of its gaping mouth. There seems little to be done about the risk except be aware of it. Be reassured too: babies bounce. Adults who fall down the hatch often break a leg, but I have yet to hear of a baby who was not back on his feet within half an hour.

While the boat is under way, be careful to ensure that a tiny child cannot be toppled down the companion ladder when the boat lurches. The solution to this one is simple: keep the bottom board in place.

Below decks

The cabin of a yacht at anchor is a marvellous 'Wendy house' for a child, but if he is to remain safe and happy while the boat is bobbing about on the sea, certain criteria must be met.

Aboard *Maamari*, I planned all sorts of fittings which would convert the saloon into a baby friendly environment. There were to be grab rails here, handholds there... and all of them at a height suitable for a midget. We never got round to making any of these brilliant ideas concrete. Like mountaineers scaling a rockface, the kids managed with whatever existing fingerholds came within their grasp. Your boat may be cluttered with

nooks and crannies at knee height, or you may find that you need to fit the odd brass drawer handle or towel rail (or a teak one, if you have that sort of yacht) in a suitable place, but I would suggest that before going to any great trouble you get the kids to test the existing arrangements under sail.

The ladder

Companion ladders are often quite an obstacle for a small child, and seeing one's tot teetering at the top of the ladder while the boat is lee-rail under is quite a heart stopper. When my children were tiny I used to immobilise the ladder, in a rough sea, by placing a board (such as a locker lid) against the bottom half. Nick and I could step over the board but the kids could not.

Children of all ages should be taught to descend the ladder in the proper sea-manlike manner, facing the steps. There is almost always a 'grab' of some sort on either side of the companionway, at the top of the ladder. As adults we use these all the time, scarcely noticing what we are about. A child may also need handholds. If the steps have no back to them, he can hang on to each one in turn, but if the ladder abuts onto a locker or onto the bulkhead it may be necessary to cut slots into the frame. Of course, a certain amount of scrambling and climbing is actually no bad thing; why make life easy when, as we all know, children like nothing better than a climbing frame?

The galley

Now that we have descended into the cabin, the first and most obvious hazard is the cooker. A cooker is a potential source of danger to a child in any environment, but nowhere more so than in a small yacht at sea. Boiling a panful of soup or a stew while the boat rolls or pitches is an operation which entails a considerable risk of scalding for the cook. To a child toddling about below the level of the pans, the risk is even greater; small kids must be kept out of the way. A toddler who will not do as he is bid and stay out of the galley must be restrained in his bunk.

Even in less exciting circumstances the average yacht's cooker is a tool of the devil. It is much lower than the household cooker, well within the reach of a stagger-ing baby's inquisitive fingers, and when the child grabs hold of it, it gives; it swings away from him. Even if the cooker is not in use this is bad news for the baby. As he topples and lets go, it lunges back and clobbers him. If the kettle is on the stove, all the worse.

If the cooker is sited along the side of the hull, as is usually the case in a modern yacht, then it will certainly need to be gimballed, otherwise, when the boat is heeled, your dinner will pour out of the pan. But does the cooker necessarily have to be aligned to the side of the boat? No: it can be placed facing for'ard or facing aft, and if the boat is sufficiently big and beamy and the cooker is reasonably close to the centreline, you may find that you can do without gimbals.

The cooker aboard *Maamari* was not gimballed. It is true that when we made cookies while the boat was heeled hard over, all the dough used to end up at the lower end of the tray – but at least it stayed in the oven. Frying also presents something of a challenge if the boat is well heeled. However, I never had any trouble boiling, baking or steaming things in any kind of weather, I never had to resort to wearing oilskins for an apron; and with our new yacht, *Mollymawk*, I chose the same arrangement.

While we are on the subject of safe cooking at sea, a pressure cooker is invaluable. Aside from saving you gas and time, a pressure cooker can save your dinner from ending up on the floor. Its lid can be locked in place – the contents do not have to be placed under pressure; the valve can be left open – and if the lid is on, then no matter how rough the sea, the contents cannot escape. Even if the pan jumps off the stove, and I have heard of this happening with a gimballed cooker, your dinner will remain aboard and no one will be scalded.

How much space is there in your galley and how big is the worktop? If you will be living aboard, then you may want to consider whether there is room for your children to join in with the cooking and the washing up. For those who have no intention of making cruising their way of life, ensuring that the children cannot get at the cooker will be a greater priority than making space for them at the work-top. The stove top can often be reached by standing on a seat in the dining area. In this case, a piece of fishing net artistically arranged in pub décor style will put culinary affairs beyond the reach of the toddler without unduly obstructing air-flow or segmenting the cabin.

The allure of the knobs on the front of the cooker should not be overlooked. Little children love to twiddle knobs. One can hardly expect them to make the connection between their twiddling and the funny smell which follows, but that 'smell' is more deadly than the mightiest ocean storm. One does not often hear of a yacht exploding as a result of a gas leak, but this is because most yachtsmen take the risk very seriously. Butane gas is heavier than air and any that is 'spilt' sinks down into the bilge. A sufficient or repeated spillage will gradually and invis-ibly fill the bilge and the cabin. Our bilge aboard *Mollymawk* is bone dry, but we pump it regularly to get rid of any gas which may have accumulated.

When the children were very small, we put the cooker beyond their reach by placing a wooden door immediately in front of it. If there is no scope for fitting a door in front of your cooker, other precautions will be necessary. One idea is to install a tap in the gas pipeline right by the stove, but this only works if the crew can be disciplined to use it, turning off the gas every time they finish cooking.

Of course, gas is not the only fuel suitable for cooking. For those who can afford it, there is now a fancy diesel-burning cooker on the market, and for those who cannot, there is always paraf-fin, the old-fashioned solution. There can be little doubt that paraffin, being infinitely less volatile, is less dangerous than gas, but it is also messy and smelly and still not exceptionally safe. I once met a guy who lost his boat to a paraffin stove (it's a long story). I prefer to live with the dangers inherent in using gas. The risks are considerably reduced with a modern cooker, whose burners are equipped with flame failure devices.

Water taps and light switches

While the gas taps should be kept from the reach of children, the water tap is best placed where they can work it themselves. I have some reservations in saying this; drinking water is inevitably in short supply at sea, and if the yacht's system is fitted with an electric pump it might be all too easy for a child to drain both the tanks and the batteries by leaving the tap open. A small proviso, then: a tap which operates with the use of an automatic electric pump should, ideally, be placed beyond the reach of very small children – but there should also be a manual or pedal operated pump which the child can reach and work. I make this point ▼

specifically because we did *not* have such a pump aboard *Maamari*. At first Nick or I had to go to the children's aid each and every time either of them wanted to have a drink or wash their hands. Eventually they worked out a system whereby one stood on a stool, holding the cup under the tap, and the other operated the foot pump. Very good training for co-operative living.

The same arguments apply to light switches, but in this case the question of whether to place the switch within or out of the reach of your child will depend upon his age. Toddlers just love light switches. And 12V strip-lights are not very robust and do not like being turned on and off *ad infinitum*. On the other hand, a four-year-old will surely have outgrown his switch fetish and you and he will both be less inconvenienced if the cabin lights are within his reach.

Needless to say, all children are negligent about turning the light off when they leave the cabin. Vigilant nagging saves the ship's batteries but a young child will not understand the concept of flat batteries, and a night without the power to light him to bed is more instructive in the long run. (Choose a night when you do not need the nav lights!)

Cabins, bunks and bedtimes

A boat with an aft cabin is definitely more suited to cruising with children than any other. Whether you mean to camp aboard for the weekend or spend the foreseeable future afloat, an aft cabin is a great advantage if you will be sleeping aboard your boat.

None of the yachts that I sailed in my childhood had an aft cabin. My dad's first cabin cruiser was a 23ft bilge-keeler with a porta-potty under the V-berth in the forepeak. My sister and I shared this desirable en suite facility. My parents kipped on bunks on either side of the saloon and my elder brother took his repose on the floor between them. Looking back, I would assume that this arrangement was intended to stop us three kids from talking/bickering all night. It also meant that Susie and I could be packed off to bed earlier.

Many other families have also cruised blissfully (?) in this makeshift style. I believe that the intimacy of such living strengthens bonds but camping in this way is not everybody's cup of tea and for long-term adventures afloat a certain level of privacy becomes essential. The aft cabin is the answer to this need.

Aboard an ocean-going cruising yacht, occupation of the aft cabin is an adult privilege. The kids get possession of the forepeak. The only exception to this rule occurs at sea; at sea the forepeak is often unuseable. When our yacht is on passage, Nick and I tend to use the pilot berth, each in turn, and if the weather is rough the kids move aft into the big bed.

Children who live aboard and cruise tend to enjoy certain privileges unknown to the landlocked infant. One of these is their parents' mellow attitude towards bedtimes. Like children living in traditional societies, most cruising kids go to bed whenever they feel like it. The parents of children living in the mainstream of modern life are obliged to put them to bed at a reasonable hour, as they need to get them up again in time for school. If the bedtime ritual must be carried over to time afloat, a secluded cabin with a door is essential, for children who have been packed off to bed against their wishes can hardly be expected to fall asleep easily while within earshot of their parents' chatter.

An entirely independent aft cabin with its own entrance from the cockpit offers the ultimate in opportunities to shut the kids away, but an internal passage, leading along under the sidedeck or the cockpit coaming, provides safer access at sea. (Ideally, the aft cabin should be accessible both from the saloon, via a passage, *and* through its own separate hatchway. An aft cabin without its own hatch could become a trap in the event of a fire in the saloon.)

Aboard a smaller yacht, lacking the facility of an aft cabin, things can be a little bit tricky. Tales have been told of couples who, for the want of a separate cabin in which to place their kids, take it in turns to visit the pub while the other keeps a lonely silent vigil in the darkness of the cockpit. 'One or two rainy evenings brings home the value of a cockpit tent,' says Helen Watson, mother of two, 'And the absolute luxury of a stern cabin.' Personally, I think that what Helen really needed was to relax the rules – at least on Friday and Saturday night and during the holidays.

Oddly enough, as children get older their requirements as live-aboards or week-enders are reversed. Teenagers weekend-cruising with their parents are fine crashing out on the saloon floor or even in the cockpit. On the other hand, older children, unlike little ones, do need privacy. They

can forgo it as easily as us for a couple of days, but living aboard they need their own space. For a long-term cruise to be successful, each teenager must have his own cabin, and the more space he is afforded, the happier (and longer lasting) the cruise will be.

In anticipation of a voyage lasting many years, we gave *Mollymawk* a big forepeak and divided it in two. One half was intended for Caesar and the girls were to share the other. Already it has become clear that this is not good enough, Xoë wants her own space, and so we have had to reconsider. Under the new scheme, the twin cabins in the forepeak will be for the girls and Caesar will take over a chunk of the saloon; the chunk where the hanging locker and chart table were to have been built. Acquaintance with other cruising families with children in their teens has shown that a generous attitude towards their accommodation contributes *more than anything* towards a happy home.

Friends cruising aboard a 36ft Endeavour gave the forepeak over to their 15-year-old daughter and a double cabin to their son, aged 13. This left only one cupboard-sized single cabin – which was indeed used as a cupboard – and a cramped wheelhouse saloon. Most couples, I feel sure, would have claimed the double cabin for themselves and told junior to lump it in the single, but our friends had realised that they needed space and privacy less than the boy. They slept on the saloon sofa.

By contrast, other friends cruising with four children in a 43ft Bruce Roberts jammed the kids into the for'ard end of the boat and preserved the aft cabin for themselves. This worked well when the

Thought should be given to the effect
that a 20-degree angle of heel may have
on matters.

children were small, but as they grew
older the situation became intolerable. At
ten, the youngest child was still reasonably happy to kip in what was little more
than a cupboard, but his 12-year-old sister
resented sharing the forepeak with the
sailbags, the anchor chain and Dad's
workbench; she wanted somewhere to pin
her popstar posters. Meanwhile, at 15 and
18 the older boys were fed up with having
to share narrow bunkbeds opposite their
little brother's billet. This family had to
give up cruising because the kids simply
refused to play the game any more!

Of loos and lockers

When considering the suitability of a
particular yacht for the purpose of sailing
with small children, it would pay to take
said children along and let them loose
aboard. See for yourself what mischief
they might get up to. What effect will a 20-
degree angle of heel have? The position of
the loo, for instance, may seem perfectly
well planned, but will it still be possible to
use the thing while the boat is under way?

A toilet placed so that the user faces
for'ard or aft is a liability, even for an

adult. Whichever way the boat heels, he is
going to be falling sideways from his
throne. Naturally, a small child will have
even greater difficulties here than someone who can at least touch the ground
with his feet and so keep his balance.
There is a lot to be said for carrying a
potty aboard ship, even when the crew
seem to have outgrown its use. When
thrashing to windward or rolling home
after a good lunch one is often disinclined
to risk going below.

Besides making a gymnastic challenge
out of a visit to the bathroom, tipping the
cabin on its side also alters other features.
My kids are still finding new ways to
exploit a radical angle of heel and when
they were small they particularly enjoyed
the novelty of climbing up surfaces, such
as the cabin doors, which were normally
sheer. On one occasion this gave them
sudden access to certain items which I had
thought were safely beyond their grasp.

Finding a place to hide away dangerous
goodies, such as the first-aid kit, can be
quite challenging aboard a small boat. Most
of the lockers will not be beyond the reach
of a child; they will be behind seatbacks and
under cushions. Aboard *Maamari* we fitted
a lock onto one cupboard and put the first
aid kit inside, but there was much else on
board that could have posed a danger to
the kids.

Happily there was a simple solution
to this problem. Our lockers were fitted
with 'birdie catches'; little brass catches
with a spring and a lever (the lever being
shaped like a bird). The catch is fitted to
the inside of the door and is operated
through a fingerhole. All we had to do to
make our lockers completely childproof
was to move the catch along, away from

the hole, until it could only just be reached by the adult finger. (Incidentally, birdie catches are more secure in heavy weather than the usual brass drawbolt. We have found that the latter is occasionally shaken open.)

Toddler proofing

There are other things, besides the medicines and the thinners, which ought to be kept far from the reach of small children. Yacht designers have yet to take account of tampering toddlers in their positioning of the navigation instruments and other similarly attractive toys. The VHF, the GPS and anything else which beeps and blinks will be irresistible to a tiny tot, particularly if he is male. Mount what you can in brackets on the deckhead; aboard *Maamari* our radar, VHF and the tapeplayer were all deckhead mounted.

The ignition switch is another problem. It is often placed on or near the companion ladder at exactly the right height for a two-year-old. It is often red, too, perhaps for good reason but inevitably attracting the infant eye: 'Press me!' it yells. Sometimes the battery switch is close alongside, another big red switch, of the twisting sort this time. It might have been designed as a Toddler Activity Board.

➤ Removing, elevating or concealing the electric and electronic toys is only one aspect of toddler proofing. Top of the list are the flares and the fire extinguishers, which – naturally – are generally placed so that they fall easily to hand. ➤

Short of discovering one's infant in possession of a loaded gun, there can be few things more alarming than to find him fondling a flare. Flares, besides being a useful means of attracting attention, are deadly weapons. They have been used both in self-defence (by cruising yotties) and to commit murder. The likelihood of your child injuring himself with a flare placed readily to hand is vastly greater, I should say, than the faint possibility of your needing one at such short notice that you do not even have time to open a locker and grab it.

The EPIRB, if you carry one, is another safety feature easily open to abuse by a child. Small children are *often* responsible for activating the yacht's EPIRB (Emergency Position Indicating Radio Beacon). I know of two instances where this has occurred; two instances which I actually overheard on the VHF. The first occasion was in Emsworth marina, in the English Channel, the second occurred in English Harbour, Antigua.

The accuracy with which the emergency services can pinpoint the position of a vessel sending out radio signals is truly amazing. We were alerted to the fact that there was an EPIRB winking away in English Harbour by an impassive announcement made after the morning weather forecast: 'Could the person who has got his EPIRB switched on please turn it off.' It was not us, incidentally; it was our neighbours, whose two-year-old son had flicked the switch on the device 'yet again' (his mother's words). In this case the affair was of no consequence and even raised a chuckle, but it would have been no laughing matter if the little fellow had happened to transmit his Mayday while the yacht was in mid-Atlantic. Aside from the embarrassment (which would have been colossal) I would not be at all surprised if the parents of the guilty party had to go some way towards footing the bill for the needless diversion of ships and planes to their aid.

McMurdo, operating under the name Pains Wessex, now manufactures a 406 EPIRB (the type audible to certain satellites) which cannot be operated unless it is first removed from its bracket, a feat which would be beyond a toddler. It is good to know that there is one designer, at least, who acknowledges the presence of infants in the crew.

Hubble, bubble, toilet trouble

Small members of the crew can effect sabotage of a type which might cause their commanding officers to believe themselves to be in peril. If you are sailing along and suddenly find the cabin sole awash, do not immediately hit the panic button. First check your toilet seacocks. If the toilet bowl is below sea level, whether permanently or while the boat is heeled, then it is possible for water to continue siphoning up the inlet pipe even after the pump is no longer in motion. If you find yourself paddling down below, check the heads before you call out the cavalry. If the pan is overflowing, you have your answer – and if there is an under-five in the ship's company you have your prime suspect.

Marine toilets are such a nuisance that some people decide to manage without.

When we are in England we sometimes sail with a very dear friend whose yacht does not have a loo – or rather it does, but one is not permitted to use it. Our friend's yacht is a beautiful creature; a classic example of an Edwardian gentleman's plaything, maintained in mint condition. The loo, by contrast, is a piece of ugly plastic junk fitted by a previous, less fastidious owner, and the new skipper simply refuses to acknowledge its existence. For us The Facilities consist of a 500g margarine tub. This has to be used while squatting precariously under the low foredeck, in the chain locker – beside the offensive plastic loo.

Purists are not the only ones to disdain marine toilets. Some people prefer to use chemical porta-potties and others go for the old-fashioned, reliable bucket-and-chuckit system. I find porta-potties more disgusting and tiresome than I can say. Buckets are fine in the cockpit, provided the company is broadminded, but in the sort of weather where oilskins are necessary, a bucket in the cockpit is simply an invitation to disaster. The ocean has a malicious sense of humour. The first wave to break over the bow will hurl itself aft while you are about your business, and you *will* be caught with your trousers down; I can guarantee it. Using a bucket below decks in heavy weather is also an undertaking fraught with danger. We did not have a loo when we first launched *Mollymawk* and endured some very rough trips with a bucket our only (in)convenience. The kids had several near-disasters.

The ultimate in sea-side sanitary facilities is the long drop. No levers or stopcocks, no holes in the boat, no blocked valves, no pumping, no rinsing –

no fuss. But no fun in a rough sea either, and no use in a marina or a crowded anchorage. Like it or lump it, for all its ills and intrinsic liabilities, the marine toilet is the only fit solution to this problem and is a very necessary evil.

Sailing with friends

Discussion of other people's boats and their eccentric facilities brings us on to the subject of taking our children to sea in vessels other than our own. Now that I am responsible for three other lives I have become rather finicky. Before I embark my kids aboard a vessel, I like to have a little surreptitious sniff around.

Just as you cannot judge a book by its cover, so too you cannot assess the seaworthiness of a yacht by its appearance alone. If she is a long-keeled yacht she will be steady and sure, and if she is a fin-keeler you could be in for a lively sail, depending on the weather conditions, but you cannot tell at a glance whether the boat is sound. Paint covers a multitude of sins and, by the same token, peeling varnish does not necessarily point to rotten planking. I deliberately assume the worst and judge the vessel on the facilities available for coping with disaster. Being prepared sets the survivor apart from the apparently luckless. I am the sort of person who checks under their seat in the aircraft, to see that the lifejacket really is there, and I do the same when I go to sea. When you are prepared for the worst, you can relax and not have to worry about bad luck.

Man the pumps

Top priority when I embark my offspring in an unfamiliar yacht is a decent bilge pump. Every cabin boat should have at least one manual bilge pump. I do not set much store by electric or engine-driven pumps. In the only instance where I have ever had to pump for survival, the engine and the electrics were both awash.

If there is no bilge pump – well, if you are only pootling around in the harbour you might settle for a bucket. A bucket is an essential part of any yacht's equipment anyway, its uses ranging from wine-cooler, fish hold, baby bath, fire extinguisher and potty to baler. Even a high-capacity manual bilge pump is not infallible; bilge pumps block. Buckets are utterly reliable and no boat of any size should put to sea without at least one bucket.

I do not want to labour the point too much, but there is nothing dumber than letting the boat slowly disappear from beneath your feet simply because you did not have anything with which to bale out the ocean. Nick and I have even been known to carry along our own Gusher 25, complete with 12ft of 2in diameter hosepipe, when we found that the 40ft catamaran to which we were entrusting the lives of our little ones was not equipped with a bilge pump of any sort.

Man the boats

Again it may seem pessimistic to mention the fact, but a liferaft or dinghy is a handy thing to have around if the worst should come to pass. To set off across an ocean without a liferaft of some kind is folly. To count on luck and outside assistance when sailing inshore and amongst other yachts is perhaps just a touch irresponsible, but bearing in mind the cost of a liferaft, the inconvenience of towing a dinghy, and the space needed to carry one on deck, it is also understandable. By way of a compromise, many people carry the dinghy half-inflated on the coachroof. A half-inflated dinghy is a great deal better than nothing in an emergency. You can inflate the other half, by mouth if necessary, while clinging on.

Bring your own

If you are invited to sail with your children on an expedition of any length, a cross-Channel passage, for instance, then I think it is quite reasonable to ask what safety equipment the yacht carries, and to offer to supply any lack. A friend who crossed the Channel in our company a few years back examined our kit and then added to it by bringing along a large supply of 'space blankets'. Each to his own paranoia. (Another brought along a bottle of disinfectant, which speaks volumes for his faith in our standard of shipboard hygiene.)

When I embark my kids aboard a vessel of unknown seaworthiness my own supplies are enough to fill a small ruck-sack. I take a couple of flares, a handheld VHF (and/or a mobile phone), a torch, a chemical lightstick (which withstands the wet), a soft-wood plug, my knife, my whistle and a small first aid kit. My son carries his own kit which includes fire-lighters and a pocket saw, for fear of being wrecked Robinson Crusoe style.

Another thing which we invariably carry when we sail with others is our own lifejackets. Although he may have a couple of spare adult-sized lifejackets, it is unreasonable to expect your host skipper to provide jackets or harnesses for your children. Even if he has kids of his own, do not be satisfied by the vague assurance of 'plenty of lifejackets'. Lifejackets must fit. Men are generally not as safety-conscious as women and are apt to feel that the pile of slightly mildewy Mae Wests to be found somewhere in the fo'c-sle ('try under the storm jib; it's under that crate of beers') ought to be enough for anyone. 'After all, we aren't going to need them! Har, har!' If you are dependent on this kind of offer, find out, *before* you sail, whether any of the unclaimed lifejackets will actually fit your child.

Equally, an adult harness will not fit a small child. A good one can be adjusted to fit a ten-year-old, but a smaller child will need a special harness. A set of webbing reins will restrain a toddler but should not be relied upon to hold his weight if he goes overboard. Child-sized harnesses are a comparatively new thing. Indeed, even adult harnesses were unknown when our parents were kids. Merchant seamen of yore used to lash themselves onto their ship with a rope, and this is how Nick recalls being tethered to the boat when he was small, with a bowline around his chest. For want of a harness, you can improvise in this way. If the loop threat-ens to land around your child's ankles, add lines over the shoulders.

Do not touch

My warnings about toddler proofing also apply aboard an unfamiliar vessel. Unless there are kids in the regular crew, there will certainly be things within reach of your youngsters which would be better kept beyond them. The key which starts the engine, the log reset button and the echo sounder are all likely to be readily accessible, as is the switch panel. Many is the skipper who has been hailed by another and told that his nav lights are burning at midday. Sailors find this humiliating; it is not the same as leaving the car sidelights on. To be sailing along with the fenders still in place or the nav lights blazing is considered a demonstration of poor seamanship. If you want to be invited back for another sail, mind that your children keep their fiddling fingers away from the knobs and buttons.

Boat owners are also rather precious about what goes down the loo, and for good reason. Disassembling the sea toilet to unblock it of wads of kitchen tissue and worse is the most loathsome job. 'Don't put anything down the lavatory unless you have eaten it', is the popular maxim. See that your youngsters obey the rule.

Hidden dangers

One final word of caution about taking your children sailing on a friend's boat: they are far more likely to fall down hatches or tumble overboard while they are on unfamiliar territory.

Chloe Weiss, of *Blue Water Gipsy* fell overboard from a friend's boat. Her father, who was sitting in the cockpit, saw her go and such was his urgency to save his baby girl that he leapt up and brained himself on the boom. Somebody else had to go to the rescue.

Caesar also fell overboard while visiting friends. He was four at the time. He was accustomed to being aboard a boat with a net on the guard rail and was not used to the radically inclined sidedecks of our friend Gustavo's boat. He tripped and rolled under the lower rail – splash! Gustavo had fished the little fellow out again before I even knew of the accident. Caesar was quite unperturbed but returned home for a change of clothes. 'Mummy,' he asked me, 'How does Jesus walk on water? I can't do it.'

As we have seen, there may be dangers lurking aboard the vessel itself. There are bound to be flares and fire extinguishers, and perhaps other equally unwholesome things such as a foil pack of paracetamol, carelessly left on a shelf. Eight-year-old Nigel Weiss once fired another yachtsman's can of self-defence spray straight into his own face. The canister was cleverly disguised as a key fob, and the boy found it lying on the chart table.

Some cruising yotties carry more deadly weapons. We once paid a visit to a singlehander who lived aboard a well-appointed Jeanneau. Like all children, Caesar and Xoë welcomed the opportunity to explore this new environment, and having made a thorough tour of inspection they picked on the owner's en suite cabin and his double bed as a suitable place to play.

'Is this okay?' I asked anxiously. The children were very young at the time, and I was afraid that they might break something. 'Relax,' said our host. 'Leave them be.' Half an hour later he happened to mention, in passing, that under the pillow of the bed where my kids were playing he kept a loaded revolver.

Getting it right

Sailing is statistically very safe, but we can make it almost 'as safe as houses' by making sure that we choose a suitably seaworthy boat for our adventures afloat. Some kinds of boat are more suitable than others for family sailing but any boat can be child-proofed, making it safe both for and from the infant.

When visiting other yachts and sailing with friends you are back to square one. Take your own gear if you need to, and sit on the kids. A few hours of such fraught living are quite salutary. When you get home to your own little ship, you will appreciate just what a good job you have done of making her fit for sailing with children.

3
Baby on Board

Singlehanded sailing? ● **The safety seat** ● **Pushchairs v baby carriers** ● **Getting ashore** ● **And so to bed** ● **Bathtime** ● **Feeding habits** ● **Nappy days** ● **Babies to toddlers** ● **The mother's point of view** ● **Stories of cruising couples** ●

My first child was born in the West Indies – he was named for a hurricane which was rumbling around at the time of his conception – but despite this promising start to life's adventure, his first excursion under sail was made not on the azure, sparkling waters of the Caribbean, but on the miry inner reaches of Chichester Harbour.

Eager to introduce him to his grandparents, we flew Caesar back to England when he was but four weeks old and during our stay one of Nick's old school friends invited us to come for a spin in his Contessa. The plan was for nothing adventurous, just a little jolly. Naturally, we accepted with enthusiasm and without a pause for thought. As it turned out, however, Caesar's first sail was an educational one.

Having been born and bred to the sea, I have always taken an active part in working any boat on which I have sailed, and my first lesson on that chilly May afternoon was the demonstration of my new status; I could hardly lend a hand with the running of the ship when my arms were full of baby. I realised suddenly that I was now no more than a passenger.

The cockpit of a Contessa 26 is a small place and as we got under way I discovered, to my chagrin, that I was actually worse than useless: I was in the way. Our host kept looking at me in a manner which suggested that he thought I ought to put the baby down, and I would happily have done so and joined in the fun – except that there was nowhere to wedge the carrycot. I could not tuck it away on a bunk, because the bunks were not fitted with lee cloths. More to the point, perhaps, Caesar was the sort of baby who wakes the instant he is laid in his cot and cries piteously until his mum relents and picks him up again. So there I sat, straitjacketed into miserable uselessness by a one-month-old baby.

But the men were enjoying themselves. Being quite without need of the assistance that I was so eager to give and wholly indifferent to my ill-ease, they soon had the boat scurrying along nicely. With the tide under her and a fairly stiff breeze on the beam, she

● One hand for the ship, one hand for the baby.

slipped quickly from amongst the clutter of moored yachts and we were already well down channel when it became unpleasantly clear that my little one's nappy needed attention. I took him below.

The chart table looked like the best place to perform the operation and so I undressed the baby and laid him down on his changing mat. As I did so the skipper decided to harden up. He put the helm down, the boat answered – and the cabin, the chart table and little Caesar were suddenly tipped to an angle of what seemed like 45 degrees. I grabbed Caesar's heels and stopped him sliding all the way from the Mixon, along the Solent, and down to Old Harry.

Well, I had started, so I would finish; I had no choice, really. With my free hand I unfolded a nappy, congratulating myself on the fact that I had brought along a paper disposable and did not have to do origami with a terry square. Did I wash the baby's bottom? You must be joking. Mother and child both had to be satisfied with the bare minimum on this occasion. A quick wipe – I had spun the baby round so that the mess was no longer sliding up his back, towards his hair – and now all that was needed was the clean dry wrapper. But at this point the skipper stuck his head down the hatch and said, 'Ready about.' A statement rather than a question, but I answered it anyway: 'No, not really.' 'Ah, well. I'm sorry but we're running out of water. Lee-oh.'

In a clatter of sails and sheets the boat swung through the wind. Caesar and I were now on the windward side, so that I had to hold him onto the table while also holding myself in place. And, of course, he was head over heels again. 'Sorry about that,' the menfolk called down to me, gaily, 'But it will only be for a moment.'

Oh, help! I had just turned the baby around again and was now fumbling with the nappy fastenings. Maddening, the way they never peel off properly when one is in a hurry. I was still struggling to do them up when we reached the far side of the narrow channel and tacked again.

As for Caesar, he kept on gurgling happily throughout the whole silly rigmarole, but after it was over he announced a desire to be fed. That had to be done in the cabin, as there was nowhere comfortable enough in the cockpit, and by the time it was over we had turned for home and were picking up the mooring again. So I missed the whole adventure. Or rather, I missed the sail.

Caesar's first sail was a rude introduction to the delights of boating with baby. Perhaps it ought to have awoken us to the reality of what we were planning to do. But it didn't. With our heads firmly buried in the sand, we just went straight ahead with our live-aboard lives. Xoë was born a year and a half after her brother, and when she was three months old we set off from Antigua, sailed up through the Caribbean island chain, and crossed the Atlantic to Europe. And throughout it all I changed the nappies and was little more than a passenger aboard my own ship. But that is only half the story. While I catered to the needs of our infants, Nick had to meet those of the boat, day after day, night after night, on his own.

Singlehanded Sailing?

Sailing with a baby *is* singlehanded sailing:

Mummy and Daddy + Baby =
Only Daddy (or Mummy) to sail the boat

This is really the first and *most important* lesson to learn about sailing with babies, and before we get onto the subject of cots and nappies fit for maritime use, we should look at it in detail.

Even the textbook baby is a demanding, time-consuming creature needing constant maintenance. Ashore, one can fit in the daily chores around his schedule of feeds and nappy changes. Afloat, things are different. It is much harder to find somewhere secure to prop the baby while you cook supper – but that is just for starters.

The real problem is that aboard ship even the household chores are just something to be fitted in, when time allows, around the needs of the vessel. Often, at sea, there are things that need to be done very urgently. There are sails that suddenly need reefing, and bearings which suddenly need taking – and the squalls will not wait, or the shoals stand by, while your baby finishes his feed.

None of my children were textbook babies: the sort who sleep sweetly in their cots or sit contentedly in a high chair. My lot were non-conformists who broke all the rules of babycare as established by Dr Spock and insisted upon traditional methods. Cots and other such contrivances were out; they wanted to be in my arms, full-time. Regular feeds were fine, just so long as they were interspersed with frequent snacks. Determined not to compromise on the theory that 'baby knows best' about his own needs, I let them lay down the law. But even if I had not – even if I had conditioned my offspring to accept a schedule of four-hourly feeds and compulsory naps – I would have had my hands full. The routine would still have impinged upon time when, by rights, I should have been helping to sail the boat.

Sleep deprivation

Regardless of whether you intend spending a weekend away or are casting off for good, if the plans include overnight passage-making, a baby will very definitely cramp your style. The ideal skipper for a family cruising yacht is one who can get by on a total of four hours' sleep taken in short snatches throughout the day or night. He should, however, be able to manage on as little as two hours if necessary.

Nick is just such a man. He can sleep anywhere, at any time of the day or night, regardless of disturbances. He has even been known to fall asleep on the deserted floor of Maimi airport's departure lounge and to wake, four hours later, to find the place so crowded that people were stepping over him. He goes out like a light as soon as his head touches the pillow (or the floor) and yet one has only to tap him on the shoulder and say, 'Squall coming', and he is on his feet like a jack out of a box.

This robot-like ability is a gift from on high. Alas, I am not so blessed. On the contrary, I need my full eight-hour ration, preferably at one stretch, to be taken during the hours of darkness, please, and in a comfortable bed. I am therefore not a very good ocean sailor, for sleep is what it's all about on a long-haul passage. Slept up, you are doing fine; deprived, you are heading for stupid decisions. Ultimately, if the deprivation is sufficiently great, you will arrive at a state of temporary insanity and will suffer hallucinations. Some sailors see brick walls in front of the yacht, and these evidently encourage them to go below and kip, but other people have been known to step off into the sea, imagining themselves to be moored alongside. And all for the want of a good night's sleep.

Caesar was two years old and Xoë six months when we crossed from the Bahamas to the Azores, and throughout the 30-day passage Nick seldom got four hours sleep in one session. Essentially, his naps had to be timed to coincide with the baby's. In theory, I took the 'early watch', managing the boat from eight in the evening, when supper was finished, through till midnight. Nick and I had always split the night into two long watches and I had always taken the first shift, but whereas in the good old days I had often started at five in the afternoon and carried on until two, I now found that babycare drained me. Often, I just could not keep my eyes open for long enough to see in the new day. When my yawns grew too frequent, I had to wake the boss.

On a good day, Nick would get six or seven hours' sleep, some of it in the early hours of the night, some of it in the morning and some in the afternoon – but the good days were few. The evenings when I could not settle my toddler before nine o'clock were plenty, and Xoë invariably chose such nights to wake at 10.30 and

'Zoë's eaten the deck log.'

bawl. Added to this, Nick's morning sleep was often interrupted by the baby's need to feed. As this business takes half an hour or more, it is not compatible with keeping proper watch.

Navigational warning

The skipper's nap was also routinely disrupted by the need to ascertain our position. We were still living in the pre-electronic era aboard *Maamari,* and our existence therefore revolved around the taking of sunsights and the long-winded calculation of their meaning.

Until you have tried it, you can have no idea how difficult it is to navigate with a small child under your feet. Navigation is an art which places high demands on most of us. We have to think hard; we have to concentrate; and I find that these things are not possible if there is a toddler trying to shin up my leg. That is not all they do, either. I came on deck one morning and asked, 'How are we doing, then?' 'I don't know,' came the reply. 'Xoë's eaten the deck log.'

In the glorious past I had always done my share of the navigation and enjoyed it, but under the new regime navigation became solely Nick's preserve. Even for him, what had once been a pleasure became an exceedingly tedious chore. It takes time to calculate your position using a sextant. From start to finish, the taking and the computation of three sights and the plotting and extrapolation and calculation which follow can easily take two hours. This is normally a pleasurable pastime; it keeps us in touch with reality and entails a vague sense of our relationship with the great clock in the sky. It is also a skill, and just as musicians gain satisfaction from the playing of a tune, so navigators get pleasure out of performing their little feats of mathematical conjuring.

Push-button navigation, on the other hand, is absolutely soulless. Where is the pleasure in being told your position by a machine? Just another confounded gizmo, offering the sweet temptation of saved time and trouble, that was how I used to view satellite navigation systems. Spoilsport inventions, stealing all the fun.

Actually, I still hold to that view. But with a baby aboard, the fun was gone anyway. Having been awake all night, the last thing Nick wanted to do was spend time at the chart table, and nor were our infants willing or able to amuse themselves while I did the necessary. For those who cruise with their infants, flick-of-the-switch GPS navigation is a lifesaver. It buys the skipper another two hours of sleep.

Catnaps

Once in a while, on that passage to Europe, Nick got only two hours' sleep in 24 and on such occasions the only way to make up the shortfall was by catnapping. We had always promised ourselves that our vessel would at all times be under command, with one or other of us keeping watch, but this now proved impossible. Nick simply *had* to sleep – and I simply could not stay awake.

Catnapping is a technique employed by virtually all singlehanded sailors and by many cruising families, but it only works if the watch-keeper really can be relied upon to wake after an absolute maximum of 15 minutes. If there are ships around then catnapping is obviously out, and nor can one doze if the coast is close by. Many a singlehander has lost his boat that way. Bernard Moitissier even lost two. Plainly, too, one can only catnap if the boat is fitted with some kind of self-steering system.

Even when the yacht is on the open sea, poor visibility may make catnapping, and even the usual watch-keeping routine, unsafe. There were times, on that crossing from the Bahamas, when even five-minute lookouts were not enough. When the wind got up and the weather clamped down, rain and spray fogged the view, then we really needed to be on deck and alert all day and all night. Needless to say, that was impossible with two small infants in the crew. I could hardly have abandoned them to their own devices while I kept vigil.

On one occasion I went on deck to find a huge, grey ship looming a quarter of a mile off our stern. It had just passed us. It is possible that it had altered for us, but in reality I doubt whether the crew, snug in their lofty bridge, had even spotted our white yacht amongst the white-caps that patterned the sea.

A quarter of a mile. Less than five hundred yards. Our closest near-miss ever. And it happened while our children were aboard and, effectively, *because* they were aboard.

Look, no hands!

Various ease-of-handling devices make short-handed sailing less arduous, but none more so than a self-steering system. Less appropriate in coastal waters, a self-steering system is absolutely essential aboard an ocean-cruising yacht. However much you enjoy sailing, you do not want to be chained to the wheel for hours without end, day after day, and for a crew of two to do so while also attending to the needs of a baby is virtually impossible. (Believe me, please; I've tried it.) Self-steering leaves your hands free. You can change the baby's nappy, make bread or play with your toddler, while still keeping an eye on the yacht's heading and watching out for ships.

There are two basic types of self-steering. One contains an electronic compass which sends signals to a motor and thereby moves the wheel or tiller, keeping the boat on a steady heading. The other consists of a tiny sail, or vane, which is connected either to the main rudder or to an auxiliary. By careful alignment of the vane, the yacht can be made to steer at a set angle to the wind. A wind-operated vane system is by far the most reliable and suitable kind of self-steering for an ocean-cruising yacht, but an electronic autopilot is more useful in inshore waters, where a fickle wind might send the boat surging merrily towards the cliffs.

Although autopilots are commonplace aboard yachts cruising in home waters, a surprising number of blue-water adventurers leave home without any kind of self-steering. Lest anyone reading this book be tempted to discover the hard way just how essential it is to have something of this sort, I offer the following moral story.

The dumbest thing we have ever done

The setting: the Mediterranean Sea. The boat: a well-designed cruising ketch. And we had undertaken to deliver her from Ibiza to Gibraltar. The distance, then, a mere five or six hundred miles, but there were two little details which promised to make this easy number into a tough assignment. For one thing, this was to be a family undertaking and the family now included a new baby, Roxanne. For another, the boat did not have any self-steering.

We left Ibiza in a moderate breeze. The sun shone, the boat danced along and the crew were in grand spirits. On the second day out it was my birthday and Caesar and Xoë wrote a letter 'to the dolphins', inviting them to come to the party. Within five minutes we had an escort riding on the bow-wave, and the children, being only seven and five, were not the least surprised. Things could not have been finer. And then the wind got up.

Even before the wind got up, the new baby had been keeping her mother busy. Roxanne was nine months old and needed a lot of attention. Certainly, she could not be expected to sit and suck her toes all day, allowing Mum to take the helm. While I sailed the boat, Roxanne sailed with me, sitting on my lap or on my hip, but her endurance for such inactivity was not great. Nick therefore found himself handling the boat with only the barest minimum of assistance from me. On our first night at sea he had only managed to snatch three hours' sleep and on the second night, with the wind bowling us along and the baby wakeful and clingy, his score was even lower.

In spite of this difficulty, our third day at sea dawned happily. Bearing in mind that Nick was owed some sleep, I suggested that we ought to put into harbour for the night. Nick vetoed that idea; he preferred to press on.

Within an hour the wind returned, but this time it came from ahead and it kept on coming until we could not make up. Again I suggested putting in for the night, and this time the skipper approved the plan; there was nothing to be gained by thrashing to and fro in a gale. We bore off a point and reached in towards the coast, 12 miles distant.

As we closed the coast, the wind continued to rise. The waves were quickly becoming big and they were very disorderly. Nick, who was on the helm, was getting a thorough soaking, but the rest of us were tucked in behind the sprayhood and were having a grand sail. Eventually it dawned upon Nick that he did not know this coastline well, and he went below to study the chart and select a port of refuge. Meanwhile, I took the helm.

At first I tried to sail the boat with Roxanne perched on my hip, as I had done the previous day, but it soon became obvious that I could not manage the wheel in this sea with only one hand. Nick therefore abandoned, for a moment, his perusal of the chart and took the wheel while I got Roxanne below and fastened her

into her chair. The kids were detailed to amuse hcr – something at which they were not particularly efficient – and then I went back outside to resume my sailorly duty.

Up to this point, all was still well. Although things were becoming a little bit tricky, in an hour or two, I reasoned, we would be home and dry somewhere. Between the two of us, we could easily cope with the boat and the baby for an hour or two.

However, Nick returned from the chart table in an entirely different humour. The shore which we were approaching with such confidence did not parallel the wind, as he had believed. It was a lee shore. And we were surging towards it on the wings of a force nine. To judge from the information that Nick had gleaned from the pilot book, the lights list, and a rather inadequate, small-scale chart, none of the places ahead of us would be safe to enter in such conditions.

Well, to cut a long story short, we spent the rest of the day clawing our way back out of the hole we had so stupidly dug. The wind continued to rise and the seas became truly alarming. They were not massive, probably no more than 20ft tall, but they were short (ie the distance from crest to crest was short) and they were unbelievably steep. They rose up suddenly on our stern, or on the starboard beam, and dangled slobbering tongues of foam above our decks.

But greater than the danger of the waves was the danger brought upon us through Nick's lack of sleep. I could cook supper and check to see that we were not becoming embayed, but I also had to look after Roxanne. With the boat leaping about in a fashion to which she was wholly unaccustomed, she was safe only if she sat on my lap or in her chair, and the chair was very soon out of favour.

By nightfall we were free from the snare and faced a new decision: we could either carry on beating to and fro, aiming to hold our own until the wind eased, or else we could bear away and run down to Alicante. Alicante was round the corner, so to speak, and was 70 miles distant, but it was the nearest place for which we had a good chart. You can surely guess which option I favoured, and for once Nick was with me. We bore off.

Neither of us got much sleep that night. Roxanne was restless and woke every time I tried to relieve Nick at the helm. And because, for the want of a self-steering system, Nick could not leave the helm, I spent quite a lot of the night at the chart table. Ocean cruising has a lot to recommend it, I decided. No lee shores and no need to fix one's position every hour.

By the time we reached Alicante, at two the following afternoon, we were both so dog-tired and spaced out that we could not even work out how to go alongside the jetty. We just kicked the anchor over the bow in the middle of the marina, and waited for officialdom to come and tell us to move.

Just for the record, we recently made a two-week passage in a yacht whose self-steering system was out of order. A scant sail wardrobe made it impossible to balance the boat downwind, but despite several days of fairly heavy weather (force seven to eight, with 5-6m swells and breaking seas which regularly pooped us over the quarter) we experienced no difficulty in managing the ship efficiently. We were at all times perfectly 'slept up' and

even managed to find time to do a few sunsights and bake bread. We were doing flexible watches of approximately eight hours on, eight hours off, followed by four hours on, four hours off (with Nick generally doing the bulk of the night watch) but each of us occasionally did ten hours at the wheel. Blistered hands, from turning the wheel, and backache, from standing for so long, were the only problems which we suffered, for by now our kids are old enough to fend for themselves. The contrast between sailing with a baby and sailing with over-fives is huge.

The Law Of Sailing With Baby On Board

On the face of it, daysailing with a baby in the crew ought to be a piece of cake, for surely any salt worthy of the name can manage the boat on his own for a few hours at a time? If sleep or the lack of it is the big deal, why not stick to pottering for a couple of years?

This is not such a bad idea but, even so, things may not be all plain sailing. Daytrips with a baby or a toddler *are* comparatively easy – for the skipper, that is. For the person who does the baby-minding there is little improvement. Still, before we get onto that, let us just take one last lingering look at what is actually implied by singlehanding with the family.

On the face of it, the thing is quite simple. Here it is again, the first law of sailing with babies:

The skipper of a yacht with a baby in the crew should regard any assistance that he gets from the baby's minder as a bonus.

The skipper of a yacht with a baby in the crew should regard any assistance as a bonus.

Carve that one on the main beam, or nail a plaque above the chart table. Make sure your captain learns the rule by heart.

With the law as our guardian, we can relax. Settle down now, and give the baby his milk. Daddy will take care of things; that is his job. Our job is to take care of the crew of the future. We are sailing According To The Act. Unfortunately, however, we have overlooked the small print.

You have doubtless heard the expression 'worse things happen at sea'. Well they do; life on the ocean wave or up the muddy creek is full of little dramas. The 'argument' with the ferry; the accident with the roller-furling (which necessitated the skipper's going aloft); the time we mistook this lighthouse for that, and nearly

went onto the rocks; the night we spent on the mudbanks after someone-who-shall-remain-nameless went the wrong side of the channel marker; that awful day in the fog when we could not find the harbour entrance; the time the lower shrouds parted and the mast nearly came down... these are the bits we talk about afterwards. There is not much you can say about a nice, uneventful sail on a nice day – but how many of those have you had?

Once you have a baby, however, you start to see these happenings in a different light; they start to look positively life-threatening. And of course, they invariably prove the rule of singlehanded family sailing – your singlehander needs all the 'bonus' he can get during a crisis. What is more, crises always seem to occur at the worst possible moment.

Take the case of Helen Watson, who was on the helm of the family cruiser at the close of a daysail to Ilfracombe. Her husband, Bill, had gone for'ard to clear away the anchor. The only other crew-member was the couple's baby daughter June, who was asleep in her cot in the forepeak.

Contrary to Helen's expectation, this, the couple's first cruise with their child, had gone very well. Bill was evidently congratulating himself; he had always said that a giant lee cloth, a set of reins, and a miniature lifejacket and oilskins were the only things needed to make sailing with a toddler perfectly straight-forward. Now, at the close of the quiet adventure, he was irritatingly smug.

In response to Bill's gesticulations, his wife nudged the gear lever towards neutral, but the gear lever apparently had other ideas and would not go. At this moment

June, woken by the heavy footfalls above her head, decided to climb out over the top of her lee cloth, and with visions of her daughter landing head first on the cabin sole, Helen rushed below.

Bill, of course, was unaware of all this. He remained unaware until two small boys in a rubber dinghy came alongside and told him, very loudly, 'It's getting shallow where you're going.'

➤ This is another lesson worth pinning to the bulkhead: *for a mother, the baby will always come first*. It does not matter that the boat may be heading for disaster, and that the baby's interests would be best served by sticking to the helm. There is nothing logical here, it has to do with instinct and overriding urges. The mother is *bound* to answer her infant's cries and will always rush to his aid. ➤

Divided loyalties

When we took *Maamari* down through the canals, Roxanne was just two weeks old. As with most tiny babies, her main occupation was sleeping, but sucking came a close second. Naturally, whether she slept or woke this new little person was the focal point of my life – but now I had also to concern myself with locks. There are 198 locks between Rouen and the Mediterranean and somebody had to scale their slimy walls and handle our lines. I could have avoided this duty, but only by taking on that of manoeuvring the boat into the locks; not my forte. In any event, neither chore would have left me with my hands free to hold the baby.

Try as I might to ensure that Roxanne slept while we passed through the locks, I found that I could not always manage this

– on certain stretches the locks come thick and fast – and if the baby started to cry as I was climbing the ladder to make fast our mooring lines, it was all that I could do to keep myself moving upward. However – and here we come to the nub – once I was out of earshot, as I invariably was at the top of the bigger locks, the knowledge that the baby was crying had less power over me. Being aware of her needs I was still eager to get back to her, but this was a matter of the intellect.

It is difficult to be out of earshot of the baby on a small yacht. The skipper should therefore be aware that he can no longer rely on the mate to behave in the ordinary, rational way. She is programmed to respond to the baby. Her loyalties are divided.

But we also need to turn the equation on its head. As we have seen, sailing is *full* of little crises. If no one is available to lend the skipper a hand, a little crisis can easily become a very big one. Sometimes a mother just *has to* overrule her instinct and abandon the baby to his own devices.

The dramas referred to above were all real ones, and all but one occurred whilst sailing with children. When the roller-furling broke in mid-ocean, I had to hoist Nick aloft – and never mind the cries which came from my infants, left strapped in their chairs in the cabin. When the bolt that secured the lower shrouds snapped and the mast slumped to one side, I could hardly abandon the helm to go to the aid of the frightened one-year-old, who was sobbing and screaming hysterically in the aft cabin. In that particular instance, because she was not restrained and could climb out of her bed, the baby ended up in the cockpit in my arms! One can laugh about such things afterwards, but they are not so funny when you are not sure that there will be an afterwards.

Be prepared

Taken as a whole, sailing is a relaxing pastime. A great deal of our time on the water is spent sitting about doing nothing much. Those unscheduled dramas are evidently designed to make sure that we do not doze off altogether. However, sailing does also entail the occasional moment of pre-planned frenetic activity. It is at these moments that your single-hander will look to you, once more, for his 'bonus'.

Leaving the mooring or weighing the anchor, hoisting the sails or getting them down again, these are activities which *can* be accomplished by one person, but they are a lot easier if there is somebody else to keep the boat pointing the right way. With a little communication between the sailing department and the domestic one, these moments of activity can usually be timed to occur after the baby has been fed and put down, or while the toddler is having a snack or is otherwise engaged. With a bit of effort the captain can be trained to be considerate in this matter, but Mother Nature plays by her own rules and often deals most unkindly. For instance, you might go to sleep in a quiet anchorage only to wake at dawn and find the boat rearing up and down like a frightened horse. This is just the sort of minor crisis that can easily become a major one, and just the time when the skipper needs his mate. Naturally, it is also the time when the baby wants to be fed and the toddler wants a story.

One of the tricks of Successful And Happy Sailing With Little People is to

have a little something up your sleeve – or, at any rate, in your oilskin pocket or a convenient locker. Small treats suddenly sprung on your infant in the moment of crisis will always buy you time and distract him from the fact of your departure. Those chocolate eggs which contain a toy are ideal for slightly older children, but because they contain small pieces they are not suitable for anyone who still explores the world with his mouth. If time allowed I used to make some popcorn (a three-minute job) or knock up a snack of raisins and other bits and pieces which take an age to pick up one by one. In an emergency I resorted to my 'stocking-filler' stash and produced a matchbox car, a board book, a rattle or something else small and inexpensive and suited to the age and temperament of the child. Then I would leg it up the ladder and away, to deal with the crisis.

A new toy buys at least five minutes of rapt attention from a baby, and forgotten toys can be recycled. Small children have stunningly short memories. I used to remove from the toybox any items which had fallen from favour, and would then spring them on the child anew a few weeks later. A baby can also be fobbed off with whatever unexplored but wholesome piece of chandlery comes to hand. A small block will do nicely. Things with moving parts have the most appeal, shiny is more stimulating than matt, and brightly coloured lumps of plastic will be more attractive than the nice wooden things which please an adult. Bear these qualities in mind while gathering your ammunition.

Of course, when push comes to a hard shove and a major drama presents itself for your resolution, a Special Treat is not enough. It may win you enough time to reef down, but it will not be of much value if, for some reason, you are required to take the helm for a couple of hours. In these circumstances the baby will have to be abandoned – and it is therefore essential that you have already, in advance of the crisis, identified or created somewhere 100 per cent secure where he can be placed. Unless a mother is completely positive that her baby is physically safe, she will not be able even to *try* to ignore his screams and concentrate the least part of her mind on the task in hand.

The safety seat

This is the first and most essential item of babycare equipment aboard a yacht. It is the most obvious place to keep a baby secure from harm, and likely to be the most acceptable to the child himself. Whether you are out for a year, a week, a weekend or a few hours, this item of equipment will be utterly invaluable aboard a yacht. (It is, however, NOT something which ought to be used aboard a dinghy or any other kind of open boat; rather the reverse. Nobody should be fastened to a dinghy or open boat, which can disappear below the waves faster than seems possible.)

Kiddy car-seats, with their integral harness, might have been designed for yachting. Plastic car-seats are the best because they do not rust, and the kind which can be adjusted to various different angles is absolutely perfect. A baby who can sit will want to be upright, but it is handy to be able to recline the seat when he falls asleep, or he will lurch to and fro as the boat rolls and yaws.

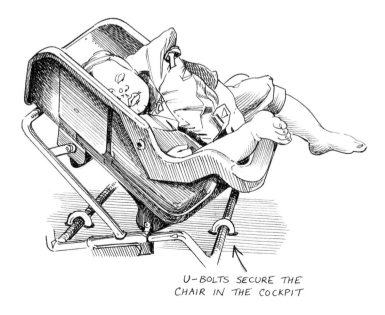

U-BOLTS SECURE THE
CHAIR IN THE COCKPIT

The most useful piece of baby care equipment aboard ship is a kiddy car-seat.

Your child will not be happy to spend more than a few minutes in his seat, however, unless you are sitting close alongside. You therefore need to find a way of fastening it securely in the centre of the action. We used to have three sets of fixing points for the baby chairs; one at the for'ard end of the cockpit (in fact, one each side in our case, as we had two chairs on the go), one in the saloon, where both chairs could be secured, face to face, behind a lee cloth, and one (one only) on the galley worktop. The saloon location was the heavy weather one – the place where I had it in mind to lash the kids if the going ever got really tough.

A car-seat is certainly an encumbrance aboard a small yacht. Even on a fairly big yacht it is something of a nuisance. We put up with carting two around the ocean for as long as we could stand it and for as long as the advantages seemed to outweigh the burdensome nature of the thing. The kids were very fond of their seats, and when Xoë was small hers doubled as a feeding chair. When the weather was hot, we stripped both the child and the chair of their coverings, which saved a great deal of washing. She could plaster herself in puréed apple to her heart's content, and chair, child and cockpit were easily sluiced down afterwards with a bucket of sea water.

Caesar was two years old at the time of our passage from Antigua over to Europe and preferred to sit in his seat than to sit anywhere else. He was steady on his feet and had learnt to play on the leeward side of the cockpit, for safety's sake, but he could find nowhere in that hard, angular pit to rest his little body. Cockpits are generally not particularly ergonomic, especially to a person who is less than 3ft tall. Caesar could not brace himself with his legs, as an adult does; his legs were not long enough to reach from one seat to the other. Only in his chair, purpose designed to a little body like his, could the child be truly comfortable.

All three of my kids agree that if they could only have their own seats now, they would be delighted. And come to think of it, I would like one too. If cockpits were equipped with comfy chairs, more women would enjoy sailing, I am sure.

Other paraphernalia

People generally seem to think that a baby requires a huge amount of auxiliary equipment, but in my experience babies do not need half the paraphernalia that retailers would have us believe to be essential. Playpens, cots, prams and highchairs are all things without which we have managed very happily aboard *Maamari*. Netting around the guard rail turns the whole boat into a mega-playpen, as already discussed. Cots and prams we will consider in a moment. A highchair would be an utter liability afloat. Yotties use a more suitable, less cluttersome item; a compact foldable chair which clips onto the table.

Eminently portable, the clip-on feeding chair can also be taken on outings to the restaurant, should you be inclined to brave such an undertaking with a tiny tot, and it also comes in handy when the toddler wants to draw or do jigsaws, but it cannot be used at sea if the boat is hard on the wind and well heeled. In such situations you will need to have the baby on your lap while you eat. And what a feat of balance and gymnastics is concealed in that innocent sounding suggestion!

Pushchairs v baby carriers

Prams, it need hardly be said, are an utter liability aboard a yacht – and who needs them, anyway? Babies much prefer to be carried, but most new parents automatically assume that a set of wheels is essential.

Some sailing families make room for a folding pushchair in the forepeak or the lazarette – the umbrella-fold variety does not take up a lot of space – but finding room for the thing is only one aspect of owning a pushchair. Try getting a pushchair *and* a baby over three other yachts and up the ladder on the side of the quay. Try keeping it dry while you row to windward and land on the sand, in the surf. And once you have got it ashore, try shoving a pushchair along a bumpy gravel track.

Nor are pushchairs particularly safe for use around a marina. If you use a pushchair on the jetties your child should NOT be strapped in. Many readers will recall the well publicised incident in which two children drowned in Brighton marina after their mother lost control of the handcart in which they were riding. The children were wearing lifejackets, but they became trapped under the cart. A freak accident, perhaps – but accidents happen, and a child strapped into a pushchair would fare equally badly if it slipped off the edge of the jetty or quay.

We tried pushchairs, and on the whole we decided that there are better means of carrying a baby; means more suited to the sailing lifestyle and which also suit the baby better. The simplest form of baby transport is a large piece of cloth. Women from different cultures and various parts of the world tie their babies onto their backs with a piece of cloth. I have come across live-aboards who wore their babies lashed onto their backs in the African style, but I have never got on very well with this method and prefer to use either a well-designed, purpose-made baby carrier or else a simple baby sling.

Xoë spent much of the first ten months of her life in a sling. She moved almost directly from the womb into its cosy confining folds. While she was still tiny I could feed her discreetly as she lay there, and when she grew older she sat on my hip, perfectly supported by the taut cloth. Weather permitting, I could even take the helm and have Xoë with me if she was in the sling.

Roxanne, however, hated the womb-like restrictiveness of the sling, nor would she ride upright on my front in a conventional baby carrier. From day one she insisted on being carried on my back in a carrier.

A sling baby carrier is useful ashore and aboard.

A well-designed baby carrier has to be tight. The baby should be lashed to his mother (or father), not allowed to dangle from her shoulders. Even a three-month-old baby is already too heavy to wear hung from your shoulders. A carrier is also far more comfortable for the wearer if the straps are well padded, but most of the baby carriers on the market are not well designed in this respect. The Rolls-Royce among soft baby carriers is the Wilkinet, recommended by both La Leche League and the National Childbirth Trust, and available by mail order. (The address is given at the end of the chapter.) The Wilkinet can be used with the baby on your back, your front and even on your hip.

I wore the 'Wilkie' aboard almost as much as I wore it ashore. I even used it while we were travelling down through the canals, carrying three-week-old Roxanne with me up some of those slimy lock-wall ladders. When it rained, I cut a slit in the back of a cheap, oversized plastic jacket, added a plastic hood for the baby, and so created an Eskimo-style oilskin for two.

Besides taking up very little space, baby carriers are far more suited to life afloat than is any wheeled contraption. Instead of struggling up a ladder with a pushchair under one arm and then subsequently climbing again with a baby on your hip, you can strap junior to your back and mount with ease. And imagine trying to push a pram up the side of a mountain. Most people, when they arrive in a new venue, want to explore. Our day-long hikes in the Cape Verde islands, our treks through the African savannah, and our strolls along miles of untouched sandy shore would have been impossible with a baby and a toddler if we had not had the sling and the carriers.

Getting ashore

While we are on the subject of getting ashore with a baby, we should consider other aspects of this matter. This task can present quite a challenge – and occasionally the challenge is best refused. I have almost lost count of the number of times that we have flipped the dinghy getting ashore. (Incidentally, when the dinghy flips, a flying pushchair will only add to your worries, whereas it is quite possible to swim with a baby strapped to your back in a 'Wilkie' or backpack.)

Even the apparently simple business of getting from the mother ship to the dinghy, or vice versa, can be quite tricky with a baby in your arms. If you are

● Getting into the dinghy is much easier with the baby on your back than in your arms.

operating alone, the dinghy must be tied both fore and aft before you climb aboard with the baby. If there are two of you around, things are much easier. A small baby is unable to support his head and should obviously be treated like cut glass, but an older one can be swung from one partner to the other by his arm. (Grip the forearm, not the wrist or hand.) This may sound like rough treatment, but the kids themselves seem to enjoy it, and we found it safer than a handle-with-care exchange, particularly in a rolly anchorage.

Ladders

Children from the age of 18 months are capable of using a boarding ladder if the anchorage is calm, but if there is any swell it is best to lift them over the rail; the stronger partner stands in the dinghy and does the heavy (arms aloft) half of the lift. Even when they were capable of doing so, we never allowed our toddlers to climb over the guard rail but habitually lifted them over, so as not to encourage the thought in their heads.

The tot who can manage the boarding ladder can also scale rusting iron rungs set into the sheer concrete wall of a quay 20ft tall, which makes shore going a lot easier. Nick and I always played safe, one or other of us ascending or descending below the child in 'catcher' position.

Ladders are actually a lot more dangerous ashore than afloat, and this is something to bear in mind while your boat is on the slip. Caesar, at 16 months, nimbly ascended a 12ft ladder up to *Maamari*'s deck while I was looking the other way. And imagine my surprise and horror when, standing in the unbuilt saloon of our new steel boat, I heard the voice of 20-month-old Roxanne outside the unglazed port. She had climbed over the fence of her playpen-prison, which stood beneath the boat, and was now balanced on the top rung of a 15ft ladder, singing a little ditty to herself!

And so to bed

Cots are another encumbrance which we found wholly unnecessary aboard *Maamari*. Before Caesar was born, Nick made him a beautiful little cot and I painted it up to look like a Noah's Ark, with animals peering from the portholes. Friends declared that it would become a family heirloom. Actually, it became a toybox; Caesar refused to sleep in it.

For almost five months we persevered with the idea of parking the baby in his own bed, although I was having to get up four or five times every night in order to nurse him back to sleep. After five months, we did the obvious thing and took the baby into our own bed.

The night that we brought Caesar into the bed with us, our lives changed forever. I slept through, for the first time in five months. Caesar did not sleep through – he nursed at least once – but it did not wake me.

The family bed is a lifestyle issue – but overseas cruising is very much about changing one's lifestyle. Weekend sailors and those cruising in home waters will be less interested in experimenting or in breaking with the well-established routines around which life ashore revolves. Still, if your crew includes a child who is fearful of the sea and uneasy in his own little cot, you may like to consider making the boat the one place where you do all share a bunk. Sailing may then come to be seen by him in a very much more positive light.

Naptime

Even if your baby shares your bunk at night, he will still need somewhere to sleep by day, and so you will still have to buy or to create some sort of shipboard cot. In the earliest days, a carrycot or a Moses basket will answer the need. Wedged tightly in place behind a lee cloth it will be secure in almost any event. So far, so good – but by the time he is four or five months old the baby will have outgrown this little cocoon. Worse, he will be beginning to pull himself up, becoming a threat to his own safety. At this stage, parents generally consider that something more secure is needed.

Some seafarers find space in their forepeak for a conventional camping cot. Strong mosquito netting placed over the top of the cot serves the dual purpose of keeping small creepy-crawlies out and the larger one in. Most of us prefer to make do with what we have, however, rather than bring specialised items of furniture aboard an already cramped and crowded ship.

Tall lee cloths are a popular solution to the problem of keeping the baby captive in his bed; popular with adults, that is. Babies do not think much of waking to find themselves trapped behind a tall wall. Recognising this problem, Muriel Weiss used a fishing net that reached right up to the deckhead to keep her young son holed up in his berth aboard *Blue Water Gipsy*.

The idea was that if he could see what was going on, then the baby would be much happier. Tough plastic mosquito netting might have been more suited to the purpose. As it was, Muriel glanced down into the cabin just in time to see her six-month-old son scrambling over the top of the net, in true assault course style.

Aboard *Maamari* we did not construct any kind of secure cot for our infants. They took their naps in an ordinary berth, fitted with a normal lee cloth. Plainly, this is a place from which a baby can readily escape – but the odds of a baby waking and going on deck, unseen, *in the hours of daylight* are fantastically remote. Surely, one or other parent is likely to be either in the cockpit or in the saloon?

It seems to me that the opportunity for a child to wake from his nap undetected and come to grief is almost impossibly remote. The odds of his injuring himself in making a determined escape from his high security prison-bunk are far higher. Recall Helen Watson, who rushed below to save her daughter, leaving husband and boat to plough on merrily towards the mud. If the baby's bunk had not been fitted with a dangerously tall lee cloth, she could have hopped out of bed and come to join her mother in the cockpit and there would have been no story to tell.

As for night-time escapes: again, it could hardly happen at sea, when there would inevitably be someone on watch (or so we very much hope) but it could occur while the yacht is in harbour. A tale was once told to me of a child who disappeared in the night, never to be seen again.

The best way to prevent such a tragedy is with an obstruction on the companion ladder, or with a door or a half-door (preferably the latter) across the entrance to the cabin where the toddler sleeps. Although our children shared the big bed, we still had such a door and we invariably used it if the boat was at anchor. The door bolted on the outside, in a position which we could reach without the least difficulty but which was completely inaccessible to the kids. Personally, I think this arrangement was far more satisfactory for all concerned than a gigantic, see-through plastic lee cloth.

A ship-shape solution: a hammock

Security only becomes relevant once the baby has become mobile. When our kids were still tiny, just like any other small fry, they needed a snug, cosy place to nap. Caesar's cot having been a dismal failure, we aimed to come up with something different for the next baby. One solution was the kiddy car-seat, and Caesar and Xoë napped in their seats on a regular basis, both in harbour and while we sailed, but we also hit upon a far better idea: the ultimate marine cot, and the obvious one. A hammock, of course!

● The MkI hammock in action.

Xoë's first hammock was a very simple affair consisting of a piece of cloth, not very much longer than her, with wooden stretchers at either end to hold it open, and net sides to stop her from being tipped out. I do not think that she could really have been tipped out, but the nets set my mind at rest. This little hammock was an incredible success, but by the time she was three months old Xoë needed something bigger, and so we created the MkII.

The MkII hammock was really quite sophisticated; a sort of cloth box, with stretchers at the bottom as well as the top, and with net sides and a net top to keep the baby aboard even if the hammock or the boat, or both, looped the loop. The MkII was intended to be a tiny bit less snug than its predecessor. It allowed wriggling room and was more airy. Once again it was a tremendous hit and Roxanne, in her turn, had a hammock identical to the prototype MkII but made of pretty, hand-woven cloth.

One benefit of the hammock is that, when not in use, it takes up very little room. Its main advantage, however, is in the way it rocks with the boat. Traditionally a hammock is slung athwartships, but we abandoned tradition and slung our babies fore and aft (length-ways down the cabin) so that they swayed to and fro as the boat rolled. We rigged the hammock on a sort of double halyard, with lines leading from the stretchers at either end and running through blocks on the deckhead. The two falls led together to one cleat on the bulkhead. The system was similar to that of using peak and throat halyards to raise a gaff sail. As the child grew, raising and lowering her became more difficult, but a stopper knot tied in the combined fall made it impossible for baby-and-all to come tumbling down all the way to the floor.

When not in use the hammock stowed on the deckhead, a couple of bungy-line gaskets holding it in place. A neater, more practical and appropriate solution to the cot problem it would be difficult to find. During our crossing from the Bahamas to the Azores we had a gale on the quarter – it hurried us along for over a week – and the motion of the boat was so violent that the stretchers on Xoë's little hammock used to bang on the deckhead at either side, thud, thud, thud, thud, yet the baby never stirred.

Alarming

One gadget worth considering if you will be sleeping aboard your yacht is an intruder alarm. An intruder alarm is no bad thing in its own right, but if there are small children in the crew it also serves the purpose of an *ex*-truder alarm. I have already mentioned the possibility of a child going over the side at night, while the boat is in harbour. If you can bear to sleep with all the hatches shut then you will not need to take special precautions, but most people find sleeping in an unventilated cabin fairly claustrophobic. Yachtsmen cruising in the tropics invariably leave all the hatches open, including the companion hatch.

The potential for disaster is there. A Belgian yachtsman whom we met in the Cape Verdes claimed to have gone on deck in the night, in answer to nature's call, and to have found his baby daughter floating face down beside the boat, 'with the air trapped in her plastic pants keeping her afloat'. She was still alive; in fact, by the time the tale was told she was eight. I took this story with a pinch of salt – it does not seem to ring true – but the point is that it *could* happen. A secure cot or a half-door on the toddler's cabin are the most obvious first line of defence and ought to be adequate, provided you are absolutely certain that your system is 100 per cent foolproof. A cheap, battery-operated motion detector buys extra peace of mind. We installed one across the companionway and in five or six years of regular use it gave us only two heart-stopping false alarms. Highly recommended for every over-anxious mum.

Bathtime

Bathing the baby is a big deal; over much of the western world women wash their babies every day. To be honest, I have never understood how anybody *could* need bathing every day, least of all somebody so small and incapable. It is true that the nappy business can be a nasty affair, and regurgitated milk also makes a stinking mess, but one can clean up these local disasters with just a cup or two of tepid water. Why insist on total immersion?

It is difficult to defy the system while one is still living within it, however, and few people even want to. Certainly, if my kids had been raised in the mainstream of society they would all have slept in cots,

● A baby bath is cumbersome. Your toddler will be just as happy to wash and play in a bucket. A miniature inflatable dinghy is another space saving option. (Think laterally: put the water in the boat.)

every night at six o'clock. But we escaped.

I am not knocking anyone who *wants* to follow the usual routines. Babies love water and if you have enough of it, by all means indulge your infant daily. All you need are a plastic bathtub, a kettle to heat the water, and a yacht with enormous water tanks. The Weiss family, aboard *Blue Water Gipsy*, managed to bathe the baby daily – but they had a watermaker which they bought specially.

My own children, when they were babies, were lucky if they got one fresh-water bath a week. However, they all used to love water, and as the fresh stuff was in short supply I would fill the tub from the sea. Caesar used to spend hours each afternoon sitting in his bath in the cock-pit, surrounded by beakers and boats and bottles.

For weekend sailing I would certainly not bother carrying a bath; they take up a lot of space. At a pinch you can wash the baby in a bucket – I have even washed mine in a mixing bowl – and a bucket will also suffice for playtime use.

been weaned long before they could toddle, and would have enjoyed a bath

Feeding habits

Feeding a baby is essentially the same at sea as it is on land, but certain considerations dictated by the sailing environment may affect a cruising mother's decision in the breast versus bottle debate.

We all know that breast is best, medically speaking. Breast milk contains exactly what the baby needs. Cow's milk contains what a little cow needs, and no matter how it may have been modified it still falls far short of being the ideal

nutrient for human infants. Informed mothers revert to using a bottle only when the use of the natural method becomes inconvenient, and so we need look at the matter only from this point of view. Which method of feeding is the most convenient aboard a yacht?

Bottle?

The principal argument in favour of the bottle is that anyone can wield it. Before they crossed the Atlantic to the Caribbean, Mike and Helga Pratt weaned their six-month-old daughter from the breast so that either one of them could feed her (*PBO* April 1988). Other yachtsmen and women have weighed up the odds and arrived at a similar decision. One couple told me that they had switched the baby onto the bottle 'in case something went wrong'. In the event of the milk suddenly drying up, or Mother disappearing into the oggin, Dad and the baby would still be able to cope.

There is obviously something to be said for the fact that either parent can meet the demands of a bottle-fed baby, but I have noticed that the thing seldom works out in practice. As Mike Pratt admits, 'Either one of us could give the feed, but Mother was definitely pre-ferred!' And if the idea is that the skipper can do the night feed, letting the mate sleep on, I'd like to know who is minding the ship in the meanwhile. You cannot feed a baby and nurse it back into oblivion in five minutes flat.

In the matter of preparing for an emergency, it is true that if his mother were to be lost overboard then the baby would need to be fed from a bottle, but surely the time to make the change is *if* that unlikely event ever occurs and not before! When sailing offshore with a breast-fed baby always carry a supply of Infant Formula and a feeding bottle; if he had to make the transition from one method to the other at short notice the baby might be exceedingly displeased, but at least he would not starve.

Losing his mother overboard is an incredibly unlikely scenario, but a shipwreck of some sort is a possibility, though still a fairly remote one. A bottle-fed baby would fare extremely badly in a liferaft. Even if there happened to be sufficient water and a supply of powdered milk, facilities for sterilising the equipment would almost certainly be lacking. By contrast, provided that his mother got enough to drink, a breast-fed baby would be in no danger either of starvation or other ill-health.

Many first-time mothers fear that their milk might suddenly dry up and give this as a reason for abandoning the breast prematurely. In the normal course of events the breast will continue to be replenished, provided that you do not get pregnant again, and provided that the baby is encouraged to suck regularly and for as long as he desires. If a woman were suffering from extreme dehydration, perhaps as a result of chronic seasickness, then the milk in her breasts would dwindle – but again, the time to worry about this is when it happens. We don't launch the liferaft just because there are rocks shown on the chart!

... or breast?

As I see it, bottle-feeding has little to recommend it afloat. Breast-feeding is far more convenient. Breast milk is available on demand in the boat, in the dinghy, at the beach or halfway up a mountain, without any kind of planning. It is always at the right temperature and is always hygienically prepared and packaged. I really do not think that I could have coped with sterilising bottles at sea.

Even under the more ideal circumstances of a well-equipped kitchen on an even keel, bottle-feeding carries with it the risk of infection and specifically of gastro-enteritis. Gastro-enteritis occurs as a result of alien bacteria entering the digestive system, and the bacteria which breed in warm milk are evidently amongst the most dangerous to an infant. Gastro-enteritis is a life-threatening condition and in mid-ocean would definitely constitute a medical emergency. Bottle-feeders venturing offshore must therefore be scrupulous about hygiene. Why make life so difficult for yourself?

One thing guaranteed to make the experience of breast-feeding unpleasant is the lack of anywhere comfortable to sit. An armchair is ideal, but most of us do not have room for an armchair in the saloon. I managed to squeeze in a folding chair. When in use it wedged tightly between the table and the bunk opposite. Back support and support for the arm which holds the baby's head are the foremost features of a comfortable nursing station. It is worth considering this requirement and identifying a suitable corner in advance, before you sail, as the difficulty becomes greater once the boat is heeled.

There are two other things to be said against breast-feeding. First, it is tiring. Secondly, some of us find that we are more prone to seasickness while breast-feeding. Caesar and Xoë were both breast-feeding when we crossed the Atlantic and this undoubtedly put me under greater strain.

If you decide to opt for the bottle you should give some thought to the supply. In home waters there will obviously be no problem, but when you go foreign you will encounter different brands. In some countries Formula is unavailable; we would not have been able to find it in West Africa, for example. Equally, powdered Formula can be hard to obtain in America as the natives all use the ready-mixed, refrigerated variety. Think hard, therefore, before you throw in the towel. It is very easy to wean a child onto the bottle and very much harder, if the man-made supply fails, to get the machinery working again. Be sure that you know what you are doing before you give up nature's gift to mothers.

Nappy days

That just leaves nappies – and by now it will come as no surprise to the reader to learn that I favour cloth ones over disposables. The production of paper nappies consumes an estimated seven million trees each year in Britain alone, and their disposal creates 800,000 tons of waste and causes further environmental grief. However convenient, disposables are, in the long run, much harder on the purse. Once again the use of this provenly sinful product comes down to the matter of

convenience. But are they more convenient than cloth aboard ship?

Even I am obliged to admit that paper nappies come into their own aboard a dayboat or weekend cruiser. Dealing with half a dozen highly odoriferous, sopping wet cloth nappies and transporting them home in a half-washed state would be beyond my organisational skills. I *always* used disposables for daytrips.

Aboard *Maamari* I almost invariably used cloth nappies, partly because they cost less, both environmentally and financially, but also because I found them to be perfectly convenient. There is nothing convenient about lugging a massive pack of paper nappies home from some distant supermarket. There is nothing convenient about finding space for 240 paper nappies (five weeks' supply) in the lockers of an average-sized cruising yacht. There is nothing convenient about running out of disposables in mid-ocean, as Muriel Weiss of *Blue Water Gipsy* did when her daughter Chloe was small. Certainly, there is nothing convenient about carrying a dustbin bag full of sewage on your aft deck – worse still if your cockpit is aft and you have no deck to leeward. Some people dispose of paper nappies at sea, but this practice is not only disgusting (paper nappies float and will therefore end up on somebody's beach somewhere), it is also illegal.

Cloth nappies, by comparison are relatively trouble-free and sanitary. After use the paper liner with its offensive load *can* be legally and legitimately dropped over the side, if you are at sea. (If you are in harbour it must not go over the side: use a sealed bag or a small bin and DO NOT TRY TO FLUSH IT DOWN THE SEA TOILET! The liner will block the pump.)

The nappy itself is simply dumped in a large bucket of 'nappy brew'. Some people stream the nappies behind the boat on a long string and let the sea wash them clean, but I was always perfectly happy with my bucket system. I found the use of Napisan and other bleach products completely unnecessary. Salt water and a dose of white vinegar works just as well (one cup of vinegar to one 20lt/5gall bucket of sea water). Salt water is much better for the purpose than fresh; nappies steeped in fresh water are inclined to ferment in tropical temperatures.

After soaking for 24 hours, the nappies are rinsed thoroughly in more salt water. Some people then hang them out to dry without more ado. The wind is supposed to shake the salt out of the cloth. In my experience, it does no such thing. In fact, if you are at sea the wind is likely to introduce more salt. I always gave the nappies a cursory fresh water rinse before I hung them up to dry.

Now I promised to discuss the difficulty of changing a nappy at 45 degrees. Not an easy number, this. The chart table is definitely not the best place. The best thing to do is lay the changing mat on the floor, fore and aft, on the leeward side. Once the baby can stand, changing nappies in a seaway is often easier with him standing on his feet. If he is still at the stage of needing to hold onto something, so much the better; he won't be able to get away!

'Pram-hoods' and biminis

Two other things are useful when sailing with babies and small children. One is a bimini or sunshade. The other is a sprayhood (a dodger, in the American language of the sea, but dodgers are something different on an English yacht).

It is said that you can tell how long a yachtsman has spent at sea by the size of his sprayhood. Certainly you can tell whether he has sailed offshore or not. In my gung-ho youth I looked with scorn on these 'pram-hoods', which shelter the sailor from the worst of the weather. If you needed a sprayhood you were soft, I reckoned. How could the helmsman feel the breeze on his face if he were hiding from it? The ignorant are ever the most outspoken.

My first ocean passage was a delivery from Chichester Harbour to Estapona in southern Spain. I was 19 at the time, and so knew everything. Within two days of leaving England, we were battling it out in a gale in Biscay. The waves were mountains and our tiny craft sat, now on a lofty summit, and now in the depths of a low valley with the peaks towering above her. Life was so wet and wild on this roller-coaster ride that at first I was scarcely aware that the sprayhood, which I had so derided, was shielding us from the worst of the wind and water. Without the sprayhood, the situation in the cockpit would have been scarcely bearable.

Even in less exciting conditions a sprayhood is a godsend. A sprayhood can convert a miserable wet ride into a lovely one. There are times even in home waters when the motion of the boat throws up sheets of cold spray, and these are just the times when most of us do not want to have to go below.

If the sun is for'ard or overhead then a sprayhood also acts as a sunshade, but as often as not the sun will not co-operate with your course and something more is needed. A bimini is essential when sailing with infants in the tropics. Sunblock, hats and sunsuits are poor alternatives.

Sunblock will not provide adequate protection for a baby for even half a day in the tropical sun, and hats are pretty hopeless things afloat. Please do not ask me how many hats I have seen blow overboard; pin a tape onto the back of your child's hat and pin the other end

● A sprayhood protects from the sun and sea and also provides the kids with a little den.

onto the collar of his t-shirt. This works better than an elastic chin-strap. Elastic under the chin is regarded with ill-favour by most small people.

If the children will be spending any length of time in the cockpit, an awning is the best answer to the skincare problem. Few yachtsmen go to the length of fitting a pukka bimini on a metal frame, because a bimini tends to get in the way of the mainsail. Aboard *Maamari* our 'bimini' was a square of lightweight canvas with an eyelet in each corner. It was lashed to various different things, at the angle dictated by the sun. When the sun was low, for instance, the shade would need setting with one edge down near the deck, made off to the lower guard rail, and the other up in the air under the boom. The mizzen shrouds and the mizzen mast itself were other convenient lashing points.

Babies to toddlers

That would seem to cover every aspect of physically caring for a baby on a boat. Sleeping, feeding, carrying, changing, bathing and sheltering have all been dealt with. But a baby also has emotional needs. Can we keep him happy on a boat? How do babies feel about spending their day, or their life, all at sea?

Most mothers agree that six weeks is the ideal age to take a baby sailing. As Helen Watson puts it: 'Strap their carrycot to a bunk and they're no trouble.' Muriel Weiss also found this age group to be problem-free. So far as she was concerned, babies were no trouble until they became mobile. Libby Purves, who is the mother of two children, feels that 'the first year is easiest and can lull you into a false sense of security.' For her, babies are 'undemanding shipmates'. I beg to differ.

My babies were all highly demanding individuals from the day that they first joined ship, and sailing in their company placed me under considerable strain. Perhaps I was a mug to give into their whims and feed and carry them all day. When I read of the ease with which other people coped with their tiny offspring, I begin to feel rather inept, but I also find myself wondering whether these folk might not be viewing the scene from afar, through the fogs of time. Perhaps they did not all keep diaries...

But it is true that the babies themselves were perfectly happy. The view from the cot, or from his kiddy car-seat, appeared to suit Caesar just fine. His physical needs were being met and that was all that mattered at this stage.

The creepy-crawly stage

When he began to become mobile, Caesar's attitude to sailing underwent a radical change. In brief, to quote from my diary: 'He hates it. He cried almost non-stop from one anchorage to the other.' As one anchorage in this case was in Antigua and the other a whole day distant, in the island of St Kitts, this was very unsatisfactory for all concerned.

Caesar's objection was not to being aboard the boat. He was used to being aboard; the boat was home. What upset him was the way his home now lurched from side to side. He could not understand why it was that the floor was inclined, and he persisted in trying to crawl up and down surfaces which were now quite beyond his scope.

Not every creeping, crawling baby reacts to sailing in this way. At seven months, Xoë saw the incline as an amusing challenge. If it threw her off her feet, she considered the matter uproariously funny. When she first began to walk, at ten months, rushing around the boat while it leapt through the waves was one of her chief delights. In the middle, between these two poles, are the babies who merely decide that caution is the watchword, and who resign themselves to spending the day in their chair, or on Mum's lap.

A child's enjoyment of sailing will naturally be affected by his physical state. Xoë never once suffered from seasickness, whereas Caesar did. On the return trip from St Kitts he threw up six times. Roxanne was also prone to seasickness and I remember having a lot of trouble with her on a rough daytrip in the Golfe du Lions when she was about eight months old. We were short-tacking into a force six and as this particular boat had no spray-hood and conditions were cold and wet, I thought that I had better take her below.

Below decks mother and child both felt queasy. When I feel queasy, I like to lie down; this saves me from further distress. Alas, the trick does not have the same effect on babies, who seem if anything to be even more inclined to puke when prone. We lay down – and Roxanne was very soon sick; all over the bunk, all over her clothes, all over my woolly jumper and even in my hair. Yuck.

Xoë's opinion of sailing was clearly demonstrated on our passage from the Bahamas to the Azores. She was six months old when we left and not quite mobile. She was perfectly happy with her lot just so long as I stayed by her side, but if I so much as put my foot on the ladder to go outside she would begin to wail and cry. At the time I assumed, somewhat vainly perhaps, that she just hated to be parted from her mother. Retrospectively, I think she was probably also eager to get outside. The weather was pretty abysmal much of the time, but on the few occasions when I bowed to pressure and took her along – one hand for the baby and one for myself – Xoë would squeal with delight. She simply adored the feel of the boat bucking wildly in the waves and she loved it when the spray broke over us. Definitely an ocean sailor in the making.

Just the same, I believe that at seven months old Xoë would actually have found life ashore more enriching. When, after a month, we reached our destination,

she at first appeared unable to see the place. It was not until we stepped ashore that the kids finally noticed the change in our environment. Xoë was in the sling for the first time in a fortnight and was about to drop off to sleep – and then a car went by. She opened her eyes and struggled to sit up. Another car went by and she followed it along the street with her eyes. Another car, and another, from opposite directions. Little Xoë's head spun to and fro and her eyes fairly bulged.

When we reached the cafe, and our destination, Xoë discovered other people. She was so pleased and amazed that all she could do was laugh. For the past month – for as long as she could remember – the world had consisted of the four of us on a tiny island in the endless sea. She had been perfectly content – but this was something else!

When we left the Azores, after a fortnight's stay, Caesar slipped easily into the old routine but Xoë, although she could not voice her complaint in words, made her disapproval abundantly clear. She was very clingy and hard to please. And when we next reached terra firma, in Portugal, the child went berserk. She could not sleep – a calming stroll around the marina only increased her excitement – and it was two in the morning before she could even be persuaded to lie down. This from a child who had never before given us a disturbed night!

I am pleased to say that in the ensuing months Xoë got the hang of the cruising life, but it would seem that her reaction to making port after a long passage was not untypical among babies of this age. Arriving in Antigua after crossing from the Canary Islands, seven-month-old Susie

Pratt 'freaked', to use her father's word. 'She was totally over-stimulated, laughing and giggling at everyone and everything, and she could hardly sleep at all that night.' Babies of this age are generally happy wherever they find themselves, but they certainly appear to like shore life better than the cruising world.

Up and running

According to accepted wisdom, toddlers are a liability on a boat. 'Very tricky,' says Libby Purves, and she suggests that one way around the problem is to sail by night. Helen Watson tried this. She and her husband, Bill, decided to sail from Dartmouth to Guernsey during the hours of darkness when the children would be asleep and out of the way. The passage was evidently uneventful, although Helen writes that she treasures the memory of their damp and dark entrance to St Peter Port, 'with Bill, holding a torch between his teeth, turning the sodden pages of the pilot book and helming'. Helen was below, feeding the baby, of course. The crisis occurred the following day. 'The children, fresh from a good night's sleep, wanted breakfast followed by a run ashore.' Their parents wanted only to sleep. Night sailing only works with kids if one parent has a good nights sleep.

Muriel Weiss, aboard *Blue Water Gipsy*, also found toddlers to be more of a handful afloat than small babies. She had four in succession to practise on, so her opinion is worth heeding. Mike and Helga Pratt decided to confine themselves to making passages of two or three days only, when their daughter reached the toddling stage.

In the face of so much negativity, and in view of the difficulties that I found in catering for a baby at sea, I regarded our future with some trepidation – but as it turned out I actually found sailing with a toddler to be pretty straightforward. By and large, the toddlers seemed to like it too.

When the going gets tough, a toddler is in the way, but provided that things are going well his parents may even have time on their hands and he can benefit from the extra attention which they are then able to give. As Muriel Weiss said of her youngsters: 'They've got me on tap while we're sailing, and they love it.' The problems begin when Mummy and Daddy want to relax and do nothing. If you are doing 'nothing' with a novel or the sight reduction tables in your hand, then your attention is up for grabs so far as the toddler is concerned. You need to adjust to this idea and kiss goodbye to the mere notion of relaxing at sea.

Another thing which people who sail with toddlers complain about is the loss of their evenings. 'The first marina to offer a child-minding service will never want for trade,' says Helen Watson. Well, I hate to seem argumentative, but we never had much trouble with this one. When we want to go ashore for the evening, we go *en famille*. It is true that dining out with under-fives is not even half so nice as dining out without them... but normal service will be resumed in a few years time.

Long-haul passages with a toddler

Daysailing with a toddler is a very different thing from passage-making, and the toddler who entertains himself happily on a day's excursion might take a dim view of going offshore. This lesson was brought home to us very clearly when we set off to journey from Anguilla to the Turks and Caicos. The distance between these Caribbean islands is about 700 miles, or seven days.

Up until now, all the sailing that Caesar knew or remembered was in the form of day-long excursions. He appeared to have taken to sailing like the proverbial duck and he would often play make-believe sailing games in harbour. Since he had adapted so easily to life on the ocean wave, we anticipated no trouble on the little run from Anguilla northwards. The child was used to sleeping on the boat; he was not troubled any more by the motion; he entertained himself with little input from me; what difficulty could there possibly be in extending the daysail to a week-long expedition?

Beaches. In a word, they were the difficulty. Caesar had grown up accustomed to spending his afternoons playing on the beach. He did not resent the odd afternoon afloat, but once the novelty of sailing had worn off he wanted to get back to his old familiar pursuits. Had we been more sensitive, Nick and I might have caught a whiff of the impending mutiny before we set sail. There are some nice beaches in Anguilla. We had spent the previous few days anchored off one of them – a lovely, pristine strip on an off-lying island – and Caesar had fallen in love with it and made it his very own. When he realised that we were tearing him away from his little heaven, our bright and cheerful boy became sad and sulky.

To add insult to injury, on the second day out Caesar was seasick and for the next 24 hours he could keep nothing down. Even after he was fully recovered his opinion of our adventure remained low. 'Caesar not like sailing,' he announced listlessly on the third day. 'He is a pain in the butt,' I wrote unsympathetically in my diary. 'He whines all day and has to be amused – insofar as it is possible to amuse him – for every waking moment. What a contrast he is to his usual self!'

When, after seven days, we finally sighted Grand Turk, Caesar refused to even look at it. As we sailed along its shore he continued to whine and sulk, and it was only when we reached the anchorage and rounded up to drop the hook that he finally allowed himself a glance at the place to which he had been brought. Then, 'BEACH!' he cried, and before the anchor was even set he was standing in the cockpit with his bucket and spade and armbands at the ready.

The truth is that while a toddler can enjoy time spent under sail, the cruising life is not really ideal for this age group. This is the age of imprinting: of rooting oneself to the home. Toddlers like to be among familiar faces and familiar things. They need to belong somewhere. At the age of two, Caesar ignored strangers – but if we encountered someone twice, he was a bosom friend; *our* harbourmaster, *our* lady in the village shop. He latched onto people and places with almost desperate eagerness. And always we tore him away from them.

Three-year-old Rose Heiney put it very neatly when her parents dragged her off on a whistle-stop tour of Britain. 'Why do we always leave harbours as soon as we've got there?' she asked. Significantly, my notebooks from this stage are stuffed full of ideas about community living, and of the needs of the child in this respect. 'The nuclear family is a disaster. Toddlers need grandparents, aunts and uncles...'

Having made this discovery, many live-aboards decide to hole up for a year or two, but Nick and I had just spent two years holed up in Antigua. Moreover, we were not in a position to hole up in the Bahamas; the hurricane season was upon us and we had to flee the area fast. A few weeks after our unhappy voyage from Anguilla we set off across the pond. As you may imagine, I had considerable misgivings about the journey ahead but, as it turned out, Caesar took the whole thing in his stride.

This time I made sure that Caesar understood what was going on, and just in case the explanation was beyond his grasp I also drew him a little book in which our past and future exploits were graphically portrayed. This made the situation abundantly plain, even to a toddler. He could see where we had been (naturally he could not recognise the places from my hasty scribbles, but we identified them for him) and he could see where we were going. Several pages were filled with nothing but sea, but there was land at the end of the journey. Little children can understand a great deal more than we give them credit for, *when* we allow them the chance.

Caesar was his old self again on that Atlantic crossing, but this did not mean that he needed no attention from his parents. On the contrary; entertaining a toddler on passage is quite hard work, but it is nothing compared to the ordeal of entertaining and caring for a toddler *and* a baby. Sailing the Atlantic in the company of two tiny tots was the hardest thing I have ever done in my life.

Fifty things to do with a toddler

The thing that a toddler likes best is to join in with whatever Mummy or Daddy are doing, and in the normal course of events a mother spends quite a bit of time washing clothes or dishes or doing the shopping with the 'help' of her little one. By comparison, being entertained is relatively boring for the child; almost as boring, indeed, as it is for the adult doing the entertaining. You can buy enough rattles to sink the boat, but they will not amuse for very long.

Unfortunately, once the anchor is weighed and the boat dancing her way across the sea, letting your little ones join in with the chores becomes much harder. It is still the number one amusement, however. One just has to be a little more inventive in creating opportunities. Here are 50 toddler amusements that have been tried and tested at sea.

1 Caesar and Xoë's favourite pastime at sea was baking bread, which occupied about an hour each morning on our month-long crossing. In order to involve them in the business I had to sit the children on the galley worktop. Xoë sat in her car-seat, which wedged behind a fiddle and lashed to a robust shelf. Even when the galley was to windward, she was held securely in place. Caesar had no need of a chair at his age, but when *Maamari* was heeled hard over and the galley was on the uphill side he had to brace himself, with his legs outstretched and his feet pushing hard against the same fiddle. It was a good strong fiddle, fully two inches high, and it needed to be.

With the kids occupying most of the worktop there was little space left, but I used to put the bowl between us, in the sink, and we would all muck in: five hands pouring, mixing and kneading (two each of theirs and only one of mine, for while the boat was heeled I also had to hang on, to the same fiddle). I generally tried to distract Xoë from the game by providing her with a series of seductively shiny measuring spoons and suchlike, things which could be 'mouthed'. Otherwise she mouthed the dough.

Bread-making at this time was a messy affair, but in the long term it paid dividends: Caesar and Xoë both bake bread on their own now.

2 Washing up is another chore which can sometimes be shared with the baby, but you may need to apply some lateral thinking. Ideally, the baby sits in his chair again, or on the draining board, but if the boat is heeled the wrong way then the safest place for him is in the sink. Yes, I know; the dishes are supposed to go in the sink. Don't worry, you'll manage somehow. Part of the fun of sailing lies in its many challenging aspects.

3 Small children also love to help with the navigation, but save this for when you have already done the real navigation. Caesar set great store by being allowed to sit on the chart table and examine the parallel rules, or peer into the radar. This may even explain his current interest in navigation.

This is not a suitable pastime for babies; babies eat charts. Nor is it a good idea if your chart table is one of those modern navigation stations, surrounded by alluring LCD displays and bleeping buttons.

4 Anything adult is desirable, so a calculator, a radio, a broken camera, mobile phone, GPS, or any other such 'toy' covered in switches is guaranteed to amuse.

5 All little children love picture books. If you read the same old stories over and over, the child will soon know them by heart and this is the first step towards reading. We only had three children's books with us on our crossing to the Azores and by the end of the month Caesar knew them all by heart and recognised most of the words, both in context and in isolation.

Avoid reading to your children or allowing them to study the print or the pictures on the first day at sea. Like drawing or any other activity requiring close scrutiny and concentration, this may disturb the body's balance mechanism and promote feelings of nausea.

6 Painting keeps a toddler happy for half an hour or so; roughly the same amount of time that it will take you to get everything set up and to clean and clear away afterwards. Finger paints are ideal. Painting is *not* such a great idea if there is a small baby in the crew.

7 Play-doh is excellent for a toddler (but, again, not suitable with a baby around). You can make a perfectly acceptable dough using flour and oil and water. Some people add large quantities of salt, 'to make it inedible', but I have never seen the sense in this. Flour and cooking oil and water are nourishing. Salt, on the other hand, is said to be bad for a baby's kidneys – and yet little children love to eat salty things. Nor do I add food colourings.

The dyes used in food colourings were originally intended for cloth, and they stain.

Once the child has got all the fun he can from handling the stuff and you have tired of making dough-men, the game can be extended by using bits and pieces of hardware (large nuts and bolts, etc) to emboss the dough. Pastry cutters are obviously ideal if you have any aboard.

8 Paint them up with face paints. Gives you the chance to do something creative and expressive for a change, while they keep quiet. Alternatively, let them paint themselves. Greasepaint crayons are best for a small child. Xoë and Caesar used to have a hilarious time smothering each other's bodies like savages. He was three when they discovered this activity, she was 18 months.

9 Play 'Simon-Says', or 'Monkey See, Monkey Do'. You lead; they have to copy your actions. Can be very funny when the boat is bouncing about.

10 Produce a couple of hand-puppets. You can knock them up out of a pair of socks. Use buttons for the eyes; the mouth you make with your hand. Do not worry if the end product is less than professional; a child has a far better imagination than an adult and can make-believe almost as well with an ungarnished sock. (My girls, having had comparatively few 'real' toys, amuse themselves endlessly in this way.)

You do not need to be a ventriloquist, young children are always enthralled by a puppet, a doll or their teddy talking in a silly voice. Every member of our motley crew of dolls and bears and other furry animals speaks with a different voice. The giraffe is a real toff, the rhino is a bruiser and one of the mice is French. I have never been able to figure the thing out; the children obviously know who is doing the talking, and yet they allow themselves to be utterly taken in. Guaranteed to stop tears in an instant and to amuse for as long as you can keep it up.

11 Let the child rifle through a locker and take everything out. He will have a lovely time, examining each item in turn. You get to put it all back again afterwards, of course.

12 Gather up all the crayons and pens that you can find – all except the permanent marker – and let the child explore the different mediums. Teach him to take rubbings. Again, this is not a suitable activity for a baby; babies make short work of wax crayons even before they have their first pre-molars.

13 Let him dress up in your clothes. Outsize shirts, shoes, hats, goggles and sunglasses will all be received with delight.

14 Lego Duplo is an essential part of the inventory of any ship with children aboard. In fact, Lego in its various guises is in my view the *only* essential toy. Duplo kept Caesar amused for up to an hour each day on his first crossing and was just as valuable on his second, two and a half years later. The same large bucketful is still providing endless hours of fun for Roxanne.

15 Recite poetry to him. No, not Tennyson, nor even Masefield; AA Milne is more popular with the under-threes. Hilaire Belloc's cautionary tales will amuse you, too. I have found that small children will sit and listen with rapt attention while rhymes are recited for their benefit. With sufficient repetition (which children love) they will soon know all the words.

16 Sing to him. I had to sing 'Nellie the Elephant' umpteen times a day for 28 days. Unfortunately, 'The House of the Rising Sun' and 'St James Infirmary Blues' were less well received.

17 Coloured pipe cleaners are useful for all sorts of games. Caesar liked to have them wound around his wrists or his ankles. He also enjoyed watching me make pipe-cleaner men. Before you give the little man to your child be sure to fold over the ends of the wires so that he cannot scratch himself.

18 A set of alphabet flash cards was very popular with Caesar. If you can't get hold of a set of cards, make your own using pictures from magazines. Scissors and glue are things of great interest to a toddler and he will enjoy 'helping'. In fact, you may find yourselves producing a collage instead of flash cards. It all helps to pass the time.

19 Teach him to count, using buttons or cotton reels or anything else which comes to hand.

20 Fill a bucket with water and give him some containers with which to pour. This is a cockpit game, of course.

21 Give him a kazoo. (But for safety's sake make him sit down while he is playing it.)

22 Make some finger puppets, from felt or paper.

23 Let him loose (in the cockpit) with a packet of split peas or dried lentils. Be sure to rinse them all down the drain afterwards, or the cockpit floor will be as safe as a skating rink.

24 Hold a tea party for all the cuddly toys.

25 Give him the whistle from his life-jacket. He will not be able to blow it very hard and the noise is less aggravating than hearing him whine.

26 Fuzzy Felt is popular with most small children.

Pipe cleaner man.

27 Your turn now, Daddy. Allow him to rummage through your toolbox or let him sift through an assortment of nuts and bolts. (Not a suitable occupation for anyone who still explores the world with his mouth.)

28 Small children like posting things; in fact, they are almost obsessive about this pastime. Ours have each in turn discovered the fingerholes on our locker doors and have enjoyed posting in all manner of goods. Also popular was a shoebox with a slit in the lid, into which Caesar posted used phone cards. Another favourite consisted of a tube lashed diagonally over a large, empty coffee tin. Toys and items pilfered from the galley were deposited into the top end of the tube and arrived with a satisfying clang at the bottom.

29 Put all the bunk cushions on the floor and create a 'padded cell' for a tumble-tot.

30 Go through all the action rhymes; 'Round and round the garden', 'This little piggy', 'Insy-winsy spider'... Though personally I hate these; I would prefer to hear my kid whine than do the action rhymes.

31 Make him a jigsaw puzzle by cutting up the front of, say, a cornflakes packet. Let him see what you are doing, and do not make it too complicated. Start with six pieces. You can always halve them. If even this seems too difficult, or if the project does not enthral, use a photograph of the child himself and slice it in three.

32 A packet of gummed paper will provide amusement, and stickers are always popular.

33 Teach him to recognise a matching pair of cards so that he can play snap with you. This is entertainment in its own right but is also very good for the development of reading skills.

34 Play 'Kim's game', commencing with just five or six items to be studied, covered and recalled. Small children are quite astonishingly inept at this memory game at the outset, but they improve rapidly.

35 Give your child a piece of line. This is a complete taboo in every babycare book, of course, but I am assuming that you will watch to see that he does not hang himself. He will enjoy tying elaborate knots all over the boat. (Roxanne's favourite pastime from the age of two to four, and still a popular activity.)

36 Put his harness on him and send him outside to catch fish, with the same line. Erling Tambs' little boy Tony spent whole days fishing in this way. Caesar also found it fun.

37 Give him an empty matchbox – kids like matchboxes – and encourage him to find things tiny enough to put in it.

38 Blow bubbles for him – incredibly popular! And babies love bubbles even more than toddlers.

39 My children all liked playing with little plastic animals. Buy in advance and issue a new one each day.

40 Let him try on all his clothes. Perhaps because they are supreme egotists, toddlers love putting on their nicest

clothes and gazing at themselves in the mirror.

41 Make him a cardboard doll to dress. Use a winebox, or something similarly stiff. Colour it to look like the child, himself – or at least tell him that it is his effigy. The clothes are cut from paper and attach over the shoulder, with tabs. Once again, a high standard of craftsmanship is superfluous.

42 Quite the most successful of all the games created, through necessity, on passage was a fishing game. Children of all ages love it.

The fish are made from cardboard. A cereal packet is perfect; paper is less effective but will do if you have nothing else. Make your fish of different shapes and sizes and colour them, if you have the time, making them as different from each other as possible. Next you need to attach a piece of metal to the mouth of each fish. Paper clips are ideal, but for want of a packet of paper clips I used pins. (Staples would also do the trick but are almost as scratchy, and you would probably need to put several, side by side, on each fish.) For the fishing rods you need a pencil, 2ft of string, and a small magnet. The magnet is your 'hook'.

Caesar, aged two, found this game very exciting. You can make it harder for older children by marking the fish with letters and asking them to catch their name. They should also have to use a longer line and catch heavier fish than smaller competitors. I used this version of the game at a children's party, and the kids all loved it so much that we could not get them to stop! They lost all interest in passing the parcel or playing musical chairs.

43 If the weather is rough, cut some boat-shaped pieces of wood or foam plastic, give each boat a matchstick mast and a paper sail and race your fleet down the incline of the table. Daddies enjoy this one.

44 Teach your child to sew. Use a blunt sailmaker's needle threaded with whipping twine. Punch holes in a piece of cardboard (preferably around the outline of a picture), tie one end of the thread to the first two holes, tie a stopper knot in the other end (on the far side of the needle) – and off he goes. You will need to be on hand to unravel the inevitable tangles.

45 Story tapes are wonderful things. Record some in advance; read your child's favourite stories onto a tape, together with some new ones. A Walkman makes the experience still more absorbing. Brilliant therapy for a seasick child.

46 Teach him to thread beads. If you have no beads, use cotton reels, shackles, spare parrel balls, or anything else that you can think of.

47 Make him a paper dart. You will probably have to throw it, too, but he will enjoy running to fetch it.

48 Make him a little den, by draping a sheet over the table.

49 Make him a submarine and tow it behind the boat. This is one to plan in advance; you will not find time to knock up a toy submarine while you are sailing with your kids. It is not my own idea. I found it in a book of sailor's crafts by Bill Beavis.

For the body of the sub you need a piece of softwood roughly 2ft long. Shape it with saw, plane and rasp, and add a conning tower. In order to submerge, the vessel will need ballast, so fasten a piece of scrap iron or lead onto the bottom. The boat must float, but only just. To help it back up to the surface it needs hydroplanes at the bow, and these and the rudder are cut from tin. Bill suggests using a biscuit-tin lid. Glue them onto the body of the submarine using epoxy. Paint the vessel white, so that it will show up under the water and then, lastly, add a towing eye.

This is the one entertainment listed in this book that I have not tried and tested, but Bill assures us that it will keep the kids' attention riveted right the way across the Atlantic. As they haul in on the towline the sub will surface, and as they slacken away it will dive. But before they go hanging over the stern, be sure to dress your participants in their harnesses and see that they are properly hooked on.

50 Finally, try a bucket swing. This may not sound like the ideal amusement aboard a yacht but it can be used at sea when conditions are calm, and in harbour it works a treat.

When at anchor we used to hang the swing in the foretriangle. I have some super snapshots of Xoë, at 12 months, soaring high up into the sky. She loved it. But it was when we hung the swing below decks that it really came into its own. It worked in the same way as the hammock: within five minutes of climbing aboard, Xoë would be sound asleep – at last!

The mother's point of view

So much for the baby, and his needs. Mummies have needs too. In the interests of harmony in the floating home, we can forgo them for a while – indeed, a woman is conditioned by society to subjugate her needs to the demands of her family – but if our needs are for long unmet then we are bound to feel aggrieved and frustrated. Does cruising with babies work from a mother's standpoint?

Daysailing with an infant is one thing. Making an extended cruise is quite another, and as the reader will have gathered, I found it very tough.

Caring for a baby is a full-time job. Ashore, the business is shared; there are grandmothers to babysit for an hour or two while Mum shops or spends time on herself, and there are mother and baby groups where a new mum can socialise with her own kind. The cruising life, by contrast, leaves us out on a limb. I was utterly tied to my kids – Xoë was over three before she ever spent a moment away from my side. During this whole time, and for the preceeding year and a half of Caesar's infancy, I never had one single hour for myself. I loved my children dearly, but I was acutely aware of the fact that my needs were not being met.

I am pleased to be able to report that things did get better with time. I adjusted, Xoë got a bit older, and Grandpa joined us for the next long-haul trip. A very happy trip it was, too, with an extra hand to keep watch and (better yet) to read *Pig Gets Stuck* again and again. By the time we made our next major voyage, Caesar was three and Xoë two and they needed little input from me while we sailed.

But this is only one sailor's view on the subject of cruising offshore with small fry. Other women have crossed oceans with a baby tucked under their arm. Let us see what they thought of the experience.

Stories of cruising couples

Pioneering parents

In 1929 a young Norwegian couple sailed from the Canary Islands to the Caribbean with no crew other than their mongrel dog and a six-week-old son named Tony.

Various 'meddlesome' people had declared that it would be nothing short of murder to take a baby on this trip – one very concerned individual had even tried to buy him for £600 – but Tony's father, Erling Tambs, had scoffed at the doom-mongers. He felt, he says, a little bit different a few days later when the yacht was surrounded by 'towering seas, leaden and menacing'.

Mr and Mrs Tambs took turns at the helm, for there was no such thing as self-steering in those days. At night they hove-to and slept. You can get away with heaving-to in the middle of an ocean – or at least, you could in 1929.

During the day Tony slept in a cot in the cockpit, beside his parents, and on one occasion when a sea broke into the cockpit he was set adrift 'like Moses'. About the only other thing we hear about him is that he woke once each night for his bottle, and that he took a cold sea-water bath each day. I suspect that we might have heard more if Mrs Tambs had penned the book, but Erling had a very easy-going attitude to life. His journey was one long series of near-disasters and his attitude to navigation ineffably laid back. When unsure of his position he would simply follow a passing steamer.

The wrong age for ocean crossing

Another couple who have crossed the Atlantic with a baby are Mike Pratt and his wife Helga. Their daughter, Susie, was six months old when they set sail for Antigua.

Mike and Helga had equipped their boat with all the usual baby paraphernalia. They had a cot which fitted into the forepeak, a clip-on feeding chair, a plastic bathtub, a large supply of nappies and plenty of baby milk powder and sterilising solution. All appears to have gone well in terms of caring for the baby but, once again, entertaining her was a big deal.

I would go so far as to say that six months is exactly the wrong age to cross an ocean with a baby. With a smaller baby you have only to cope with the basic physical requirements, and a child who is fully mobile is less of a handful and also more easily amused. Mike and Helga Pratt went to sea armed with plenty of toys, 'But still,' as Mike says, 'there was not a sufficient stock to keep us all from being thoroughly bored long before halfway.'

The weather was too rough for the baby to be taken on deck and so the double bunk was converted into a playpen, but – not surprisingly – Susie demanded that one or other of her parents play with her most of the time. As ever, the brunt of this duty fell on Helga, who consequently spent a lot of the time feeling queasy. Mike, of course, found himself singlehanding. He got the best deal, in my view.

Down under

Another man who has spent plenty of time sailing offshore with his wife and kids is Aussie Bray. Aussie feels that it is very hard, even in port, for the mother of a small baby to get enough rest, so that sailing with such an infant is bound to be arduous. In view of this, he suggests that extra crew should be taken. This is not a bad idea, but it is not everybody who wants to go cruising in a nursery and nor does every couple welcome the idea of inviting a long-term guest into their cramped cabin. Relatives are the most likely candidates for the post. Some families take on a hitch-hiker, generally someone who will pay his way, but one mother I heard about hired a teenage girl to ship as nanny.

A big mistake

Mary and Albert, a young Dutch couple, were cruising around the world aboard a GRP production yacht and when I met them had been out for four years. They were now on their way home and, as they told me, could not wait to get back. Their adventures had been brought to a premature close by the arrival of two cherubic infants. Matthias, now three, had been born while the boat was in Samoa. His little brother Nathaniel had joined the company in Thailand and was now ten months old. Sweet little boys, but – 'We think that we have made a big mistake,' their father said. 'Sailing with children is too difficult.'

Regardless of the fact that the family had just arrived from a very rough passage lasting five days, their yacht was immaculate; as clean and tidy as if she had come from a showroom. The toys were all in the toybox, the dishes were all washed, and Mary had already found time to wash the clothes which her baby had soiled the previous afternoon (and none of this was for my benefit as my visit was impromptu). This young couple would undoubtedly have found sailing with babies a little bit easier if they had been willing, or able, to lower their standards.

Time out

Laslo, a Hungarian sailor, had been cruising for some time aboard his yacht, *La Chamade*, before he met and married his South African wife Petra. The couple's first child was born in the Comores and they named her Kippy.

Kippy's arrival did nothing to cramp Laslo's style, and when the baby was but a few months old he and Petra decided to sail their boat up to the Caribbean. Kippy was nine months old by the time they arrived. Petra's opinion of crossing an ocean with an infant can be judged by the action which she took immediately upon regaining terra firma. She declared that she and Kippy were sick of the sight of each other, and she packed the child off to a playgroup.

Laslo junior was born 18 months after his sister, in the island of Grenada, and having learnt her lesson Petra very sensibly decided that the family needed to take some time out from cruising. When last we saw them they were holed up in St Maartens. This is, indeed, one common solution to the problem of cruising with infants. Many long-term live-aboards take the arrival of a baby as a cue to stop for a while, and to find work with which to replenish the coffers. Babies are only babies for such a short while, and a few months in harbour may be all that is needed to transform a hell-ship back into a happy one.

So, are you up to it?

Catering for the needs of a baby or toddler aboard a boat requires far more preparation than accommodating any other age group – and I am not talking only about blue-water babies; babies require an organised approach even if you are only daysailing.

If the boat has not been child-proofed, a mobile baby or toddler is apt to be a liability. I often wonder if the floating winch handle is not the first example of a designer recognising the needs of yachting parents, for who but a toddler would lob a winch handle overboard? And they do worse things than that.

One of the most miserable days that I have ever spent afloat was aboard my father's 28ft Countess. Nothing wrong with the boat or the skipper; no, the problem lay in the fact that the boat was not geared up for sailing with tinies. Xoë was crawling – or she would have been if there had been enough space – and I had very cleverly forgotten to bring along any toys, so that there was nothing else for her to do. Within half an hour she was bored and fractious.

Caesar, then two and a half, fared a little better. He spent an hour exploring every nook and corner of the cabin and discovered the fire extinguishers, the flares, the switch panel, a packet of pills, and the battery switch, among other delights. There are few words more guaranteed to provoke an unpleasant scene than 'don't touch that' – particularly when the phrase is repeated over and again, parrot-fashion.

Sailing with infants on a boat which has not been child-proofed has zero appeal. In such circumstances, sailing equals entertaining and restraining the child for hours on end in a room full of taboos. Throw in a touch of seasickness and you have hell.

But on the right boat, with the right preparations, boating with a baby or toddler is... bearable. And at times, between finding him another toy or helping him to use the potty, you can actually fit in some genuine, hands-on sailing. My final advice: survive the season or make the crossing, and then award yourself a medal for endurance and sit back. Wrap up the boat for the winter, or find yourself a tranquil tropical island and hang out for a while. When the visa runs out, or spring is sprung, and boating beckons again, you will discover that your baby has become a small child – and a far better shipmate.

Useful addresses
- The Wilkinet Baby Carrier is available from Sally Wilkins, PO Box 20, Cardigan, West Wales SA43 1JB.
- For information about cloth nappies contact The Real Nappy Association, PO Box 3704, London SE26 4RX.

4
Sailing with Children: Midshipmen or Mutineers?

A word to the wives • **Selling the idea of sailing** • **Careful handling**
• **Midshipmen** • **Mutineers** • **What do you expect?** •
The making of a midshipman • **Hot tips** • **Port pursuits**

If I have made sailing with infants sound horrendous, that is because, by and large, it is. The only thing worse than sailing with infants is not sailing – an unthinkable scenario! Sailing with tinies is terrible, but there is light at the end of the tunnel. Having survived the era of changing nappies on the chart table and spoon feeding while you navigate, you can claim your just reward. Sailing with slightly older children is great fun, or at least, it can be.

As we have seen, the chief problem about sailing with babies and toddlers is the amount of attention that they require in their general upkeep and in their amusement. Over-threes, by contrast, are independent little beings. By three a child has reached the age of relatively reasonable behaviour, tantrums not withstanding. By three he no longer needs somebody else to pump the loo and zip up his lifejacket, and when you rush on deck to reef or drop anchor he understands that you will be returning shortly; he no longer requires to be bribed or distracted.

Whereas a baby accepts the adventure of sailing without question and without comprehension, an older child is awake to what is going on in his environment and he judges his experiences, rating them pleasant or otherwise. However, until he reaches the age of 12, or thereabouts, the child still takes his lead from the adults around him and his opinion of a particular place, person or activity will be strongly influenced by his parents' ideas. Essentially then, sailing with children is fun, *if* they have decided that they like it, and so far as younger children are concerned, their mother's attitude is often the determining factor here.

Young children generally do what is expected of them. Psychologists have observed that if his mother's attitude encourages a small child to believe that he will fall into the swimming pool, or down the companion ladder, then he is more than likely to do so. 'If you play near the edge you will fall in,' is tantamount to an instruction, it seems. Equally, if Mummy and Daddy show by their attitude that they expect their child to loathe sailing and to be bored out of his mind, then he will oblige by conforming to this expectation. If, on the other hand, their behaviour makes it obvious that sailing is fun, and if their remarks carry no hint that it had ever occurred to them that anyone might think otherwise, then their child is likely to be perfectly content with his lot.

A word to the wives

One thing more readily guaranteed than any other to cause unhappiness among smaller members of the crew is a negative vibe coming from the mate. If Mum has a must-I-go-down-to-the-seas approach to sailing, then you can bet that any under-eights in the company will also catch the malady.

There are various reasons why women are generally less fond than men of spending their weekends on the water. Much of sailing is very physical and tends towards the macho. Winching up the anchor and grinding in the genoa are great for the biceps – but not all mothers are into building up their muscles. Likewise, women tend to be less enthusiastic than men about having buckets of icy salt water thrown down their necks. Men appear to find this character building, but we women do not feel the need to have our characters enlarged and we tend to look upon an icy shower bath as a deliberately spiteful action on the part of the sea.

Women who love sailing are seldom very image conscious. Concern for hair-dos, fingernails and frocks rather prohibits one from partaking fully in the management of the vessel. I once knew a live-aboard who had to call her husband home from work when a mooring line wanted adjusting in a gale. She 'couldn't do it, of course,' as she might have damaged her long pointed talons. (Interestingly enough, although she hardly knew which

end of the boat went first, this woman loved living aboard and cruising.)

The problems of navigation also seem to be more suited to the male psyche than the female. Fewer women than men appear to have an aptitude for mathematics. Those of us who are determined to get to grips with the art in its marine form often have to grapple hard with the figures. Mending the engine, climbing the mast and diving to fit a new anode on the prop are pastimes which the competent sailorman takes in his stride; he even seems to enjoy such opportunities for demonstrating his skills. Few women are adept at these sort of activities. For my own part, I cannot manage any one of the three.

And I suspect that fewer women than men are attracted to the romantic side of sailing: to the smell of manilla ropes, to the notion of a ship brought to life by wind and sea, and to the whole jolly-Jack-tar image. After all, there were not many jolly-Jills in the glorious days of sail.

One other thing sets women apart from men in a boat. We girls are far more likely than the fellas to suffer the curse of seasickness – and it is difficult to enjoy the day, still less to convey a sense of pleasure to one's children, while throwing up.

A great many women are driven and dragged into sailing by their men. Naomi James was even persuaded by her husband to sail singlehanded around the world.

She also raced around Britain with him aboard his trimaran, a radical racing machine. At the end of it all she wrote, 'If I liked sailing – which I do not...'

Compared with Naomi's, the sufferings which the average pressganged sea-wife must endure are nothing, yet with a little care and consideration an inveterate salt can make his pet passion his lady's favourite pastime too. And if Dad really wants to make sailing a family affair, he *needs* to start by getting Mum onto his side.

Selling the idea of sailing

Men are sometimes very clumsy about the way in which they introduce their second love to their first. Sailors are, anyway. I feel sure that mountain-men do not drag their girlfriends up a sheer rockface, or get them to abseil, before they have kitted them out and taught them the rudiments of the game. Women, as a rule, are not impressed by wild, wet, exciting reaches across the foam-capped sea; not, at any rate, until they have grown accustomed to the quieter moments of sailing and have understood that the sport is really quite safe. And what goes for girlfriends and wives goes for children too. Softly, softly is the way to sell sailing to any hesitant newcomer.

I was once the owner of a lovely old tub whose iroko cabin sides and mahogany planked bulkheads made her endearing to anyone with the least bit of the romantic about them, but which sailed about as efficiently as a packing crate. She had practically no keel. I was therefore quite astonished when I put her on the market to find that amongst my enquirers was an expert dinghy sailor, accustomed to thrashing about the harbour in a Finn. So I was somewhat embarrassed when he and his wife came to take *Serenus* for a test sail, but I dutifully hung up the sorry-looking rags which passed for main and jib and waited to hear them denigrated. I was just relieved that the couple had chosen a day of no wind for this investigation; after all, no boat can be expected to shine in a calm.

We motored along – and pretty soon it dawned on me that this choice was, in fact, no accident, and nor did the lack of keel or the disgraceful appearance of the sails matter two hoots. As the afternoon unfolded I realised that I was not selling my boat to this man; he was selling sailing to his wife.

The lady had never set foot in a boat before. She boarded *Serenus* very nervously and awkwardly, but one glimpse of the varnished iroko and mahogany below decks had been all that was necessary: 'Ooh, she's lovely,' the lubber had cried. And that had clinched the deal.

I forget the fellow's name, but he was a clever man. He had the sense to lure his wife, oh, so softly into sailing. A week or so later I saw them putt-puttering down the harbour (sails still safely furled) – the man, his timid but very excited wife and their two completely over-awed, wide-eyed, mop-headed children.

I saw them again, seven years later, by which time the kids were teenagers. The family had long outgrown *Serenus* and now they sailed a nondescript GRP cruising boat. By now the lady was a confident, competent sailor with pride in her ship (she had just made new cushion covers for the bunks) and the children were old enough to pull their weight too. It would not surprise me to find that the skipper was still carefully and cautiously advancing towards a performance fin-keeler.

Teach us...

Besides luring her into the game with tact, a man can also improve his wife's opinion of messing about in boats by teaching her how they work. Many women do not know how to get the best from the boat and regard that as their captain's business. A friend, now in her thirties, has sailed for several years but still hardly knows a jib sheet from a halyard. Because her husband treats her as if she knows it all, this woman is somehow ashamed to reveal her ignorance and blunders on as if all were well. I suspect that her situation is far from unique.

Anyone is likely to enjoy an activity more if they are actually taking part in a meaningful way. The family man can make sailing much more appealing by enlightening his crew – every one of them – as soon as they are amenable to seeing and hearing how the ship is handled. Some husbands are better at this than others, and many women prefer to learn from a qualified instructor at a sailing school. Many sea schools offer women-only courses. Similarly, children sometimes learn better from an outsider, often making a greater advance during a weekend spent in the care of an RYA instructor than they would otherwise manage in an entire season under Father's guidance.

Fussing about inappropriate footwear may be interpreted by your crew as precious-mindedness.

... Don't forget that it's OUR BOAT...

When a couple are both keen sailors they take an equal interest in their yacht. They share the enjoyment of planning passages and both contribute ideas and energies towards the upkeep of the vessel. Unfortunately, this sharing situation is far from inevitable. Men are often very possessive of their little ships. They may also seem to their crew to be very precious.

One gentleman of my acquaintance took his girls to sea aboard his brand new Centaur and then had a fit when the elder child bled copiously over the mainsail. He was not the least bit concerned about his daughter's cut hand; and so far as I am aware, the girls never sailed with their father again.

Fussing about toilet seacocks and battery switches and inappropriate footwear on the deck can be offputting for the novice. If you really want your family to share your pleasure in sailing then it is your job, Captain, to see that your motley crew are brought to order through education and inspiration, rather than with irate remarks and peevish complaints. When I hear a man speaking of 'my boat' then I know that his family are not with him wholeheartedly.

... And give us something to do

Another thing which men do well to recognise is that they are much better than women at doing nothing. My husband and my son both have an endless capacity for doing nothing; they can sit in the cockpit for hours on end – *days* on end – and do nothing else. I lack this ability; I have to be doing something – but as my boat is also my home this is not a problem for me. There are always dozens of things to be done. For a woman weekend-sailing, this is not the case.

A woman who has 'a hundred and one things to do' will not appreciate the idea of wasting her day sitting in a cockpit. She is much more likely to want to be aboard if there are also things on the boat which beckon. Sailing itself is one such thing, but there are other draws which a talented man might promote. Read on.

Pink sails and lace-edged lee cloths

Mere lip service to the principle of Our Boat is not enough; if the yacht belongs to all, all must have a say in what goes on aboard. Just as men and women have their own fields of endeavour in the home, so we also tend to have our own strengths and weaknesses afloat, and I am not suggesting that the average couple would want to share decisions about changing the engine oil or even about general

handling and navigation, but there is more to boating than being under way.

Among the many hundreds of sailing couples that I have encountered, only one reversed the usual roles, making the wife the skipper (and, significantly, this couple had no children). In every other instance that I have come across – even where the woman was sailing first – the man has been the Master of the vessel. Few men are autocratic about this, but in the end somebody has to have the final say as to whether the boat goes left or right. In most cases, the man makes *all* decisions relating to the navigation of the yacht (albeit, usually after discussion with his lady). The deck is a man's domain, then – but when we pass below decks we leave this arena and enter upon a domestic one.

It takes a woman to turn a house into a home, so it is said, and this being the case she should also be the interior designer aboard the boat. A skipper who denies his wife the opportunity of choosing new fabric for the curtains and re-covering the cushions contradicts the principle of shared ownership. He thwarts a nest-building instinct and in doing so jeopardises his mate's interest in the boat.

I once saw a magazine article written by a woman who had transformed a Westerly into a sort of tart's boudoir. The cushions were covered in plush red velvet and the curtains were of pink satin. There were lace curtains around each bunk and, if I remember rightly, there was a pink crocheted cover on the loo seat. The overall effect was... devastating. What the lady's husband thought of the décor we were not told – but at least he had an enthusiastic crew member who was *eager* to be aboard each weekend.

Interiors with the appropriate nautical flavour and spick and span caravan-style cabins are, however, more the norm. Women and children almost always enjoy the Wendy-house aspect of owning a boat and a man can easily promote this interest by positively encouraging his crew to consider the cabin their own especial domain.

What goes for a reluctant sea-wife in some measure goes for the children too. If the boat is 'Daddy's' it will hold small interest for his offspring. If they are to enjoy time spent aboard, then they need to think of the boat as a home from home; they need the chance to love her in the way that their parents (both, hopefully) do. Personally, I would try to discourage my kids from painting the forepeak shocking pink or day-glo orange – but only because I would regard this resistance as part of their education. (Tastes are acquired, not inborn.) Like his bedroom, the forepeak is the child's private HQ. In principle at least, my children can do as they like in their own quarters, decorating the place with posters and glow-in-the-dark dinosaurs and whatever else takes their fancy and makes them feel that they want to be there. This I would do even if we were not living aboard, and I would also encourage them to fill the place with their toys and games. Why would they want to spend time on the boat if none of their favourite things were to hand?

Careful handling

As I have said, one does well to introduce a newcomer to the sea quite gently, and no new sailor needs more careful handling than a child. It is not only the first sail which can be upsetting. Even if he has been messing about in boats since the day that he was born, the memory of last year's exploits will invariably have dulled in the mind of the young child, and the first sail of the season may come as quite a shock, especially if the weather turns out to be rougher than expected.

One of my earliest sailing memories is of embarking in a little lap-strake pram dinghy which my father had built. I knew and loved *Sprite* well, but several months had passed since I last sat in her. Now, on this blustery April morning, the new season was beginning and the racing dinghies were setting out from the hard en masse. Dad was between boats, I imagine, for he was crewing in a Sharpie, and whenever he sailed with others in this way my mother would row the three of us across to the other side of the harbour in *Sprite*.

My little sister Susan was about one year old at this time and I would have been two, going on three. My brother must have been six; he probably paddled out and climbed aboard the dinghy. Susie and I were lifted in, and then my mother stepped aboard.

This is the bit that I remember most; the sudden violent lurch of the dinghy as Mum boarded her; the horrid feeling of being suddenly tipped sideways; the definite impression that we were about to capsize. That instant of my mother's stepping aboard is frozen like a snapshot in my mind. I can still see her yachting red trousers, rolled up to just below the knee, and I can still see the water, a scant two inches below the gunwhale.

I also remember my shrill scream. 'Shut up,' said Mum brusquely. She denies that she would ever have said such a thing, but it was surely her unexpectedly callous reaction which has caused the moment to remain with me – and I can even recall the brief chiding which followed, to the effect that I had been sailing long enough to know that the dinghy would not capsize, and that I should not make a fool of myself in front of all the other people.

I have told the tale to illustrate the fact that even a child with experience of sailing merits careful handling after a period of absence from the sea, but there is also another moral. My mother's curt reaction eased my fears completely, whereas soothing reassurance would only have reinforced in my mind the idea that this tippy little boat was dangerous.

I have used this 'trick' often to bring reassurance to a frightened child. It works when there actually *is* danger too.

Faith dispels fear

A gentle introduction is even more important where utter novices are concerned. Babies and toddlers do not appear to have a sense of danger – so long as Mummy is there at their side everything is hunky-dory – but children of primary school age are often not so easy-going. The skipper should take his cue, not from the height of the waves or the wind's measure, but from the faces of his crew. If the crew look bored, by all means stoke up the action, but if they are quiet and a little wary, let it be a warning sign. What seems to an old hand like a thoroughly nice, lively sail, for

example, may strike terror into the heart of someone who does not realise that keel boats cannot fall over.

Most young children have faith in their parents and will not be unduly alarmed by an exciting sail, provided that Mummy and Daddy are not alarmed, but your child's best friend, or any other child who is not your own, may find it all too easy to doubt the capabilities of both boat and captain. I should like to dredge up another story which illustrates this point.

Once, when I was quite young, my father invited a French business colleague to come sailing in our Wayfarer. The gentleman brought along his two little girls, shy little *mesdemoiselles* in pristine white cardigans and cotton dresses, and being of like age I was pressed into the company. Not that I ever needed pressing to go sailing; I was always eager.

One image alone from that afternoon remains etched in my memory. The boat is heeled hard over and I am sitting down on the leeward side with my hand skimming over the fast moving water. This always used to give me a thrill. I could see that my legs were beneath the level of the water as it lapped at the Wayfarer's broad, varnished sidedecks – but it never quite came in. Never. My father never once capsized his Wayfarer, although I later did so several times.

While I sat there, only inches from a dunking but supremely happy, the two little French girls perched on the weather rail with their father and mine and squealed in terror. I was quite astounded at their silliness. The possibility of a capsize never even entered my head. I had absolute confidence in my daddy, who was grinning down at me.

I often look back on that day and think of those two children. They had no reason to trust the man on the helm – and they did not. It must have seemed to those girls that they were in real danger. If they recall that far off day at all it is probably with a shudder. I often wonder if they ever sailed again or whether this first adventure frightened them off for life.

Hydrophobia

Besides rough weather and a radical angle of heel, there are other, less rational things which can disturb a new sailor. The mere fact of being far from the shore can upset a child – or an adult, for that matter. Some people are inexplicably stricken with panic when the land falls away over the horizon; others cannot abide the thought of there being two miles of water under the keel. To me either of these situations brings only feelings of immense pleasure and relief, but I have witnessed the phobia in others; the latter in an adult who was crossing the Atlantic, the first in a child of about ten who joined us, one glorious summer's day, aboard my dad's first yacht.

Dad and I were enjoying an excellent sail in the new boat. The sky was blue; the breeze was on the beam; our little craft was skipping along merrily. We had decided to take her out of the harbour for the first time and make a turn around the Nab tower, a few miles offshore. Our only other crew members were my Mum, who was laid low with feelings of *mal de mer*, and the ten-year-old girl, who sat quietly in the corner while my father and I helmed and hauled the sails about. Dad was a racing man – 'Cock of the Harbour' twice

Hydrophobia.

over in his heyday – and he always sought to get the best from his boats.

While we sailed we also fished, hauling in rank upon rank of mackerel; 50 all told before we decided to quit. All in all we were keeping busy, and it was only while we were landing the fiftieth fish and telling ourselves that we must not be greedy that I noticed that our young companion was not joining in. On the contrary, she was sitting in a corner of the cockpit quietly sobbing to herself. She could give no reason for her distress except to say that she was terrified and that she wanted to head back to the shore. As soon as we were close to the shore she was as right as rain again.

This girl was an experienced sailor, she had been sailing all her life, but this was her first venture away from the vicinity of the land. As an adult she now sails happily with her husband and their children, but she is adamant that she would never wish to go offshore. For a child who had never sailed, a negative experience of this kind could be terminal; he might never want to set foot in a boat again. If your child is the least bit apprehensive or is easily unnerved, a few expeditions in calm, confined waters are the safest introduction to sailing. If he is stout-hearted and intrepid, even then be watchful and be aware that irrational fears strike at random whilst seemingly silly ones still need to be quashed by the reassurance that all is well.

Midshipmen

So long as he is introduced gently to the game, and provided that nobody dampens his liking with negative vibes, a child usually takes quite readily to sailing. Boys, like men, are generally more enthusiastic than girls, but girls with no interest in sailing for sailing's sake often like the Wendy-house aspect of things, and so they too are happy to spend time messing about in a boat. To be sure, you need to bring along a plentiful supply of amusements for the littler members of the crew – too much of sailing seems to consist in doing nothing, so far as the under-sevens are concerned – but older children, if they are given the opportunity, can find plenty to do aboard ship.

Older children often fall hook, line and sinker for the romantic side of sailing. Undoubtedly one is more likely to be seduced by nostalgia for the great days of sail aboard a wooden yacht with lovely varnished blocks and manilla warps (and leaking decks), but children have vivid imaginations and are quite capable of making do with a 'tupperware' tub as they relive the adventures of Jim Hawkins or Horatio Hornblower.

To anyone who has not experienced it, the romance of sailing is hard to define. It does not consist in outright fantasy about the past; we do not act out the role of 18th-century boatswain or mate, in the manner of people who don fancy dress and re-enact ancient battles. The romance of the sea is much more subtle than that. It is the feeling of exquisite contentment at the sight of the taut curve of a sail printed on the blue sky, or a thrill of joy as the yacht rolls along, full and bye, with a bone in her teeth. It is pride in belonging to a great and wonderful fraternity which surpasses the boundaries of history and of nationality; the satisfaction of being an initiate of the clan, skilled in the arts and literate in the language of the sailor. Oh, there is plenty of nostalgia to this romance, but nevertheless it is still fundamentally a living, practical affair.

● Give advice – in small infrequent doses – but resist the urge to 'help him' or you will spoil his fun.

A 12-year-old with a passion for the sea packs his head full of esoteric lore. He knows the difference between a ship and a barque and can name every sail on either. He knows the name and meaning of every code flag and is insistent about the protocol of lowering the ensign at sunset. More usefully, our young salt can tie a monkey's fist and a Turk's head, besides all the usual knots. He carries a marlin spike in the pocket of his fisherman's smock, and a brass shackle on his belt loop, and he rows with the easy grace of a ferryman. Naturally, he is also eager to sail the boat and to learn to navigate.

If all this sounds fanciful, it is not – I promise! It was me; it was Nick; and our son is following us into the family business.

Caesar is already handy on the helm and eager to navigate, both with the modern box of electronic tricks and by the old-fashioned means, with a sextant or a hand-bearing compass. He rows well, he even tries his hand at skulling, and he can make a much better job of an eyesplice than his mum. His younger sister shows a similar bent, and their nine-year-old cousin is also in on the act. As third-generation sailors, perhaps they have a head start, but I have seen plenty of young tyros take to sailing with equal fervour. In fact, when I consider our friends and acquaintances it seems to me that the kids whose parents have themselves only just discovered sailing are the ones likely to be the most enthusiastic.

Mutineers

Unfortunately, not every child takes to sailing like a duck to water. Many are 'pressed men', who sail under duress. Few under-tens are openly hostile to the idea of spending a weekend on the boat – indeed, they may quite like the boat itself; boats make very good climbing frames and cosy dens while they are in harbour. Young children also enjoy the marine environment of jetties from which to fish for crabs and beaches where they can run and play. No, the boat and the water are seldom a problem. It is the sailing itself which sometimes leaves children cold.

To anybody who is not involved in the actual business of making the boat go, sailing must be unutterably dull. Dull, and at times also cold, wet, uncomfortable and, occasionally, scary. How many adults would relish the idea of spending a

day being bounced around on a hard, wet seat in a chilly breeze? Bearing in mind that children have a much lower tolerance than adults for boredom and inactivity it is no wonder some of them find sailing disagreeable.

Bored on board

Children who are too small to understand anything about sailing and to join in the fun are bound to be miserable unless there is something else for them to do. My little niece Rebecca enjoys sailing, but given the choice she prefers to make passages in Grandpa's boat, rather than with Mummy and Daddy. Grandpa owns a cabin cruiser. My sister and her husband own a little gaff cutter; a lovely creature but one whose only cabin consists of a pokey little broom cupboard filled with hawsers.

Aboard Grandpa's boat Rebecca can sit at the table and draw, and this is how she likes to fill the long hours of a day afloat.

Although they are happy to spend days and weeks at sea aboard their own home, Xoë and Roxanne are also apt to get bored after a few hours when we sail with friends. Having explored every cabin and quarter berth and exhausted the possibilities of the boat as a playground, they resort to reading. Xoë and her brother have both been reading since they were tiny, and at sea the ability is a godsend. If you intend cruising, take my advice and teach your youngsters to read before you go. It makes them self-entertaining. On the subject of entertainment, a sister or a friend provides much better play value than a whole shopful of toys. Couples with only one child find themselves devoting a great deal of effort and time to entertaining him while they sail.

Most amusing

As far as toys and games are concerned, many of the ones that your children enjoy at home will be just as appropriate afloat, but anything that rolls is best avoided. Cars are not too terrible, but marbles are a liability. They get lost, and then they suddenly reappear when the boat rolls. Watch the air turn blue when they reappear just under the skipper's foot as he descends from the cockpit in haste.

With older children, as with toddlers, the very best shipboard toy is Lego. Almost every family cruising yacht carries a good supply of this stuff. Lego contributes so much to the smooth running of the family yacht that it should go down on the list of essential equipment. We will know that the sailing industry has finally noticed that kids also sail when the chandlers start stocking boxes of Lego bricks and tubs of Duplo.

I would suggest that rather than cart toys to and fro between your house and the boat you encourage your child to keep some of his favourites aboard; things that he really likes and that will cause him to want to spend time on the boat. Give him his own locker, beside his own bunk, and let him keep his things in there.

Mummy, what shall I do now?

When the child runs out of toys, then he must fall back on Mother's wits. I have already made some suggestions in the section '50 things to do with a toddler'. Ideas for older children include 'I-spy' to teach a child letter sounds ('Something beginning with G. Guh, guh...') and 'Alphabet adjectives' (angry ant, beautiful bear, etc). These games get the kids thinking hard. We also play 'nautical alphabets', where everybody has to think up something 'boaty' for each letter.

'Hunt the thimble' (or the deck brush) is another game suited to small people, and one which places very little demand on the parent. 'Twenty questions' fills the hours and is actually very educational. 'Draw-my-drawing' is another game which promotes mental development. Mother can sit back and relax for this one; all she has to do is describe something unseen and the children have to draw it. 'Kim's game' also helps to pass the time while encouraging the development of memory. If you would rather promote the child's imagination, draw round his foot and suggest that he colours it in with his favourite shapes and patterns.

'The feely bag' is a popular amusement for smaller children. Caesar used to love it. I would put eight or ten objects in the bottom of a duffel bag and he would have to identify them by touch alone. Sometimes, something in the bottom of the bag would grab his hand and pull (work it out for yourself!) which left him squealing in a confusion of delight and dismay.

One thing that the children do still enjoy is a story. I am not very good at story telling; happily, the kids do not mind filling in the blanks. Poetry recitals (or to be accurate, rhyme recitals) and stories read from books are also popular. We also sing sea shanties; even Daddy joins in with our singalongs. You do not need to be musical to sing 'Hullaballoobalay' or 'Hanging Johnnie' and the words can be learnt or made up as you go along. There is nothing like a rousing chorus of ranting and roaring to lift the spirits. Nursery rhymes do not have the same effect.

Watersports

Although certain games can be converted to nautical usage, this feels like second best; it turns a passage under sail into something no better than a train journey. It ought to be possible to find entertainments derived from the sea itself.

I think we all share the fascination with foam and froth gushing by. It holds a hypnotic allure akin to that of a flickering fire. I can vividly recall the delight I felt, as a small child, in dragging my fingers through the fast-moving water. You cannot dangle your hand in the water which whooshes past a cruising yacht, but there are other things that can be trailed in the wake. Toy boats do not fare very well when dragged along at 3 knots; at sea they are a waste of time. Submarines are amusing, if you have the time and ability to make one (see '50 things to do with a toddler'). For the want of such a toy, try a ball. When my sister and I were small we each had a ball to tow. They were about the size of tennis balls but were made of plastic and had holes roughly 1cm in diameter all over their surface. When towed beside the boat such a ball behaves like a fountain, squirting water at all angles. This keeps the little ones quiet for ages, provided they have control of the string. The near end of the string should be firmly attached to the boat, of course, as should the child (unless you are aboard an open boat).

Swallows and Amazons forever

Wherever possible the seagoing child should be encouraged to find his fun in sailing itself and in things related to boating, and to instil interest there can be no better starting point than the *Swallows and Amazons* stories by Arthur Ransome.

No one who missed out on this classic series of books can consider his experience of sailing to be complete, and no child who reads them can fail to be affected; his whole perception of sailing shifts, and the effects of reading about John, Susan, Titty and Roger are carried into adult life. Ransome's code of conduct, so subtly given, becomes one's own. If sailing was a pastime enjoyed by the majority, and if Ransome were writing now, *Swallows and Amazons* would have a cult following.

After *Swallows and Amazons,* an uneventful sail to the beach is converted in to a dangerous crossing of an ocean cluttered by pirate craft (motorboats) and foreign men-of-war (Westerlies, et al, if you sail an old gaffer, and vice versa). The landing is a treacherous one, on an inhospitable shore peopled by cannibals (landlubbers). My mother, at the age of 76, is still playing this game. She probably thinks that she is playing it for the sake of her grandchildren, but her own kids know better; she was still playing it when we were in our twenties. Whereas most people's logbooks contain only dull statistics, hers are full of remarks about waterspouts and 'the natives'.

When I was a child my mother used to encourage us to make *Swallows and Amazons*-style charts of the place where we sailed. My charts were fanciful pieces of artwork rather along the lines of the *Mappa Mundi*. I was more interested in drawing sea serpents and giving names to the creeks and rythes than in making an accurate map. My brother took the job much more seriously and spent a great deal of time taking compass bearings and soundings. For him the exercise was educational, but we both derived several seasons' fun from our endeavours.

Stories about messing about in small boats were food and drink to me, but for my children tales of ocean crossings are more relevant. Arthur Ransome provides these too, and with his usual cast. Caesar and Xoë like *We Didn't Mean to Go to Sea*, the story of how John and the others accidentally crossed the Channel in a friend's yacht, but their favourite in the series is *Peter Duck*, a tale of ocean sailing, buried treasure and pirates. My children also adore Robert Louis Stevenson's *Treasure Island*. We first read

this aloud when Xoë was five, and she and her brother were so thrilled and inspired that for months afterwards they were dressing up as pirates and making treasure maps.

Treasure Island is ideal for reading aloud; it might have been designed for it. A child cannot imitate Long John Silver's accent or understand the contrast between him and Dr Livesey, but an adult reading with the proper sense of theatre can bring the whole thing wonderfully alive. The little ones squeal in delighted horror as Silver clamps his hand on the ship's boy's shoulder and leers, 'Jim, lad! Aar, Jim!' We have read the book so many times now that some of the classic lines have become family catchphrases.

Treasure trails

All sorts of activities derive from reading *Swallows and Amazons* and *Treasure Island*. Some of them are useful only in terms of their entertainment value, but others encourage the child to become involved in the running of the ship and lead him towards being a fully paid up crew member. On the entertainments side there are maps and treasure trails.

Treasure trails are best run ashore, of course, but you can make a surprisingly good one around the boat. You can make up little rhymes or invent number clues, or even write the instructions in the international code flags, semaphore or Morse. I usually use some of each type of clue, and I also try to include some geographical ones. Mizzen, Main, Anchor, Samson (post), Genoa and many other parts of the boat are scattered around the world in the guise of Mizzen Head, Anchorena, St

Samson etc. (Main and Genoa exist in their own right.) Besides these, one can also find Looking Glass, Kettle (Creek), Key (West), Table (Bay) and a good many other useful places in the index of a really good atlas. Simply record the latitude and longitude given alongside the name and you have a clue, one which provides a first step on the ladder to understanding navigation. (Naturally, the first couple of times that you use this type of clue you will have to demonstrate the method.)

For younger children the clues can be very simple. For her fourth birthday I made Roxanne a trail consisting entirely of pictures (drawn by her big sister). A picture of the kettle led to the kettle; it was as straightforward as that, but it went down very well. For her fifth birthday I made Roxanne a trail consisting of simple words, such as... well, kettle, for instance. She had to read them herself, which she was just about able to do. Another hit. Had her reading skills been better then I might have cut the words each into three pieces (being sure to bisect the letters with each cut). Dot-to-dot pictures and puzzle mazes can also be used to provide simple clues for non-literate crew.

When you have ten or 12 assorted clues, decide upon the order of the trail, number the pieces of paper, and hide them in the appropriate places. The only other things needed are a treasure map and some loot. The map can be a clue in itself; the last clue for instance, marked with an X, or with co-ordinates to mark the spot where the crisps and chocolate are hidden. (The more insignificant the treasure, the better; do not let it be a 'reward' as this will detract from the experience of the trail.) I have yet to meet a child who did

not love my treasure trails. As a bonus, the kids often end up writing trails for each other or for me.

Buoys and gulls

Identifying things is another time filler and a first class habit to encourage. Birds, jellyfish, seaweed, dolphins, clouds, stars, headlands. You will need to carry reference books to enable the child to identify the flora and fauna and ephemera. The identification of stars and of headlands is another first step towards navigation.

If you regularly sail in a busy little corner such as the Solent or the Bristol Channel, an identification guide to ships comes in handy. One could also carry a copy of *I-Spy the Sea*, a spotter's book containing pictures of ships and buoys and all sorts of other marine features.

As a full-time occupation the identification of things is a flop. The speed at which the boat moves is too slow to provide a steady supply of landmarks, and wildlife is anything but abundant. Nevertheless, if the children are not already engrossed in other things (in which case, treat as sleeping dogs) one can grab opportunities as they flit, float or flurry by.

Inappropriate intrusions

For my part, I would steadfastly resist all requests from the crew for shipboard TV, videos, Gameboys and the like, and if we were weekend-sailing I would resolutely deny my child access to the yacht's computer (if any) for all but navigational purposes, and would refuse to let him bring a laptop aboard. Surely, one goes sailing to get away from such things? An hour or two of Walt Disney will certainly act as an effective tranquilliser and keep the kids quiet while you travel from Now till Then, but what purpose does this serve in the long run? It only sets a precedent. If you want your child ever to enjoy sailing for its own sake, you will need to break him of the addiction to a mindless sedative. Do yourself a favour, therefore, and don't allow the thing on board in the first place.

What do you expect ?

A great many parents seem to expect that their kids will be bored on board. Perhaps we should not be surprised, then, when our offspring fulfil our expectations.

I can only say that, so far as I can recall, no one ever troubled to amuse me while we sailed. I amused myself. I trailed my ball in the sea, or I played in the fo'csle, or I sat and watched the shore creep by. And from the earliest age I also took my turn at waggling the tiller – which is what it's all about, after all! I was expected to enjoy our weekends afloat, and so I did.

Similarly, my children have not needed to be entertained since they were toddlers. I suspect that this is partly because they are not accustomed to being told how to fill their hours. School-going children, who are used to having their time organised for them, might have a little more trouble occupying themselves. Since they live aboard, my children also have a good repertoire of pastimes lined up, and plenty of props – toys, pens and paper – but they seldom occupy themselves with these pursuits on a daysail. While we are on passage the kids tend to want to be involved in the actual sailing.

To journey is better

One of the best ways to ensure that your child fusses and whines while you sail is to emphasise the destination. Forget the destination! Emphasise the *sailing* if you want your child to enjoy it. By pandering to questions along the lines of 'Are we nearly there?' you are only fostering an obsession with arrival; with Not Sailing.

When sailing from A to B, resist the temptation to list the delights of the latter and the rewards to be got by reaching it. The promise of ice creams and beaches and fish and chips will inevitably detract from the sailing itself. You go sailing to sail, do you not? (If your answer is in the negative, please re-read the first section of this chapter!) You are sailing because sailing is what you like to do, not because you are desirous of getting to a different anchorage, and you should not allow your child to gain any impression to the contrary. He must understand that the port of your arrival is merely the full stop which ends the poem. (Avoid the use of the word 'sentence' in this context.)

Motor-mania

Again and again I have heard people bewail the fact: 'Now that we have children we use the engine far more'. Day sailors, weekend cruisers and ocean-going live-aboards all make the same glum confession, and yet I really cannot understand this.

I can distinctly recall our friend Günter Weiss saying as he looked down at our newborn son: 'You'll see. Now that you have a child you will find that you want to get every passage over and done with as quickly as possible.' Günter had four kids. He must know what he was talking about, we reckoned, and yet... and yet we were determined that we would *not* give up sailing and become motorists.

Well, I am pleased to be able to report that our German friend was completely wrong. The presence of our children aboard ship has not caused an increase in our engine hours. I would not dream of starting the engine just because my children were nagging me – but, in fact, they never have done; they are as content to be at sea as are their parents. My children have been taught to regard the engine as a convenience in confined anchorages and a safety aid in a truly tight corner.

I have noticed that people do motor their yachts far more these days than they used to. You seldom see anybody drop anchor under sail. We usually do, if at all possible. Generally this results in comments like, 'I see you have a problem with your engine,' and a couple of anchorages ago someone very kind and considerate came rushing out to rescue us. He mistook our backed sails for some sort of handling difficulty.

A wild digression from the subject of happy sailing with kids, you might think, but I merely wish to make the point that people motor because they *want* to motor. If you are one of those who has the urge, follow it – but, please, do not use your children as an excuse, or make them your scapegoats. Children only look towards crossing the horizon, by any means necessary, if the attitude of get-me-there-quick has been taught them by their elders and betters.

The making of a midshipman

I have devoted quite a lot of space to the subject of keeping the kids content while Daddy plays with the boat, but the way towards genuine Family Sailing does not lie with artificial amusements. If you aspire to be a Sailing Family, then rather than spend hours labouring to occupy their minds with irrelevant amusements, why not make the effort to show your children the fun to be had from sailing itself? Trivial pursuits such as the ones described above are all very well, but if you want your child to grow up a sailor then wherever possible he should be encouraged, rather than spending his time in distractions, to help man the ship.

➤ Parents should be on the lookout for any opportunity to let their youngsters join in with the main activity – but please note that the word is *let*, not *get*. This is the key to sailing with kids, or indeed to doing anything with either children or adults; one must *let* them help, not *get* them to do it. As the old Sussex saying has it, 'We wun't be druv.' ➤

Flag officer
Duties for the child who shows the least leaning towards the sea usually start with the ensign and the burgee. Children, although they abhor most routines, usually enjoy being trusted with the daily responsibility for raising and lowering the flags at

the proper times. All they need is the knowledge of how to tie a sheet bend and a clove hitch, the sense not to let go of the halyard, and the desire. (In my experience, children are not capable of learning to tie knots until they are around six years old.)

Duties such as the care of the flags are useful in giving a child a sense of pride in the yacht and in himself as crew, but they do not fill many minutes. They do not occupy any sea time at all, unless you happen upon a warship and can dip your ensign to her, in the proper courteous manner.

Handy on the helm

At sea, the main occupation for a young salt should be taking a trick at the helm, but even the most enthusiastic child tires quickly of this activity. An hour on the wheel or at the tiller is quite enough for all but the desperately eager or very experienced. After an hour of such intensive concentration, a child's attention begins to wander – in fact, half an hour is generally plenty long enough for an under-ten, and ten minutes of closely supervised steering is enough for a five-year-old.

Before you hand over the helm to a novice, try to put yourself in his shoes; it must be frustrating to have someone else keep butting in and grabbing the toy again. Choose a nice clear patch of water, and steel yourself to be very patient and to quash the feelings of embarrassment which will begin to rise in you when your boat turns pirouettes and attracts the unwanted attention of other water-users. If you can manage this, your child will very soon get the hang of steering the boat under engine. Learning to handle her under sail is a different matter, and one to which we will turn our attention later.

By the time he was six, Caesar had learnt to handle *Maamari* quite competently under engine and on our journey down through the French canals he made himself very useful. Naturally, we did not trust him to take the boat into the locks, encouraging him instead to help with the sluices or to act as line handler, when this was feasible. Between the locks, Caesar often steered and was very reliable *for so long as his concentration held*. We showered him with praise, demonstrated our trust by seeming not to be keeping an eye on progress, and as his pride in his helmsmanship grew, so the child's ability also improved. A nice example of the opposite tendency to a vicious circle.

Sheets and halyards

A trick on the helm fills a few minutes, but if one is making a passage this still leaves many more minutes and hours to be filled. What else can our young sailor do to while away the time? Well, there is more to sailing than simply pointing the boat in the right direction, and one can best get this knowledge through to a child *not* by explaining the principles of lift, but by leaning on him for assistance. If he is sitting in the cockpit, getting ready to look bored, ask him to keep an eye on the luff of the jib. Tell him – show him – what you mean, and then keep prodding him, 'Is it lifting? (Is it flapping?)'

Children are innately competitive, it seems. One sure way to get them involved in making the vessel go is to interest them in the idea of staying ahead of the guy creeping up behind you, or in thrashing the fellows in the boat ahead. Make sure that the chosen competitor is one that you really can, and really *will* beat, or else the exercise will certainly backfire! Children do not like to be overtaken and nor do they like to lose a race. They are essentially very bad sports and will not play the game again if you let them lose more than twice, so choose something small and under-rigged for your first victim.

Before you begin to involve your young crew in working the boat, it may be worth finding out whether they have the least idea what is going on. Accustomed principally to travelling by car, small children may be only dimly aware, if at all, that it is the wind pushing or sucking on the sails that makes the boat go. If you are travelling very slowly or are some distance from the shore, your small fry may not even be aware that you *are* travelling. (Consider this, and the little child's frustration with the tiny, tippy, floating island becomes even more understandable!)

If your boat steers with a tiller, your child may have no notion of its function; after all, it does not look like either a steering wheel or a bicycle's handlebars, and it is at the wrong end of the vehicle.

My parents tell a tale of how, one day, my sister looked round from her habitual position in the bow of the Wayfarer and asked, with some concern, 'Who's driving this thing?' Presumably she was afraid that it might be supposed to be her.

Having ensured that the children have some remote idea of what makes the boat go, you can then begin to involve them in making her go a bit faster – and, as I say, competition gives an impetus to this activity.

Besides watching the luff of the jib to see that the helmsman does not take the boat too close to the wind, the children can also lend a hand with the actual sail handling. They can help to hoist the sails – even a slight four-year-old can tail a halyard, provided it is first run around a winch – and if the wind is not too strong or the sails too big, older children can be asked to ease the sheets preparatory to a tack, or to ease and bring them in, according to changes in the wind's strength and direction, while the skipper maintains a steady heading on a reach. This is NOT a suitable activity for a very small child, or even for a bigger one if the sail concerned is large and powerful – a powerful sail will pull a child into the winch – but in the right circumstances, where the ratio of child size to sail power is appropriate, handling the headsail is an ideal task for a youngster.

If you have two children, one can be in charge of casting off the old sheet at the right moment, as you go about, and the other, if he is big enough, can help to sheet in on the new tack. Boys of ten years and upwards will usually be keen to test their muscles in this way.

Little things of this sort are pieces in the puzzle of learning to sail, but there is another important thing that your young sailor can do while you are at sea. He can begin to navigate.

Cocked hats and cardinals

Navigation is not something to foist upon a child who finds the idea tedious and a lecture will fall on deaf ears. Even a demonstration is likely to be received with polite yawns, or worse. Spare the child the benefit of your sagacious learning, Father; save your breath. Remember the proverb:

*I hear, and the words pass me by like the
    wind.*
I see, and I forget.
I do, and I understand.

Lessons in navigation need not be formal
– indeed, better if they are not – and they
should begin with things far more basic
than the three point fix. If you make use
of a GPS aboard your vessel then your
opening gambit might be to let the child
press the appropriate buttons and discover your position for himself. Modern
navigation really is child's play. Coming
up with a chain of figures is only part of
the art, of course. If he really wants to be
able to say that he guided the ship from A
to B, the young navigator will need to
know what the figures mean and will have
to learn to plot them on the chart. He will
feel very proud of himself when he
can manage this feat, and his sense of
satisfaction will allow him to be lured into
learning more about the ancient and
worthy art of the navigator.

    Proceeding backwards, you can now
introduce your scholar to the possibility
of discovering the ship's position without
recourse to modern science, by taking
bearings with a compass. And it is worth
pointing out that this is exactly what the
magic box does anyway; effectively, it
takes bearings on passing satellites.

    At its simplest, coastal navigation is
the identification of features from which
we can establish our position. Your young
sailor does not even need to glimpse the
chart to help you with this; it will be much
more interesting for him if he does have
the chance to study the chart, but if he is
too young to comprehend its purpose, or
if he is feeling off colour, keep him on

deck and ask him to watch out for towers
and buoys and church spires.

    'I'm looking for a northerly cardinal.
Can anybody see it?' 'Who's going to be
first to spot the West Pole beacon?' 'There
should be a port-hand mark somewhere
to the north of us... Well done! But I'm
not sure if it's the right one. Can anybody
see what it's got written on it?' (Be
warned, however, that if you have more
than one child aboard, the last question
will probably result in a brawl over the
binoculars.)

    If the children are to be of any use in
coastal navigation they will need to know
the various shapes and colour configurations of the buoys, but these are so easily
learnt that a five-year-old can master them
in an afternoon. There are only eight or
nine worth speaking of and only six are in
regular use. I have heard of parents who
go to the trouble of producing a 'buoy
bingo' sheet or an I-spy game before each
passage. The children have to sight the
buoys or landmarks and cross them off as
they go. I think that this is an excellent
idea. Scanning the horizon is a good cure
for nausea, so that activities of this sort
can serve a dual purpose.

    If you are still navigating in the good
old-fashioned way, the game of spotting
salient features will lead your child swift-
ly towards wanting to take on the next
stage of the art: the actual business of
taking the bearings. From that will follow
the desire to do the plotting, too – and
once the principles have been *briefly*
demonstrated, the average ten-year-old, *if
he is interested*, will soon be knocking out
cocked hats almost as neat and tiny as
Dad's (or Mum's). In fact, once he has got
the knack the young sailor is apt to adorn

the chart with a continuous chain of fixes – so make sure that he is using a soft pencil.

Astro-navigation, although widely believed to be a black art and one of great complexity, is also well within the scope of an intelligent, interested ten-year-old. Taking sunsights and starsights and working them through are a natural part of the maths curriculum for children living aboard and travelling afar.

When we are making ocean passages, I always make a map of the relevant land and sea areas and pin it to the bulkhead. Plotting our latest position on this map becomes a daily ritual. Very young children will be capable only of making a mark in the place which you indicate, but as they grow older they will learn to translate the co-ordinates given to them, and eventually they will be able to take full responsibility for the whole exercise. Maps of the journey can give a child his first clue as to the extent of our small world. We also mark the day's progress on a globe, and this is a still more valuable aid in teaching the child about distance and time and the size of the planet.

A sound idea

Even if he is not yet ready to take an interest in the navigation or to lend a hand with the sailing, there are still relevant things that our young sailor can do to help while the boat is under way. Taking soundings is one useful and satisfying pursuit (provided that you are sailing in coastal waters!).

If they are literate, the children can start out by reading the depth of water off the echo sounder and comparing it to the figures on the chart, but the real fun is in learning the depth in the old-fashioned way, with a leadline. Children seldom give much consideration to what lies under the water beneath the boat, but when they measure the depth with a leadline they are actually making physical contact with what lies below, and that makes them pause for thought.

There is no need to go swinging the lead over your head – in fact there is every reason why this manoeuvre should *not* be performed in the confines of a small yacht. Pendulum-style swinging works just fine. The line can be kept on a drum, but before use it should be pulled off (rather than unwound from the end of the drum, as this encourages twists and tangles) and should be flaked down onto the deck in a seemingly careless pile.

Older children will enjoy perfecting the art of getting the lead to land ahead of the boat as she sails along, but for the sake of your gel coat or paintwork a smaller one should be told simply to drop the lead over the side. In this case, you will need to take the way off the boat by easing sheets or heaving to. Otherwise the lead will be trailing in your wake before it ever gets near the seabed.

For safety's sake, your child should be fastened to the boat before he swings the lead, or else he may follow after it. The far end of the line should also be secured. If he is allowing the line to pay out through his fingers, ensure that your child does not wrap a turn of the line around his hand. Also, see that neither he nor any other small crew member stands on or near the line. Since the lead only weighs 4lb, it is unlikely that even a toddler would be dragged overboard if he got caught in a coil, but he could certainly be pulled off his feet. Oh, and do not forget that the lead is simply that: a piece of lead. It is not a toy and should not be fondled by the child.

The language of the leadline

Once the lead has been swung (or dropped), then comes the business of reading off the depth: 'By the mark six', 'Deep five', etc. Lovely seamanlike cries with a tang of the mystical about them. Of course, before one can utter these words, or even their mundane equivalents ('Exactly six'; 'Five and a half') one has to learn to read the leadline code. Bits of leather, knotted cord, scraps of coloured cloth – and each with its own secret meaning.

For the romantic, a large measure of the leadline's charm comes from the knowledge that generations of true, ranting and roaring sailors of all nations have used just such a line, and sung out just such words, and have used the same sequence of leather and rag – but you do not really need to adhere to the traditional code. The genuine article is marked with two leather thongs at 2 fathoms, three leather thongs at 3 fathoms, white calico at 5 fathoms, red bunting at 7, leather punched with a hole at 10, and so forth, but you can easily adapt the method to modern usage. Since modern charts are marked in metres, it makes sense that the leadline be marked accordingly.

There was more to swinging the lead, in the old days, than the mere matter of learning the depth. A proper lead has a recess in the bottom and this is designed to hold a lump of tallow. When the lead touched the bottom the tallow, being sticky, brought up a sample of the seabed. If it brought back nothing then the bottom was rocky. Tallow nowadays is hard to find, but fortunately, margarine works just as well.

The desire for an exact knowledge of the depth of water might seem pedantic; surely it is sufficient to know that there is enough water under the keel to keep the boat afloat? Likewise, information regarding the nature of the seabed may appear of academic interest. So it is in this electronic age but in the past, when mariners were apt to be less sure of their position, a knowledge of the depth and bottom type were very useful. If you take a look at a chart you will see that it is marked not only with soundings but with terse descriptions of the bottom characteristics. Using these, a ship's captain could establish his proximity to the coast and might even be able to pinpoint his position. Those 'true British sailors' in the shanty 'Farewell and Adieu', who 'hove their ship to' (to take a sounding) and found 'forty fathoms on a fine, sandy bottom'; information that told them they had left Biscay and were in the Channel entrance. Accordingly, they 'bore off and filled away for the Downs' (a roadstead anchorage behind the Goodwin Sands).

This piece of information is quite an eye-opener for children raised on satellite navigation and sonar. Present it to them in the right way, with the lead in your hand and the song on your lips, and it can lead on to an interest in other aspects of 'what it was like in the old days'.

Historical inspiration

One of the best ways to bolster an interest in the 'glorious age of sail', and so foster an interest in the present one, is with a visit to some kind of maritime museum or, better still, to an old sailing ship such as the *Victory* or *Warrior*. From the sailor's point of view, *Warrior* is the more exciting of these two as you can roam around at leisure, try out the hammocks, sit at the tables, and do everything but climb the masts and set sail.

Warrior and the *Victory* are both at Portsmouth naval dockyard, together with the *Mary Rose*. I strongly advise against trying to 'do' all three ships on the same day. Even an adult emerges from such an undertaking feeling dazed, and for your child all three vessels will overlap into one confusion. Smaller children may even need to have the obvious explained to them; this strange, gilded building perched in this hollow in the ground is actually a boat. I mention this because Nick, when he was taken at a tender age to see the *Queen Mary*, could not see it at all; he could only see a huge black wall.

Heave the log: nautical pooh-sticks

Another time filler with its origins in the pre-technological past is the Dutchman's Log. This is a means of determining the speed of the vessel through the water, but there is more than a touch of pooh-sticks about the exercise.

Two players are needed for a Dutchman's log, and one of them must be competent to operate a stopwatch. He stands on the stern. The other player stands in the bow – suitably harnessed, of course – and lobs overboard some inoffensive item of flotsam, such as a small piece of driftwood. (Do not use a beer can or a bottle, and do not use anything made of plastic. It is illegal to throw plastic overboard, anywhere and everywhere, and bottles and cans may not be jettisoned in inshore waters.) The stick should be thrown for'ard of the boat but not into her path. At the exact moment that it passes the bow, the thrower must shout, 'Now!' and the person with the stopwatch must simultaneously start it up. When the flotsam is level with the stern he stops the watch again. In other words, his job is to time the passage of the stick from bow to stern.

That was the easy bit. Now for some mathematics. Small fry can cheat (if you approve) and use a calculator. Numerate children should be expected to exercise their grey matter. Let us say that your boat is 26ft long and that the stick took three seconds to travel from bow to stern. If we really want to do the thing properly we must involve ourselves in a hideous sum, based on the fact that 6,080 feet covered in 3,600 seconds imply a speed of 1 knot. Alternatively, rather than spoil the afternoon, we can take a short cut and use a ready reckoner:

1 Multiply the distance travelled (in this case, 26ft) by 3.
2 Multiply the elapsed time in seconds (3, in our case) by 5.
An eight-year-old ought to be able to cope with that, but he may need help with the next bit, which consists in dividing the first product by the second:
3 In our example, (26 x 3) divided by (3 x 5).

The answer, in this instance, is 5.2, so our vessel is doing approximately 5 knots; probably time to put in a reef!

By the time the children have solved the problem, the wind will have changed and the boat will have picked up speed or lost way – and anyway one ought to take the average of three shots. By the time they have done the job three times, an hour may have slipped away and it will be time for something new.

There are all sorts of other nautical measurements that can be made on passage, but most of them involve more complex calculations, and for some you need specialised equipment. Navigational party tricks of this sort should form the core of the maths curriculum for a live-aboard teenager. Unless he is of a scientific bent and loves arithmetic, the average child sailing for pleasure at the weekend will resent being given 'school work' in outside hours.

Children are far more likely to want to take soundings or to measure the speed of the vessel and do other things with a slightly academic leaning if they think that you actually need the information. If your vessel is fitted with an electronic log and echo sounder, you might suggest to your young crew that they test the accuracy of the equipment. Echo sounders are usually spot on, but logs often over-read.

Certificated seamen

Most children are attracted to the idea of winning awards. Whether this is a positive thing I cannot say, but it appears to be a fairly basic human trait; all societies promote levels of achievement, whether in winning diplomas and doctorates, or in lion slaying. If the award system helps to encourage achievement, we may as well make use of it.

When it comes to sailing the RYA might be thought to have the award

situation fully taped, but not every child likes the idea of learning to sail in a school-type environment. Besides, the RYA syllabus concentrates purely on sailing and navigational skills and therefore leaves several areas uncovered. I designed a set of challenges for my children which aimed to cover everything from sailing ability through to catering and cooking. The scheme is loosely based on my idea of the system that would have operated aboard a merchant sailing ship in the 1800s, but also owes much to the *Swallows and Amazons* mentality.

At the bottom of the scale we have the Ordinary Seaman and to qualify for this award, and therefore raise themselves above the rank of ship's boy or girl, the kids have only to be able to swim a short distance, row well enough to be allowed off the leash, tie a few basic knots, and demonstrate that they can be trusted to behave themselves both in the dinghy and aboard the yacht. Weekend sailors might also like to include a certain amount of seatime logged.

Having achieved the rank of Ordinary Seaman, the children are trusted to use the dinghy without supervision and can work towards their Able Seaman's ticket. Or perhaps they will prefer to earn a rating as Ship's Cook, or as Navigator, Bosun, or Engineer. One could also throw in Ship's Doctor and Ship's Naturalist. (Have they learnt about Darwin, who was official Ship's Naturalist on the voyage of the *Beagle*?) In order to qualify as Captain the children must earn all or most of these awards and must also have qualified as Mate.

Fear not, Father. It will be a long time before your offspring earn the chance to order you about. Since the scheme is reality-based and insists that the candidate really *can* cook, or navigate by the stars, or captain the ship, it forms quite a serious and lengthy curriculum. Indeed, it ought to see the child through from kindergarten to college, or at any rate from the age of five to 14, or thereabouts. Many of the skills acquired can be demonstrated to be National Curriculum related and much of the learning will be vastly more worthwhile than anything which could be taught in a classroom.

Incidentally, if you decide to implement this idea, then I recommend that you resist the temptation to hand out prizes for the attainment of an award. A fancy certificate is appropriate recognition of the child's new status, and you might also issue badges of rank – a penknife for the AB, for example, and a bosun's whistle for the Bosun – but a new toy or other irrelevancy will only detract and distract.

Hot tips

Certain things can make sailing with children happier, safer, and more comfortable. First on the list is the pre-departure organisation of meals.

Hot meals

Sailing cookbooks often grade meals according to the Beaufort scale. Thus on a calm Sunday we might be served cod *au gratin* or roast beef and Yorkshire pudding, but by the time the wind reaches force 4 we are down to curried corned beef, and in a high wind (force 7) we find ourselves obliged to make do with spam sandwiches. If the wind rises any further we will be lucky to get anything more than a packet of biscuits, and once a storm has been declared, prayer and fasting become the order of the day.

If the weather is fit for sailing then, once you are accustomed to the motion, cooking under way should present no problem – but you do first have to grow accustomed. Nobody likes having to go below and prepare a meal before they have found their sea legs. The best way to feed a hungry crew on the first day at sea is with a pre-cooked meal. By this I do not mean an additive-packed convenience food, selected from the supermarket freezer, but a nourishing, carbohydrate-packed meal which you have prepared and cooked in advance. My mother always used to bring aboard at least one pre-cooked, frozen dinner (which slowly defrosted inside a Thermos bag) and I adopt a similar procedure. I cannot cook on the first day at sea, and so I prepare at least one meal the evening before we sail and leave it sitting in the pan, ready to be reheated. Some kind of stew or casserole is ideal for the purpose. It should be brought to the boil and *thoroughly* reheated before you set to, as food which has only been warmed is a cosy breeding ground for bugs such as *e coli*.

When I was a child, we did not eat at sea but my mother's ready-made meal was always appreciated, and by none more so than the cook herself. The last thing a mum wants to do, after a day of sailing, is to knuckle down to preparing a nourishing meal in a tiny, ill-equipped galley, with a hungry audience who keep asking how long supper will be. Like the rest of the crew, she wants to unwind and be fed. I do not know how it was that day-sailing came to be thought of as relaxing. Relaxing is what you hope to do *after* the sail, when you have found the entrance, crossed the bar and managed, after the third try, to find a spot where you can anchor without coming up against some-body else. Having gone through all this, with the kids alternately prancing around, trying to join in the fun and wailing when they get scolded, lighting the gas is quite enough cuisine for any mum.

Regardless of whether one is planning a long passage or only making daytrips, it is a good idea to stock the boat with a supply of foods which can be prepared quickly and easily in rough weather. This makes sense regardless of the composition of the crew, but is especially important if there are children aboard. Children, even more than adults and armies, march on their stomachs. A child with a hollow tummy is bound to be grouchy, yet when you fill his belly with something tasty he can endure any kind of weather and almost any crisis. Food puts the smile back onto a tear-stained face.

Warm and dry

Besides being well-fed, our little sailor also needs to be appropriately clad. You do not have to have spent much time on the water to discover that sailing in tem-perate climes is usually chilly. Even if it was warm enough on the run down from the marina for the crew to strip down to their T-shirts, when you turn around to beat back up, the apparent strength of the

● For safety's sake each crew member, regardless of age and ability, should have their own waterproofs.

wind will have doubled. One of the things which I remember best from my child-hood sailing, and the thing which for me most typifies cruising in English waters, is the business of having to take one's jumper on and off every five minutes as the sun comes and goes behind the little fair-weather cumulus clouds.

Anyone who has ever sailed will realise the wisdom of carrying warm clothes even on what begins as a scorching hot summer's day. For children, tracksuits are the best option. Jeans are completely unsuitable for sailing. They are suitably tough but if they get wet they stay that way for a long time, robbing the wearer of heat. For a child old enough to worry about his or her appearance, cords are a reasonable alternative.

When one is sailing in the tropics the need for warm wear disappears; during all the time that we were living and sailing in the Caribbean I never once wore a jersey or trousers. But in temperate regions the sailor must be equipped not only with winter woollies but with a set of waterproof gear, and this goes for our junior crew quite as much as for those who stand in the front line facing the wind and spray.

Children get cold much more quickly than adults. You may like to imagine that when the going gets unpleasant your little ones will be snug and safe below decks. Ideally they should be – but young inexperienced sailors do not always want to be below in bad weather; not if it means being shut in behind the hatchboards, far from their mother's soothing influence. Clear Perspex hatchboards are an advantage in this situation, but if Mum is outside the kids will probably insist on being there too, come hell or high water. Unless conditions are actually dangerous, it is as well to oblige the infant whim. An unhappy, frightened child will probably be seasick in the confines of the cabin. If circumstances allow, dress him in his full waterproof regalia, see that his safety harness line is hooked on properly, and let him join the rest of the crew.

For coastal sailing, cheap and cheerful plastic macks and plastic salopettes are all that the young sailor needs. My children's first waterproofs came from car-boot sales and charity shops. For so long as we sailed in inshore waters they served their purpose well – they kept off the rain and spray – but when push came to shove, and a hard shove at that, these stop-gap oilskins were dangerously inadequate. If you are intending to spend any length of time cruising offshore in the (so-called) temperate regions of the globe (where the

weather is often anything *but* temperate) you ought to consider buying heavy-duty foul-weather gear, of the best sort that money can buy, for even the littlest member of the crew.

Before we set off for Patagonia we tried hard to find proper yachting oilskins for Caesar and Xoë, but at that time it was virtually impossible to buy anything in a size suitable for three- to four-year-olds. Crewsaver and their rivals had been producing well-styled children's lifejackets for aeons, but 'fouly' manufacturers were a few light years behind. When our yacht capsized and the hatches were torn off and the ice-cold waters of the Southern Ocean tumbled into our home, Caesar and Xoë were at a considerable disadvantage. They got soaked through. If we had needed to take to the liferaft or had been exposed to the wind, then the situation for the children would have been desperate. As it was, the risk of hypothermia was high, and it was largely for this reason that we put out a distress call.

Douglas Gill now produce kiddies' oilskins 'just like Mummy's'. Unfortunately, the price is also just like the price for the adult outfit. By way of a compromise, I recently bought for Xoë a set of Peter Storm waterproofs from Millets. These are at least half as good as the real thing and cost well under half the price.

You may like to note that commercial seafarers, such as fishermen, do not wear yotty-type nylon oilskins. Fishermen work a lot harder than yotties but do not seem to suffer the need for high-tech, breathable waterproofs. They invariably wear oilskins made from heavy duty, cloth-backed PVC. These are the oilskins which Nick and I also now prefer. They are rugged and durable; I have owned my Guy Cotten plastic oilskin trousers for more than 20 years now and I can still sit in a puddle without getting a wet bum. I cannot recall how many fancy, top-name oilskin jackets I have been through in this time. Alas, Guy Cotten do not produce these fabric-backed PVC oilies in kiddies' sizes, but they do make XS jackets and salopettes and these are suitable for young teenagers.

Hot weather

So much for wintry weather. Of course there are times, even in England, when the sun shines down fiercely, and then the younger members of the crew will feel that a pair of shorts or a swimsuit is all that they need. Skippers are inclined to feel this way too, I have noticed, and it is down to the Mate to see that they all wear some kind of protection.

We are all aware now of the long-term risks associated with sunburn, but wind chill deadens one's appreciation of the danger; the weather-beaten sailor is actually one who did not realise that he was getting burnt. Hats, if they remain on the head, will protect from the direct rays of the sun, but reflected light also contains the harmful ultra-violet wavelength. The many-faceted surface of a wave dancing past the yacht is a powerful reflector and a hat will not shield from these rays, which bounce up off the water in all directions. For total protection a child needs a high-factor sunblock. And do not forget his lips. Caesar was recently badly sunburnt on the lips. For more than a week afterwards his lower lip was sore and swollen and he now has a couple of freckles there to remind him (and me) of our carelessness.

Hot on safety

Mothers are also in charge of laying down the law concerning the wearing of life-jackets and harnesses, and a clear inviolable set of rules which govern the use of this safety gear is another thing which goes towards the making of a happy ship.

Port pursuits

There is more to sailing than travelling over the waves. Anchoring, going alongside and picking up moorings are as much an aspect of the game, and are things that children enjoy greatly if they are able to assist in the endeavour. If they are capable, teach them to tie on the fenders (to the stanchions, please; not to the rail itself) and show them how to coil a line properly and how to throw it. If you are going for a buoy and your child is old enough to be trusted to keep hold of the boathook, let him try picking it up. What does it matter if you have to have two (or half a dozen) shots at the thing? It is all good seamanship practice.

Time spent in port is very much part and parcel of the sailing business. Indeed, most of us probably spend more time in port than at sea. Quiet evenings lying on one's bunk listening to a soft rain fall on the deck, and murky days when the clouds clag down and ruin the well-laid plans for a weekend jolly – these are quite as much a part of sailing as is bashing across the briney. So too are lovely sunny afternoons when the water in the anchorage sparkles and chatters to the hull, and a gentle breeze wafts little cotton-wool clouds along the horizon.

Funnily enough, it is the grey, desolate evenings in muddy creeks that I remember with the most nostalgia, and the soft sound of rain pattering on the deck makes me feel safe and snug – probably because it takes me back to a time when somebody else had the worry of whether the anchor would drag in the middle of the night. I loved anchorages – I liked them far better than the places where one could go alongside, and I still do – but as a child I would surely *not* have enjoyed being at anchor if there had been nothing for me to do, or if I had felt that I was trapped aboard.

The first essential for a boating boy or girl in port is a suitable dinghy. The ship's own tender will probably fit the bill, but a command of his or her very own is a better thing by far, and in the case of a dissatisfied young crew member might help to tip the scales in favour of yachting. Surrounded by the sea, which beckons him to come and play, a child without access to a dinghy is like a bird whose wings have been clipped. But this is a subject so important that I have given it its own chapter. In the paragraphs which follow we shall consider more mundane pursuits, suitable for when the weather or darkness forbids fooling about in a 'rubberduck'. How will our infant midshipman fill his time aboard ship?

Monkeying about

There is one thing that my kids invariably do in port, whether we are aboard our own boat or with friends, and that is to clamber about all over the vessel as if it

● Fishing is popular, especially for boys. These small dorado were later salted and dried, and were delicious.

were a kind of maritime assault course. I once had the idea of putting a scramble net over the boom, to encourage the children in their activities, but they need no encouragement. Within ten minutes of boarding a strange vessel, Xoë will be up in the rigging. If there are no mast steps, she will have a go at shinning up the pole, and if there are no ratlines on the shrouds then she will pull herself up them using her bare toes.

People tend to feel sorry for children who spend their days cooped up aboard a boat and we have often been accused – albeit in the politest of terms – of what amounts to cruelty. 'The poor things,' strangers say of our threesome, seeming to think of them as if they were rabbits kept in too small a hutch. 'Don't they get fed up? I mean, children need space, don't they, to run and play?'

The answer is that children need to run and play but that, unlike rabbits, they do not crave to be set free and do not need very much space. Caesar has never felt the need to rush about, but Xoë and Roxanne certainly do – and they do it on deck, thundering up and down tirelessly, to the annoyance of anyone below their pattering feet.

Chris and Eddi Woodbridge, who feared that their five children would be bored aboard the family's tiny bilge-keeler, also found that the youngsters occupied themselves very happily, swarming over every swarmable surface 'and a few which were less so'. With abundant opportunity to perfect their climbing prowess and test their nerve, live-aboard kids sometimes combine monkey antics with swimming activities, using the crosstrees as a diving platform. A teenaged, terrestrially based friend of Caesar's spent a good quarter of an hour plucking up the courage to jump from the end of *Mollymawk*'s spreaders but, while I sympathised with the boy, I also found myself thinking about two far smaller children whom I had watched, a few years before. These youngsters had spent several hours chasing each other round and round their boat on a circuit which took them up the mast, off the spreaders into the sea, and up on deck again via the self-steering rudder. Gaff-rigged boats often offer splendid opportunities for such antics.

When they tire of chasing each other over the spreaders or along the boom, there are other things that the children can do on deck, the most obvious one being fishing. We once shared an anchorage in the Cape Verde islands with a Belgian yacht whose crew included an eight-year-old boy completely fanatical about fishing. This child used to fish all day and kept both his own family and ours well fed. Although less dedicated to the pastime, Caesar has also managed to provide us with supper on many an occasion, and we have met several other boys and girls who do the same. There can be few other opportunities these days for a child to contribute in this way to the family's welfare. The knowledge that they are pulling their weight gives children a great sense of self-worth and satisfaction.

What to do on a rainy day

Children can almost always find ways to pass a sunny day in port, but in the evenings or when the weather is wet the crew must find ways to amuse themselves below decks. Accustomed to letting the TV entertain them, many people are initially at a loss when denied its company, but soon discover that there is a considerable pleasure to be had from homemade fun.

Enforced togetherness and interaction might seem, initially, to threaten the very survival of the family, but in the long run time spent living in each other's pockets strengthens family bonds, and the opportunity to spend time together without the distraction of television is one which should be warmly embraced. Such occasions – ridiculously rare in the modern world – are often a source of warm memories in later life, and the togetherness which a child and his parents find while snugged down in the cabin of a little rain-lashed boat at anchor can help to create a lasting and meaningful bond.

So much for the theory – what about practical reality? What do we actually do with ourselves at the end of a long day or during a wet one? Well, when home is where the boat is there is never any shortage of things to do and, like other folk, we have to deliberately make time for Family Evenings. Without being able to define why or what, we all feel a gain from a few hours spent in playing Scrabble together or combining to create a masterpiece of rhyme.

The children occasionally try to talk us into a battle of wits on the chequerboard or a few laps of Snakes and Ladders or Monopoly, but Nick and I both dislike board games (or bored games, as I term them) and we prefer to encourage more imaginative or cultural diversions. As I have mentioned before, this family particularly enjoys reading aloud and we often take it in turns to read a few sentences or paragraphs of a book or story, each according to his ability. Sometimes we read plays. Shakespeare is still beyond us, but Oscar Wilde is a big hit and we have also tackled *Pygmalion* together. We also make up stories – idiotic stories – taking it in turns to contribute one word at a time.

At other times the children will come up with ideas which require an element of adult assistance and we will find ourselves embroiled in an evening of origami or puppet making, or something of that kind. Charades is another source of entertainment, and one which can be riotously successful if everybody is in the right mood.

Some families pass their evenings following more nautical pursuits. Learning to tie knots and making a knotboard are satisfyingly creative ways in which to fill the idle hours, just so long as your children are old enough to learn the knots without things ending in tears of frustra-

tion (yours). French cruising friends used to make a living out of selling the knotboards which they made in their evenings, and many a self-motivated cruising kid has earned his pocket money in this way.

If you are obliged, by forces beyond man's control, to spend all day in port and aboard ship, consider putting the children in charge of the galley. Let them choose what to eat and let them cook it. Like most young children, Xoë is more interested in baking than in cooking meals, but Caesar at the age of four announced an intention of owning a restaurant (which he planned to tow behind the boat) and he has a continuing interest in providing elaborate breakfasts and three-course dinners. Quite as much time is spent in planning the meal and writing out a fancy menu as in standing at the stove, so be sure to throw out this idea several hours in advance of feeling hungry.

Xoë is usually permitted to serve as waitress, and sometimes as sous chef, but the maître is a bit of a prima donna and sometimes insists on doing everything himself. (Everything except the dishes, that is.) The dressing-up bag is raided for velvet capes and net curtains, and the cabin is draped with these oddments and transformed into the children's idea of a high class restaurant (and our idea of somewhere rather sleazy). Naturally, there is a dress code and guests are expected to wear their best bib and tucker. The bill is often astronomical and we sometimes have to do a runner.

Sing-songs and socials

Quite the nicest way to spend an evening in an anchorage is with a singsong. A few choruses of 'Hanging Johnnie' and

Farewell-and-adieu' in the sympathetic glow of an oil lamp are surely guaranteed to see any young sailor off to bed in good spirits. Of course, it helps if somebody in the family can play an instrument; guitar, recorder, penny whistle, concertina, fiddle, harmonica... any of these will provide the ideal accompaniment in the right hands. Aboard *Mollymawk* we have recently acquired a melodeon, or button accordeon, which makes a suitably loud and tuneful racket.

If you hold your family singsong on deck it will probably turn into a party, with crews from other yachts in the anchorage turning up to join in the fun. Home-made music, even if purely amateur, has an allure which pulls in other souls like iron filings to a magnet. There can be few more convivial ways to pass an evening afloat than among a likeminded fraternity of seafarers, whose mood has mellowed to reflect that of the music floating over a star-speckled harbour.

I have noticed that yachtsmen sailing in home waters tend to be exclusive and keep to their own cabins. By contrast, live-aboard cruising yotties spend a lot of time to-ing and fro-ing between each others' boats. A new anchorage is a chance to meet up with other members of the cruising family, people who, as likely as not, are friends of friends. The first thing that cruising yotties do when they meet is inquire where the other has been, not so much out of polite curiosity as to establish a common frame of reference; have they been anywhere that we have been, and do they know anybody that we know? The next thing that we do is scrutinise each other's visitors books. Once you start gadding about the oceans the

world really does become quite small, and you can almost always find friends in common in a visitors book.

We know, when we row across to greet a new arrival, that we will certainly be invited on board, and if we hit it off there will be an exchange of invitations to drinks or dinner. Home-loving, house-living people would not dream of inviting a stranger through the door just because he happened to knock, and perhaps this same psychology of privacy and security pervades the mind of the weekend-yachtsmen. If weekend sailors were to open up a little and recognise each other as potential friends, then hours at anchor and wet weekends might be more sociably filled. Children are actually the best bet, in this respect; unless you are determined to remain aloof, you can hardly help but get to know the parents of your children's playmates.

Children, having spotted others of the same breed, sniff around each other like dogs and then quickly get stuck into playing together. If he is not sufficiently out-going to make these kind of moves but seems to hanker after other infant company, issue your child with a pair of water pistols. My kids sometimes resort to this tactic when faced with the language barrier, for there is nothing quite like a water pistol fight to break the ice.

Read all about it

It is not every child who needs or wants overt adult involvement in his evening agenda. Singsongs and Scrabble nights are like parties; most of us look forward to them and enjoy them very much, but a large part of their appeal stems from the fact that they are not everyday occurrences. We also need quiet moments in our lives, and a bleak, grey anchorage or a still one whose waters shimmer like black silk beneath the jewelled canopy of the heavens can bring us to a place of inner peace not accessible in the ordinary course of a typically hectic life.

If your little one has not fallen under the spell of your surroundings, or if they lack the necessary, soul-stirring ambience and yet you cannot face another lap of Snakes and Ladders, try bringing the child's mood into line with yours by reading to him. Be sure that your choice of material is suitably salty and seaworthy (ie worthy of bringing to sea).

Older children, too, may want for nothing more, at the end of the day's adventure, than to curl up in their cosy nook. Again, if they are curling up with a book, try to see to it that they are soused in sea lore. Stories of adventure under sail, read while the waters lap past, may be the spark to inflame a lifelong passion for the sea.

When I was young I had a book about a little Dutch boy whose adventures began when he slipped out of his aunt's home and let himself be stolen by the local deep-sea fishermen. I can remember nothing about the story but one image is fixed forever in my mind; that of the child waking up to find himself huddled in the dank, smelly fo'csle of the fishing boat, amongst the tarred warps and the tanned sails. Hardly a pretty image, and yet it captured my imagination. Every night for years thereafter, when I went to bed, I would make believe that I too was a ship's boy curling up beneath damp, mildewed canvas on coir fenders and coils of stout hempen rope.

Shore party

Before we pass on, it is worth pointing out that one other rather obvious way to spend a wild, wet day in port is ashore. Eddi Woodbridge suggests dressing the whole crew in their oilies and marching them off on a long walk. In Britain, almost every town has its museum, historic church or castle worthy of a visit.

If they are old enough, send the kids out to scavenge on the shoreline. Give them a list of flora and fauna to collect: one crab carapace, two seaweeds, three shells, etc; or, if you prefer: crustacean, gastropod, echinoderm, alga, and so on, depending on the children's level of education and yours (but you can all cheat, and use a textbook to find out what you are talking about). Children like to load the boat with 'interesting' stones and shells and suchlike, so that the scavenge is really just an extension to this museum-keeping, collecting instinct.

Nor need you confine yourself to barracks every evening whilst in port. Few people would spend every night aboard if they were cruising *à deux*, and yet even fewer parents consider the idea of heading ashore *en famille*. Are our children really so appallingly ill-behaved that we cannot face the drama of dining out in their company, or is this another instance of the sacred Bedtime coming to the fore and pulling a wet blanket over any after-hours ambitions? I wonder.

Enjoy it!

In the main, and in contrast to boating with a baby, camping afloat with kids is fun. Cruising with children is also very rewarding, but the difference between spending a few days aboard and living for years in a small boat is so great that I have kept my ideas about epic family voyages for a later chapter. That said, whether your skipper's ambitions and the yacht itself are little or large, life afloat is essentially similar to any other existence; your young crew still need to eat and play, rush about, relax and sleep. Just like anybody else, they thrive on a healthy balance of adventure and security.

Yachting offers a range of adventure even broader than a fairground and can meet all needs, from the tot who finds a static ride on the merry-go-round utterly thrilling, to the teenager getting his kicks on the cyclone. From drifting along on the placid waters of a sheltered estuary, to fighting for survival in a Southern Ocean blizzard, yachting has it all. As a by-product, you will find that a boat is a grand environment for personal development. Watching your child grow in self-confidence as he takes on responsibility is very rewarding, and there can be few other lifestyles which present such splendid opportunities for this.

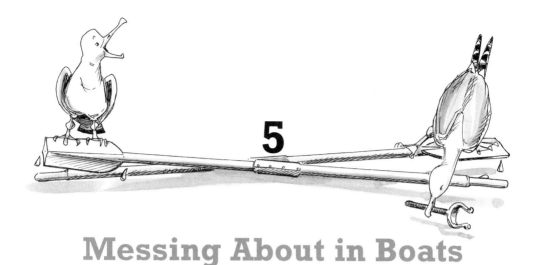

Messing About in Boats

Dinghies under oars • **Dinghies under sail** • **Sailing lessons**
• **Future sailors** •

'There is nothing,' said the water rat, 'half so much worth doing as simply messing about in boats,' and which young sailor would disagree? I do not mean crossing an ocean, or even pottering around in the English Channel. Messing about in boats, to a child, means taking the dinghy off, on his own, for no particular purpose other than the pleasure of being out on the water.

Even a die-hard young sailor, who loves the family yacht and seems to like nothing so much as helping to work her, also needs time out. To really enjoy sailing, a child, once he is old enough, must have the opportunity to do his own thing. He must be free to come and go; he must have the chance to pootle about the harbour and explore under his own steam. To be trusted to run ashore and fetch off a visiting grandfather, or buy a loaf of bread, is an activity that appeals greatly to most youngsters. And having done with excuses and explanations, the truth of the matter is this: to enjoy sailing, to really love sailing, your child must have a command of his own.

Dinghies come in all shapes and sizes, from the folding tender and the rubber inflatable, through the lovely clinker pram and the just-about rowable, just-about towable Mirror, to the super-powered semi-rigid (or RIB), and the Flying Fourteen and its modern descendants. Since our purpose here is to consider the dinghy as an accessory to the mother yacht, we can forget about racing dinghies and RIBs. Many of us would also like to forget about outboards for use by our children, but few small boys will allow their parents to forget.

Afloat, quite as much as elsewhere, children are susceptible to the 'everyone else has got one' syndrome. If one child in the anchorage has the use of an outboard, any who are deprived of the opportunity will feel hard done by. In this situation, parents are inclined to bow to pressure – but they soon find that this is not the end of the matter.

Having entered the race, they learn that their outboard is not big enough (ie not the biggest on the block).

When I was a child, most people travelled back and forth between the boat and the shore under oars, and a few of us still do. For those who prefer to burn fossil fuel rather than body fat, I suggest that you let your child drive the boat under engine while the family are to-ing and fro-ing, or if he is running an errand, but that he be encouraged otherwise to make use of either the wind's energy or his own. If you own an outboard and your child is old enough and sensible enough to operate it safely, it would be a shame to deny him the opportunity of doing so, but motoring should not be seen as better than drifting on the wind or getting about through one's own exertions. To let the child miss out on learning to row skilfully and handle a dinghy under sail would be an even greater shame.

Dinghies under oars

A rowing dinghy is the boating baby's bicycle; both a means of transport and his favourite toy, from early infancy through to the age when he can command a yacht.

A child can pick up the action of rowing even before he has learnt to walk. I have a photo of Caesar at five months, sitting on his daddy's lap with his fat little legs wedged firmly between Nick's so that he could not fall. While the old man rowed, Caesar cycled his hands with the exact same rhythm and you can tell by the look on his face that the exercise was completely absorbing.

By the time Caesar was two he had perfected his stroke and had evidently realised that the circles which he drew in the air with the handles of the oars were responsible for the action of the blades. However, he was two and a half before he had the strength to manage the weight of the oars alone. It was at this age that he first soloed, at the end of a fairly short tether, in the safe confines of a marina.

The temptation to keep a small novice oarsman safely tethered is strong, but this method of providing security is not without its drawbacks. Unless the rope used is long, the youngster soon reaches its limit and then, like a tethered goat, he must endure the frustration of being unable to roam further. This is enough to dampen anybody's enthusiasm. And if you have ever rowed a line ashore, or set a second anchor under oars, you will know that it is surprisingly difficult to keep moving against the weight of a rope in the water. Unless the line that secures your child is the kind that floats, it will be restricting in this sense also – but a line lying on the water or just below its surface is a liability to everyone else.

Aiming to keep everybody happy, we tried using a 300ft length of bright orange floating line, the idea being that other harbour users would be able to see it and avoid it. However, they couldn't and didn't; there were some heart-stopping moments. There were also occasions when the kids managed to plait the line around every pile and post and mooring buoy in sight. Finding themselves abruptly

• No young sailor should be without a command of his own.

moored, at the far end of this tangle, they did not have the wits to unwind themselves and instead used to get into a panic. Nor did the line fulfil its purpose in this situation, for we could not pull the kids back home if their tether was wound around things.

Without a doubt, the line had to go. But the children were as yet only three and five years old; not old enough to be trusted to stay safe all of the time. Either they must be chaperoned – an idea which appealed neither to them nor to their prospective chaperone (no prizes for guessing who) – or else we must come up with another solution. The other solution, the obvious solution, was a number two dinghy; a rescue boat on standby.

A two-dinghy family

If the kids are to be let loose in a dinghy, as indeed they should be, then the yacht must be equipped with two. You would feel rather silly, to say the least, if you were unable to render assistance when the kids lost an oar or got caught by the tide, and went drifting off over the horizon. There must be a rescue boat to hand, and it must be swifter than the children's own command.

No responsible parent would allow their offspring to take the dinghy without having first noted the state of the tide and the strength of the wind, and instructed the kids accordingly, but even this precaution is by no means infallible. Circumstances change and children do not have the ability to keep a weather-eye open. While your children are in the dinghy you must be watchful on their behalf, and if the weather turns nasty or they wander where they should not, you should issue a recall. This is best done with a shrill whistle or a foghorn. You can shout until you are blue in the face and your voice will fail to penetrate minds absorbed in play. (Naturally, everybody else in the vicinity will hear you yelling, however.)

● Start 'em young. Note the painter securing the dinghy and the lanyards attached to the oars.

➤ In our family we have a pre-arranged recall signal; the Morse code for the letter U, which is dit-dit-dah. This means 'You are standing into danger'. Sometimes the danger is only of missing lunch, but at all times when they hear the signal the children must return at once to the flagship. Reader, please choose a different signal; otherwise our kids will all be dashing hither and thither, in response to false alarms. ➤

A more direct aid to safety consists of a sea anchor, which can be deployed by your children when they find themselves unable to make up against a strong wind – assuming that they notice this problem. Our dinghy sea anchor came from a condemned liferaft. It is a piece of cloth 40in square, its centre punctured by a hole 2in in diameter. Nylon lines no thicker than a flag halyard are sewn right across the cloth in the form of an X, and the four ends are led a further 24in to a robust brass swivel. You and your children can play around with your sea anchor to discover the optimum scope for different wind strengths. We have had a lot of fun playing with ours in high winds.

If their lifejackets are not fitted with whistles, your young oarsmen should also be issued with one of these.

Some caustic criticism

Although there are people whose penchant for snazzy accessories extends even to their children's toys, yachtsmen are more typically inclined to think that any old rubbishy dinghy will serve the children's purpose. Figures well known and respected in sailing circles have recommended 'one of those very cheap beach toys' or suggested that 'the cheapest Campari will do', but I say it will not; it most certainly will not. Toy boats are not designed for yachting and your child is far more likely to get into trouble if his command is a piece of junk with no thwart, whose only means of propulsion is a pair of silly little plastic paddles. Anybody with the least desire to roam around and explore would be bound to get into trouble in a boat (so-called) which simply cannot be rowed properly. Moreover, your young seaman can hardly be expected to learn any worthwhile skills aboard one of these liabilities.

I think it is very important that the children's dinghy be a proper seaworthy one. Blow-up beach toys are out and so too are miniature boats. I once saw an advert for a neat little kiddy-sized dinghy made of GRP. It was about 4ft long, with beam and freeboard measurements in proportion, and the idea was obviously that it could be managed by a small child – but the wash of a passing motorboat would have swamped the vessel instantly!

Boats must be scaled to the size of the waters over which they will voyage, and not to the stature of their occupant. In any event, as we have seen, a three-year-old can manage a full-sized dinghy and full-sized pine oars. Another snapshot in our family album shows Xoë, at three and a half, transporting her father, her uncle and her 18-stone grandpa in a rubber dinghy. Progress was slow, as I recall it, but steady.

Rubber v rigid

Hard dinghies, wooden ones especially, are often pleasing and they are much easier to row than inflatables. This might incline us to want to choose a hard dinghy for our child's first command, but we must first consider the matter more closely for there are various other points on which rubber scores over rigid.

Rubber dinghies, being flat-bottomed, are very much more stable than hard dinghies; it is virtually impossible to capsize a rubber dinghy. Older children might learn from the experience of playing in a tippy dinghy – hopefully one with sufficient buoyancy to keep it from sinking if it capsized – but tiny tots are safer in something that withstands sloppy, unseamanlike behaviour (such as stepping on the gunwhale while boarding). One can load a well-designed rubber dinghy with seven small children. I do not recommend it, but as long as they do not squabble and push each other around they will be safe. I would not care to put more than three kids into a hard dinghy of the same size, and even then I would feel it necessary to nag them about not standing up or moving about unnecessarily.

If anybody does fall in the drink, it is much easier to drag them back aboard over the rounded tanks of the inflatable than to lift them in over the stern of a rigid hulled boat – although even the former is not as easy as you might imagine.

Hard dinghies also teach the child another aspect of good seamanship; the ability to come alongside without knocking the boat about. The owner of a GRP yacht might reckon this lesson a costly one if it means that his gel coat gets covered in little spidery cracks. Certainly, one ought not to expect a child under six years to come alongside tidily and carefully every time. A stout rope or rubber fender on the dinghy's gunwhale helps to reduce the impact of the collision.

Another disadvantage of the hard dinghy is its rowlocks. While the children are young it is a good idea to tie them into the boat. I can still vividly recall the hot flush of panic which washed over me when I lost a rowlock over the side from *Sprite*. Fortunately I was in very shallow water and, groping over the side, found it at once, but the experience has made me quite paranoid about losing either a rowlock or an oar. Incidentally, metal rowlocks also scar the hull with indelible reminders of poor seamanship.

Of course, the most obvious advantage of a rubber dinghy is its ease of stowage. Rubber dinghies were created specifically for use aboard small craft with limited deck space and are meant to be deflated and stowed in a locker.

In fact, although we rate them for their ease of stowage, few of us actually take advantage of this aspect of owning a rubberduck and many people leave theirs inflated for the whole season or throughout years of cruising – which suggests that this feature is not so relevant as it at first appears. It will be more relevant, however, when you start thinking about stowing two dinghies. Plainly, one or other of the duo has to be an inflatable. Deflated, the second dinghy could be carried aboard a boat towing astern, but if you do not want to put all your eggs in one basket, make room for a Number Two under the table, or in the forepeak; anywhere, in fact, but *make room*! Put up with the inconvenience of tripping over it every time you go below for the greater good of a contented young crew.

Rubberducks and rowlocks

Rubber dinghies, although superficially alike, can be very different in their detailing, and some brands are more suited to infant use and abuse than others. Some dinghies do not have proper rowlocks, some have no rowlocks at all, but most are equipped with silly little pins to which the user attaches silly little aluminium and plastic paddles. Do not assume that the boat can be rowed efficiently; many cannot. Rather, *try before you buy*.

● A small Avon dinghy is easily rowed as it has good set of rowlocks. This one was bought at a boat jumble for £30.

These days, people generally prefer to motor their rubberducks, and the dainty oars and rowlocks provided by the manufacturers are therefore little more than ornamental. They imply that the boat can be rowed when the outboard packs up, but when it comes to the crunch many prove impossible to row and have to be paddled Indian-style. Nick has more than once gone to the rescue of people whose outboards have broken down and who are in the process of discovering that their dinghies cannot be worked to windward.

Although you can learn the basic rowing stroke even in an ill-equipped boat, a decent set of rowlocks and a strong pair of oars of the proper length are essential to perfect your style. For my money, you cannot do better than a small Avon: an old-fashioned one with black rubber rowlocks. Old Avons are also virtually immortal. We have owned a couple which were over 25 years old when we sold them on.

Having knocked dinghies with pin-type rowlocks (or tholes), I must admit that some of these are much better than others. At the better end of the scale comes the Tinker Tramp, which can be rowed in a reasonably satisfactory manner. It can also be sailed, which is a big bonus when there are children around. The Tramp's big sister, the Tinker Traveller, although more fun to sail, is quite unmanageable under oars.

Dinghies under sail

If you want your child to learn to sail then you should get him a sailing dinghy, for a dinghy is by far and away the best place to learn the art. Dinghies respond quickly to whatever input the helmsman makes; he has only to waggle the tiller the tiniest bit to get a reaction, and so he quickly learns about cause and effect. More to the point, the sails aboard a full-sized yacht are often too heavy for a child to manage, whereas a dinghy's gear is on the appropriate scale. Your child may be 15 before he is strong enough to hoist the sails aboard the family cruiser, and older still before you trust him to take the boat out on his own. If he is to grow up loving sailing, he will need his own command long before this.

Live-aboard kids, especially, ought to have access to a sailing dinghy. Although we like to think of ourselves principally as ocean sailors, we live-aboards actually spend most of our time in harbour, and for a child to be living in the middle of a flat stretch of water but with no means to exploit it seems to me a great waste of opportunity. What a nine-year-old learns in a year of ocean sailing he can learn in just a week at the helm of his very own vessel.

The most popular sailing dinghy for small children is the Optimist. Scarcely more streamlined than a shoebox, and carrying a single, low-aspect gaff sail little more efficient than a bath towel, the 'Oppie' is actually a bit of a pig... but this may be of small relevance if you can fit one on the foredeck, or between the mast and the sprayhood. Even if you end up having to tow it, it will be less of a drag (sorry) than towing a bigger boat, such as a Mirror or a Topper.

Because they cannot be fitted aboard, Mirrors and suchlike are out of the question for live-aboards. A massed parade of the dinghies pressed into service and rigged for sail by cruising folk would make a motley parade, for there is seldom a pukka one, of recognised class, in the anchorage.

● These children grew up cruising but were not yet big enough to take much part in sailing their floating home. They relished the opportunity to take command of our dinghy.

Sailing lessons

You may want to send your child to an approved sailing school for tuition. If you decide to take the matter into your own hands, a little planning is advisable. If you have been sailing all your life, you may not be aware that the language of the sea is gobbledegook to the non-initiate. Even bona fide instructors sometimes make this mistake. I once watched a flotilla of children in Optimists who were being ordered about by a man with a megaphone. Over and over again this chap patiently told the class that he did not want them to gybe – yet still they carried on gybing. When I suggested that the kids might not know the meaning of the word gybe, their teacher called out, 'I want you to turn through the wind, not ahead of it.' This was as accurate a definition as one could wish of the difference between a tack and a gybe, but it made about as much sense to the kids as one of Lewis Carroll's poems.

Keep it simple, and quell the temptation to give uncalled-for explanations of how things work. Start with the basics: ask your child to steer for a buoy or other specific feature, which is downwind. Next, show him how to beat, demonstrating the way in which the sails flap if the boat is sailed too close to the wind. Do not expect him to pay much attention to your words. Regardless of whether he has

been listening, let him try for himself to sail the boat back up to your starting point. When he luffs, do not intervene. Instead, draw his attention to the problem and ask him why the sails are flapping.

Fundamental to the ability to sail is an understanding of the fact that it is the wind that makes the boat go. Pretty obvious, you might think – but not to a small child. Whenever I had the helm of our Wayfarer my dad would tell me to watch the burgee: 'Watch the burgee! Watch the burgee!' – on and on he went, like some demented parrot. Being an obedient child, I did as I was told and looked up at the little flag fluttering at the masthead, but really I thought that Dad ought not to distract me in this way; he ought to be encouraging me to look where I was going.

Eventually, my father must have realised that I had no idea of the burgee's function, and so he explained: 'Jill, the burgee shows you where the wind is coming from.' This moment would surely have been the turning point in my sailing career if I had understood the relevance of the information. However, at this tender age I was not even aware that the wind was the boat's driving force. When teaching children to sail, take nothing for granted; start with the obvious.

Future sailors

Although we are a seafaring nation, we Britons do not give our youth as much encouragement as do the sailors of certain other nations. For example, although many British clubs have dinghies for their junior members, I have yet to come across one which has a yacht kept specifically for their use.

By contrast, in South Africa almost every club has at least one 26ft Lavranos for its teenage members. These boats are managed, maintained and raced by girls and boys whose average age is around 15. Adult input is purely financial; in all other respects the kids are left entirely to their own devices. And when regatta time comes around, the juniors often leave a good many of the seniors in their wake.

Teenagers have also shown themselves to be perfectly capable of getting from one side of an ocean to the other and have even circumnavigated on their own. One of the contenders for the title of first woman to sail alone around the world was American teenager Tania Aebi. Ellen MacArthur was still in her teens when she sailed her own little boat around Britain, and another British teenager, 15-year-old Sebastian Clover, recently became the youngest person to sail solo across the Atlantic.

At the other end of the scale, there are teenagers who have lived aboard and cruised all their lives but who are still not trusted with anything more than basic watch-keeping. It is one thing to let your offspring disappear on his own with an expensive but well-insured toy, and quite another to entrust him with command of all that you own in the world. Still, if we *can* bring ourselves to let go of the leash, our kids will certainly benefit hugely from this obvious display of confidence in their abilities.

● When we give them enough scope, cruising offers children fantastic opportunities for personal development.

6
Seasickness

**Acclimatisation • Keeping your balance • Preparations
• Remedies • Coping with seasickness •**

This is a short chapter but on a subject that is of concern to a great many sailors, whether they be old hands or tyros, weekenders or ocean-going live-aboards.

At best, seasickness is a spoilsport affliction with the power to ruin a fun-filled day. At its worst, it is a threat to the safety of the vessel and her whole crew, for it is a debilitating malady. It is difficult to believe, when sitting in a rock-steady apartment or under a shady tree, that something involving no extraneous chemical or biological input can wreak such devastation on both mind and body – but it does. Seasickness can reduce a fit, competent sailor to a state of complete inability. People have been known to put out a Mayday and abandon ship, so desperate were they to escape the awful misery of *mal de mer*.

What does this have to do with children? Well, if the Captain and Mate of a family yacht are both reduced to a state of quivering incompetence, this plainly has everything to do with the child and his safety. That apart, seasickness strikes irrespective of age and children are quite as likely as their parents to suffer. Contrary to popular opinion, even babies get seasick. Caesar was already being seasick at six weeks. In an informal census of 18 under-12s, 17 children were found to be occasional sufferers, and of them four were smitten on almost every trip either with feelings of nausea or with actual vomiting. Xoë is the only child I have ever come across who is never seasick under any circumstances. She takes after her dad.

As with any other problem, the first line of defence against seasickness is prevention. And before we resort to the battery of pills and other anti-emetics we should consider safer strategies.

Acclimatisation

Very few people are seasick when sailing on flat water. It is the unpredictable lurch, pitch and roll of a boat in the waves that upsets the body's balance mechanism. It is true that there are a few unfortunate people who have only to step aboard a boat and they go green. If you have the sort of stomach which starts to heave while the boat is still tied up in the marina then you should probably think about changing your hobby. For the rest of us, all that is generally needed is time to acclimatise.

The fact that you or your small crew are prone to seasickness need not deter you from crossing oceans; you need not resign yourself to pottering about on the Broads. Seasickness is not an eternal thing. After the body has adjusted to its new environment the feelings of nausea pass. The way to happy cruising is therefore to break yourself in gently. A day or two of flat water sailing in advance of an offshore trip often forestalls the malaise. Where this is not possible, a couple of days in a rolly anchorage does the trick. Assuming that the anchorage is a safe one, the demands on the crew will be minimal and they can therefore acclimatise at leisure. A rolly anchorage is no fun at all, but it is more fun than trying to cook, navigate and manage the boat while you feel like dying, and it is safer, too.

Acclimatisation is definitely the key to conquering seasickness. If we set sail into a strong breeze, or even if we set off to roll along before it, I can pretty much guarantee that Caesar, Roxanne and I will soon be feeling grim. On the other hand, if we leave harbour in a gentle breeze, our bodies have time to adjust and we can usually survive whatever weather might be flung down a couple of days later.

A story of survival against the odds

Cruising south from Portugal to Africa via the Atlantic islands, we left Madeira on what seemed like an averagely breezy day. However, when we left the shelter of Funchal harbour we found that there was actually a northerly gale blowing. *Maamari* could handle a gale on the quarter as well as any other decent-sized, longish-keeled yacht – but could I? On previous occasions such conditions had reduced me to invalid status through seasickness. This time I was absolutely determined not to become a burden.

Xoë was barely one year old at the time of this adventure, but she was already up and running – and I do mean running. She had skipped both the crawling and toddling stages and at ten months had gone straight from slithering on her belly to running. Being fully mobile and very independent, Xoë was no longer such a drain on her mother's energy and time as she had been in the past. Having watched the town slide away in our wake, she clambered below decks and, as I recall, began to dash about the rolling cabin in great glee.

Caesar was another matter. Caesar should not really have been allowed to go below, but with the waves rumbling up

● Children who are feeling ill (or who have gone suspiciously quiet) should be encouraged to sit outside.

from astern and filling the cockpit with spume and spray there was really no option. He followed his sister down the companion and sat at the foot of the ladder, in the place where the motion was least. So far, so good, but these two infants could hardly be expected to occupy themselves all day. Soon they would require the services of an amusing, entertaining adult. That was definitely not going to be me, I decided; not today. I had been on the helm while we set the sails and I was in no hurry to relinquish control to the automaton.

My reluctance to go below and do my bit may sound selfish, but what good is a seasick mum, anyway? By going below I would inevitably have transformed myself from able-bodied crew member to extra baggage, and the skipper would have been left caring for vessel, children and casualty. There was absolutely no point in sacrificing myself. Most toddlers prefer a mother's company, and my kids were no exception, but on this occasion they were going to have to make do with Daddy.

What promised at first to be an ordeal of survival was so transformed by this contingency that it became a thoroughly enjoyable sail; one of the best I have ever had. From morning till evening I sat at the wheel while *Maamari* surged along, a chariot drawn by frenzied white-maned mares. Ten years on, I can still feel the thrill of that headlong dash south. We covered the distance between Madeira and the Canaries in half the estimated time.

Occasionally, in the course of that first day, the children scaled the ladder and cast longing looks in the direction of their oilskin-clad mother. Suitably wrapped in her own plastic foulies, Xoë came outside to nurse. When night fell the children's occasional longing looks were replaced by an insistent demand for Mummy, but by now I had more or less found my sea legs. I got the kids off to sleep by the simple expedient of joining them in the bunk, and then I went back outside and took the early night watch. I was quite sorry to stop when we reached La Palma the next evening, for I had now become fully acclimatised and was fit to sail, cook and cater to the needs of my kids for as long as we remained at sea.

Keeping your balance

You may be wondering why it is that I have begun this chapter not with anecdotes about children being saved from seasickness but with a tale concerning my own experience. This is because a child's seasickness is merely a discomfort to himself and an inconvenience to his mother, whereas the loss of an able-bodied crew member, on a vessel which is already short-handed, is a serious problem. As I have already pointed out, when Mum goes down, Dad is left to manage both the ship *and* the kids – assuming that he himself is not on the sick list. Therefore, it is to the adult problem of seasickness that we must first address ourselves.

Nobody seems to know exactly what causes motion sickness, but we do know that it has to do with the body's balance mechanism. Despite the fact that it is the stomach which is so dramatically affected, our balance mechanism is actually in our ears. This might seem to suggest that one could tune the equipment using sound, and I have heard of sound being used in an attempt to control seasickness, but in my experience sight is the sense best used to correct the system.

To conquer seasickness we must supply the brain with information about its new, unnatural environment. The worst thing you can do when you feel sick is to slouch in the corner of the cockpit or lie down. If you lie in a cosy bunk the chances of surviving with breakfast still aboard are quite good, but adjustment will be very slow. It may be necessary to spend the best part of two days prone; while Mum lounges about, taking care of her breakfast, who is looking after the kids?

The best way to fight the malady is by remaining upright and alert. Make your spine take care of your body; your spine and your muscles must adjust continually for every rock and roll of the boat. This is tiring, but largely because tiredness is a symptom of seasickness. Do not lean until you have to. When you are so tired that you simply must prop yourself in a corner, try to sit facing for'ard rather than athwartships or towards the stern. Try not to slump and, above all, do not let your eyelids droop. Scan the sea. Do not look at the foam rushing past, and do not even glance down into the cabin. Even a glance below decks is likely to bring on feelings of vertigo and a prolonged study of the cabin will cost you dearly.

If the weather is tolerable, a sailor who is feeling queasy should sit up on the cockpit coaming. From this position she (or he) will be able to get a good look at the sea all around. Gazing fixedly, and absentmindedly, at one small patch of sea will not help. One needs to scan the horizon, moving both the head and the eyes.

People who feel nauseous are generally reluctant to take the helm, which is a pity. Sailing the boat is not a sure-fire cure for seasickness, but it works for most people. If you decide to try it, do not steer on the compass. If the boat is on the wind, get the best from her that you can. If you are running or reaching, steer on a cloud or a landmark.

Deep breathing also helps. Take in huge lungfuls of air with long, deep breaths, and relax your body and mind. Anxiety causes feelings of seasickness and this is a vicious circle. If you are worried about the trip, you are far more likely to be seasick, and if you are afraid that you might be seasick, you are more likely to worry.

When you are already feeling ill, stifle any desire to yawn or cough. These two things both increase the likelihood of losing lunch and dignity. Keep warm, but do not get too hot. Eat, but do not overeat. Sip tea or fruit juice, or whatever appeals, but avoid alcohol, beer in particular. And whatever you do, DO NOT GO BELOW. Do not even go below to use the loo; use a bucket, come what may.

When you go below, your balance mechanism loses the plot altogether. This clearly demonstrates the degree to which sight is important in maintaining balance. I find that I can be feeling A1 in the cockpit, but that when I become over-confident and risk a trip to the galley, my balance machinery immediately goes haywire. The only thing that can save me now is a glimpse of the horizon caught through a porthole. That one glimpse acts like a fresh lungful of air and sets me up for the dash back up the companion ladder to the 'surface'. On this basis a wheelhouse or deck saloon, although not a particularly oceanworthy feature, would surely be an asset during a bout of sea-sickness.

Preparations

Much of what has been said above applies to children as well as to adults, but trying to persuade a small child to sit up straight and gaze at the sea is a lost cause. Children insist upon learning the hard way. You can prevent them from reading or doing jigsaws, but you cannot stop them from studying their toes. You can prevent them from guzzling, but only at a cost of hearing them whine on about their hunger. Therefore the greater part of managing seasickness so far as young children are concerned consists in preventing them from puking over themselves or the furnishings.

Adults invariably know when they are going to throw up. We watch the disaster creeping upon us and, except in the case of extreme disability, we get to the bucket in good time. By contrast, vomiting often takes small children completely by surprise. One moment they are laughing and playing and in the next they are spraying the cabin. Caesar used to puke in mid-sentence.

Even when they feel the symptoms, children do not always manage to identify them, so that it is down to their parents to be on the lookout. Coughing and yawning are classic signs, and unless your child habitually sits quietly and gazes vacantly into space, you should also regard this behaviour as a portent of doom. Some people get the urge to use the loo immediately before they are sick. A yacht's bathroom is a particularly unpleasant, disorientating space in a sea-way, and balancing somewhat difficult while the pot is bucking about. A child should not be allowed to attempt the feat before he has got his sea legs. Until then, bucket-and-chuckit must be the rule.

For heaven's sake do not ask your child if he is feeling sick. Auto-suggestion is a very powerful force. If you suspect, just get him off the bunk cushions, fast. Place a small colourful beach bucket alongside the potential offender and be ready to snatch it up and hold it in place at a millisecond's notice.

Children are obviously much more likely to be sick if they have just eaten. Unlike adults, they are also as likely to be sick lying in their bunks as on their feet. Trying to clean up a puke-sodden bunk cushion is... well, it is a very nasty busi-ness. The smell never really washes out of the foam, even after you have removed the cover and hosed the thing down. A foam cushion takes weeks to dry out; it never does dry out altogether in a salty atmos-phere, so that either you have to take it home, if you have another home, or else you wind up paying a launderette.

Preparedness is the name of the game when sailing with seasicky kids. Steal their pillows in advance of the crisis, or else equip them with cheap ones which you can dispose of without feeling distress. Cover the head end of the bed with a double layer of towels. When they ask why you are doing this, lie; tell them it is to make them feel more snug.

The first time he is sick, the child bounces back. Adults do too, for that matter. We generally feel better for getting that lot out of the system. Do not rely on your child's recovery; do not let him continue to play as he was doing. If he is not already outside, get him out (weather permitting) and be ready for a relapse. Keep the bucket close by. Incidentally, children should never be allowed to throw up over the rail. They must place their tributes to Neptune in a bucket.

After the child has been sick two or three times he begins to wilt. There is no point in trying to keep him sitting stiffly erect once he has reached this stage; the time for educating the balance mechanism has passed. If he is still small enough, pop your child into his kiddy car-seat. Otherwise, let him lie down in the cockpit or put him to bed. A walkman with a story tape is ideal entertainment for a seasick child. Time is the only cure available now and a night's sleep almost invariably brings relief.

In extreme cases, where the child is seasick repeatedly for more than a day, a mother begins to worry about dehydration. I suspect that we are apt to panic about our little ones long before they are in any danger from this cause. If the child is still producing a reasonable amount of clear urine, his life is plainly not in danger.

If you give a seasick child a glass of water he will most assuredly bring it up again within ten minutes. If you give him a glassful of sips of water over the course of half an hour, he *might* keep them down – but generally speaking he will not. Half a dozen sips, if they stay down, will do more good than the half cupful that comes back again.

Water is actually not a very good thing for a seasick stomach and it is not very good for rehydration. Our bodies lose more than water when we dehydrate and there is no use in raising the water level if you do not also provide the necessary balance of minerals. Purpose-designed oral rehydration salts (ORS) are the best thing for the job. You can buy the salts at the chemist or pharmacy and dissolve them in water as the need arises. I have to say, however, that ORS is no better on an unsettled stomach than water. The perfect ORS for a baby is breast milk. A full feed will wind up in your lap, but if you give your baby a few sips now and then, these will probably stay down.

Remedies

Seasickness has been with us ever since man first put to sea, and over the course of time people have proposed all sorts of different ways for dealing with the problem:

- Ginger biscuits and raw ginger are the cures most often proposed. They do not work for me, but they might for you.

- Some people swear by green apples. Any kind of fruit or raw vegetable invariably finishes me off if I am feeling below par, but Caesar is convinced that raw carrots help him along.
- Gunpowder and treacle was the old fashioned recipe, we hear. Kill or cure? I am not recommending it, so don't blame me if it puts you in the mortuary.
- Bacon rind is the remedy offered by Arthur Ransome in *Peter Duck*. Strawberry ice cream has also been recommended. Fine, if you have a freezer.
- Salt water is said to bring relief, but somehow I have never been able to stomach the idea. My own favourite recipe is a cocktail-sized can of Coca-Cola. I do not like the taste and I do not like the fizz, but bizarre and unlikely as it may seem, it certainly settles my stomach.
- A Russian yachtswoman once told me that chewing salty fish used to settle her stomach. I prefer to nibble a few salty crisps, or a couple of pepper crackers.
- Other things that help me to remain on an even keel are chocolate pudding (for which I am a bit of an addict) and tiny amounts of strongly flavoured cheese. I also find that a few mouthfuls of hot spicy stew are good for the condition, but it is important to be restrained; an empty, acidic stomach encourages feelings of nausea but you should never do more than take the edge off the hunger. A handful of crisps is a good thing; a packetful is detrimental. Children are not good at controlling themselves in the vicinity of food and they must therefore be rationed.

Although these things work for me, there is no reason why they should work for anybody else. The point is that my remedies are unconventional. In finding them I was guided by appetite alone and I suggest that fellow sufferers, adult or child, be allowed to do likewise. When I was a kid I was never allowed to eat either cheese or chocolate before a long car journey, in case they made me sick, and I strongly suspect that this is why they now act as cures! There is a psychological element in seasickness, I believe; perhaps if we could peer inside our own heads, we might sort things out.

Some people gain relief from seasickness by the use of acupressure. Personally, I find that acupressure bands merely focus my mind on the problem, but this is not the only non-invasive cure available. A shock works a treat. I remember once scurrying to the lee rail at my stomach's urgent bidding, opening my mouth, and in the same instant spotting a ship bearing down on us. It was heading straight for us, on a reciprocal bearing, and it was only a couple of minutes distant. The shock dissolved my nausea in an even more efficient way than the bubbles in Coca-Cola; I was cured for the rest of the trip! Perhaps doctors should experiment with adrenaline as a seasickness remedy.

Chemical treatment

I have left until last the most obvious and most popular remedy for seasickness. Many sufferers turn to the pill bottle for relief. Stugeron (cinnarizine) is the most popular motion-sickness pill. Some people take it routinely and also give it to their kids (it is not suitable for children under five years). Stugeron must be taken two hours in advance of departure – so users take it even before they know if the weather will be rough.

I have tried using Stugeron, but to no avail. Some sailors gain salvation from Scopoderm (hyoscine). Scopoderm is a stick-on patch which releases the drug into the body over the course of 72 hours. Opinions vary; some people say that the drug is brilliant, but others say that it wiped them out totally. One woman told me that Scopoderm sent her on a trip! Another who used it daily for a month-long crossing had withdrawal symptoms when she stopped. Scopoderm is not suitable for children under ten years.

Anti-emetic pills have been in production for only a few decades and we do not know what long-term side effects may be associated with their use. Personally I would rather see my kids suffer the odd bout of vomiting than put their future health in question.

Coping with seasickness

Having succumbed, I invariably continue to throw up on a half-hourly basis, until, or unless, I lie down. When I lie down I am never ill but if I have reached this stage, if I have been defeated, then the ship is now seriously undermanned. Singlehanding is one thing, but singlehanding whilst running a crèche is another.

A non-suffering child big enough to look after herself is a great asset to parents who are feeling ill, but one old enough to look after others as well is an absolute godsend. Xoë, since she is immune, has long found herself acting as gofer, and nowadays she sometimes serves as cook too. A younger child, even if he is not stricken, is a burden to a seasick parent. Indeed, a young child who is not stricken will be full of bounce and needing attention and is therefore likely to be an especial burden.

When Caesar and Xoë were small I used often to be seasick, and on the occasions when I was defeated and had to lie down I would take up residence on the saloon floor. The children could now play around me and indeed they positively *thrived* on my incapacity, as it gave them a complete monopoly over my remaining energies.

It is as well to consider in advance how you will amuse the kids when you are laid low. A bucketful of Lego Duplo is an ideal toy for this occasion as you can join in and 'play' with your eyes shut. Plastic animals and Playmobil people also come in handy; minimal input is required from Mum, who only has to supply names, confirm gender and feeding habits, etc. Stickers are popular, but little fingers being rather clumsy, I found that I had to peel off each one for each child. If asked to read a book while feeling under the weather, I used to tell a story instead. Telling stories is not my forte, but my audience was not very critical.

There is another aspect to preparing for the possibility of seasickness. The skipper will find the management of ship and crew much easier if a meal has been prepared in advance. But all this presupposes that the skipper is still fit. What happens if he too is brought to his knees by a maladjustment of something in the middle ear?

I am fortunate in being married to a complete superhero who is never seasick. Nor is my level of incapacity such that it prevents me from taking my watch. When Nick needs to sleep and I am feeling seasick, then I do my stint by visiting the cockpit every five or ten minutes, between times remaining prone on the carpet. And so we stagger along in this fashion until my stomach (or rather, my ears) have sorted themselves out. But what would we do if Nick was also sick?

Well, I can answer this question because he once was. Although Nick has never known *mal de mer*, the entire Schinas family was once struck down by a mysterious ailment one day after we left port. Caesar was the worst but Nick was a close second – he slept for a whole day – and for 24 hours the management of the crew fell to yours truly, although I was also feeling far from fit.

Xoë was first to recover, and as she was only two years old she inevitably made a thorough nuisance of herself and added further to the ordeal. Caesar gave us considerable cause for concern; for 24 hours he vomited regularly and passed not one drop of urine. When he finally asked for the potty, he filled it to overflowing and then half filled it again, with perfectly clear, healthy-looking pee. (I mention this for the sake of other mums who might some day find themselves in the same situation. Infant bladders are unpredictable!) Well, we survived our ordeal

and managed to keep proper watch throughout – fortunately the weather was undemanding – but we were mighty glad to reach our destination a couple of days later.

Without wishing to discourage anyone from sailing or the sea, I have to say that if both parents are regularly incapacitated by seasickness then they had better pick another pastime or means of travel. To be in this state with only ourselves to care for is bad enough, but to expose our children to the danger of being aboard what is, to all intents and purposes, an unmanned vessel, is gross negligence.

One day, I am sure, somebody will make a scientific study of the balance mechanism in the ears of sufferers and non-sufferers of seasickness. Or perhaps this is not a physical thing; I have a private suspicion that seasickness is in some way linked to hormonal activity. Most women, even if they are generally immune to the problem, are seasick while they are pregnant. Some women, myself included, are more inclined to feel sick while lactating, and I also believe that I am most affected on the first day of a period (to the extent that I will even feel seasick in the middle of a crossing). Perhaps it is no coincidence that fewer men then women suffer from seasickness.

One day some clever scientist will devise a cure for the ailment which has smitten seafarers down through the ages, but in the meantime the only guaranteed method of avoiding seasickness is to sit under a tree.

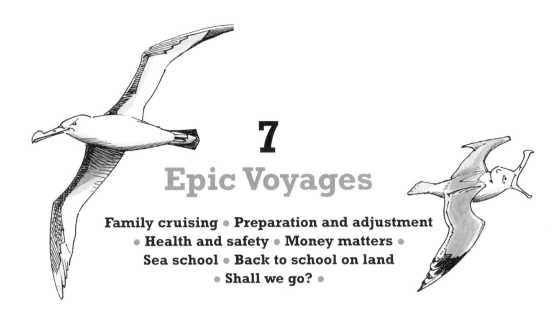

7
Epic Voyages

**Family cruising • Preparation and adjustment
• Health and safety • Money matters •
Sea school • Back to school on land
• Shall we go? •**

Cruising means different things to different people. Many are attracted by the idea of sailing beneath a tropical sun, while some feel the urge to cross oceans. A few are drawn to make a specific journey: a trip around Britain, for example, or a voyage in the wake of the Vikings. For most people, the adventure that they plan will take the form of a sabbatical lasting anything from a few months to four or five years, but one or two are casting off to travel indefinitely; it is the cruising lifestyle that appeals to these folks and their return lies far over the horizon. Perhaps they will never return.

For every adventurer who puts his plans into action, there are a dozen more – two dozen more, perhaps – who will never realise their dreams. To turn aspirations into reality you need courage; the courage to throw yourself out of the nest and see if you can really fly. Many people prefer to stay at home, where they are safe, and dream their lives away. Others are simply being sensible; they will jump in the end, but first they want to see how someone else gets on. Would-be cruisers who are also parents are especially concerned to take a good look before they leap. 'Can we afford to do it?' they ask. 'Will it suit the children? Will they be bored? Will they be safe?' and, most of all, 'Will their education suffer?'

Couples who sail regularly but who have never taken their children for a long-term, long-distance cruise tend to be dismissive of the notion. 'Temper any ideas about epic voyages,' says Pippa Driscoll, author of *Children Afloat*. 'Don't plan a cruise which is longer in hours than the youngest crew member in years.' Similar advice has been issued by leading lights in the RYA, people who are supposed to be promoting sailing! Even Libby Purves, who sailed around Britain with her husband and their children, has nothing good to say on the subject. 'You think you can sail to Cherbourg, do you?' she asks. 'Ha! You'll be lucky to get from Poole to Weymouth!'

Perhaps Libby's children were too small to enjoy their big adventure. Or perhaps they had not had much previous experience and were thrown in at the deep end. Then again, perhaps three months is exactly the wrong length of time for a family cruise;

much too long to be a holiday but just too short for either the parents or the children to adjust to the lifestyle. Whatever the reason, I can only say that from my own experience, cruising with children aged from three to 13 works very well. And hopefully, as the years go by, I will be able to adjust that second figure.

Family cruising

There is nothing new about the idea of taking children to sea. Long before the age of cruising began there were children who were raised afloat. Joshua Slocum, the first man to sail singlehanded round the world, spent his working life as a ship's captain and he and his wife raised their four children as they travelled and traded.

Another who spent her childhood afloat was Elizabeth Drinkwater. She and her mother lived at times in a house in England, but the little girl far preferred the life on the ocean waves. Coming up to date we find Günter and Muriel Weiss, whose four children were all born during a 19-year circumnavigation of the world. Muriel Weiss does not much like sailing, she leaves the sailing side of things to her husband, and latterly to the older boys, but she loves living aboard and feels that the travelling life is a good one for the children.

Roger Morice and his wife Jaqueline set off from France in 1976, and in the course of many adventures aboard many different boats they also added four kids to their crew. The Morice children are all independent, capable people. The older three have now left to do their own things; the girls live ashore, one in France, one in America, but 24-year-old Morgan has his own yacht and is still cruising.

Many others have also raised their children afloat. Finlay and Ellen Reeves are ten and seven years old and have never lived ashore. Home for 15-year-old Melissa Ruault and her younger brother Morgan has always been a 37ft sloop. And so it goes on. Raising kids afloat has been tried and tested; it works.

But as I have said, most would-be cruisers are not going to spend their lives on the ocean waves. Most view the undertaking as time out. After the experience of a lifetime they will slot back into reality, picking up where they left off, or so they imagine. Some do not make it back – some are so smitten with the cruising lifestyle that they decide to carry on indefinitely – and none pick up exactly where they left off. One cannot expect to cross oceans and still be exactly the same person on one's return!

Remington, Ashton and Sierra were aged nine, six and three when their parents decided that they fancied the idea of spending a year cruising the Caribbean. At first, little Sierra did not take happily to the life of the sailor; she was clingy and would not let her mother out of her sight. Ashton, too, was unenthusiastic during the early stages of the voyage, but by the time we met them the boys were both revelling in the adventure. They vied with one another for the privilege of raising the anchor and they liked to help with the handling of the boat.

'A year is not long enough, I'm going to do it again,' said their father, and he

● Cruising kids make friends fast. They have to, they are forever moving on.

gave his boys a sly glance. 'I'm going to do it again, without the kids.' Howls of dismay greeted this announcement and Daddy smiled. 'It's too cramped,' he explained. 'The boat is only 39ft. But the boys don't care; they just love it. They don't want ever to go home!'

But before you decide to take my word for it and set off for the far horizon, we ought to take a look at the other side of the coin. Are there people who have tried this lifestyle and loathed it?

People who go cruising can be divided into two broad categories: those who have sailed for years, and those who have bought a boat with the express purpose of doing some blue-water cruising. Odd though it may seem, the latter group is by far the biggest and some of its members do find that they have bitten off more than they can chew. Some have never sailed at all before they cast off and head for foreign shores.

Women who have been messing about in boats for years will know whether they enjoy it, and whether they are likely to want to cross oceans under sail. Women who have never sailed before very often find that they do *not* like sailing, but they almost invariably enjoy the lifestyle. They are generally very attached to their boat, they like living alongside a succession of palm-lined beaches, and they love the endless holiday which cruising is: no rush, no stress and no *News of the World*; just fun in the sun, eating freshly caught lobster and sipping rum punch. Barbecues on the beach with new friends who are drifting on the same ocean current. And a united family: Mum, Dad and the kids all sharing the same life. No nine-to-five, no ironing of suits and ties, no PTA, no

traffic jams. There cannot be many people who would not enjoy this lifestyle.

The cruising life is a good one – but do not cast off yet; do not hurry on your way. Fools rush in, but the folk who succeed in this eccentric, unorthodox, radically different way of living are the ones who have immersed themselves slowly and gently.

Negative vibes

Consider the case of a Sussex family who bought themselves a 40ft Salar. 'We're off!' they said, 'We're going to sail around the world.' Dad, Mum and their two teenage girls were equally excited and eager. 'Have you sailed before?' I asked them. 'No, but we'll get along just fine.'

I recommended that they begin the adventure with a shakedown cruise. A harbour-hopping journey to the west coast would give them time to settle in whilst also helping them on their way. The further west one heads, the less the chance of being embayed in Biscay, but – 'No,' said the gallant skipper, 'We'll leave England from Chichester.'

They left on a sunny Saturday when the Solent was overflowing with other yachts. Before they had even emerged from the shelter of the Isle of Wight, Mum and the kids were struck down with seasickness and Dad, finding himself all alone, decided to call for help: 'Mayday, Mayday, can somebody tell me where I am please? The boat's just fine, but I can't steer her and navigate at the same time in this gale.'

The RNLI towed him back into the harbour and he was given a severe dressing-down and threatened with a fine.

A week later our hero was off for the Canaries, but on his own. Mum and the girls had decided to fly down and join him. How the novice singlehander fared crossing Biscay, I do not know.

Experienced or otherwise, most people do manage to get themselves across Biscay, but a few come to grief. I recall reading, some years ago, of another family who set off without having prepared either themselves or the boat. Caught in a gale and all laid low with *mal de mer*, they decided to abandon ship. Mother, father and their young son were all successfully evacuated to a freighter, but during the transfer the yacht was holed and sunk. This family was unlucky – but as I have said before, luck is very much a matter of preparation.

Preparation and adjustment

Muriel and Günter Weiss had no sailing experience when they set off to cruise the world, but having quickly realised their limitations they hired a professional skipper to show them the ropes and get them down to the Med. Five years later they set off again, in a newly built boat, with three young children who had forgotten all about sailing. Before they left, the family spent a year living aboard the boat – and this, I believe, is the key to successful cruising with kids. If you tear them away from their home and head for the open sea in a hurry, then you can expect trouble.

Undue haste was, I believe, one of the problems which made life difficult for Libby Purves and her family on their journey round Britain. Five-year-old Nicholas and three-year-old Rose were not even aboard when their parents began the cruise. They joined ship in the first port of call and were at once whisked away into an alien environment. Reading between the lines of Libby's book, one gathers that the children were not very familiar with the boat and had never before spent a night at sea. Libby and her husband Paul were both experienced sailors and had evidently prepared thoroughly for the voyage ahead – but they had not prepared the kids.

Time spent living aboard in advance of your departure will also give you the opportunity to discover whether the family really gets along well enough to live in harmony in a very small space, day in and day out, for months and years. Families following a conventional existence actually see very little of each other; Dad spends all day in the office, while the kids pass the hours in school. The cruising lifestyle presents a dramatic contrast. How will you fare when you *cannot* get away from one another? If your children are under the age of ten or 12, then throughout the duration of your cruise they will be permanently and forever in the company of one or other of their parents. You will not be able to leave them aboard while the boat is at anchor; that would not be safe. Is this acceptable to you – or will you find it suffocating?

We spent a year living aboard *Mollymawk* before casting off from the shore, and when we finally left we did it

● On an ocean passage, fishing often provides quite a drama (and quite a dinner).

slowly. To have set off across an ocean with children for whom sailing was no more than a faint memory would have been very short-sighted. We reintroduced them to things with a couple of daysails, and followed this up with two overnight journeys, which gave the kids the chance to experience sleeping in a seaway. Having assured ourselves that all was well, we then embarked on a five-day passage, which was conceived as a gentle shake-down. As it was, we ended up riding along with a gale on the quarter, but the children took it very well. In fact, Caesar and Xoë loved it. Because the self-steering

had failed, the skipper and mate had a heavy workload, and Caesar therefore received instant promotion from ship's boy to navigator. Quite a responsibility for a ten-year-old! Xoë, meanwhile, found herself serving as cook. The ship's baby was the only one to express concern at the proceedings. Roxanne, then only four, could not quite understand the change in her circumstances. 'We will go to land again one day, won't we?' she asked.

Our next long haul was from Namibia to St Helena Island and took 14 days. Again the weather was rough, and we had problems with the boat – but not with the kids, who were perfectly content.

The voyage from St Helena to the Cape Verdes took 29 days. Our voyage thence to the Mediterranean lasted 34 days, most of which were spent beating into a light headwind. The children took all of this in their stride. There were no complaints and nobody ever asked, 'Are we nearly there yet?' Nor did the children beg us to stop at Ascension or Madeira, islands that we passed close alongside. When we were becalmed for five days, nobody mentioned the possibility of motoring; indeed, the interlude was the highlight of the journey. The children spent the time swimming and fishing and were quite disappointed when, on the sixth day, they awoke to find that we were on the move once more. When we arrived in southern Spain, the kids were pleased to be able to go ashore but after a couple of days they wanted to move on. As Xoë said, 'It's okay here, but it's nicer at sea.'

Health and safety

How safe is the cruising life? What a question! But it is one that I am asked quite often by worried mums.

Sailing is as safe as you care to make it. Buy a biggish, seaworthy boat and look after her well; stick to sailing in the tropics and steer clear of the hurricane seasons; do all of this and you can hardly go wrong. On the other hand, if you plan to cruise around Iceland or through the Straits of Magellan, you could come to grief. High-latitude sailing is relatively risky.

Cruising safety, like any other kind of safety, is a matter of perspective. Yotties are not the first people to have taken their kids into an unforgiving, alien environment. The pioneers who crossed America and those who sallied forth from the African Cape journeyed, as we do, beyond the reach of outside assistance. They faced hostile natives. At least we, as a rule, only face hostile seas.

If we want to be absolutely sure that our children are safe, then we must keep them cocooned in cotton wool. Keep them away from playschool, in case they catch meningitis; keep them off the street, in case they get run over or abducted. In fact, now that I come to think of it, perhaps the cruising lifestyle is actually safer than the landlocked one! My children are seldom exposed to those particular risks, nor is it likely that they will die in a car crash. Car crashes involving children are a familiar occurrence in the UK, and yet they seldom warrant more than a couple of lines in the newspaper. On the other hand an accident at sea has impact.

When we capsized our boat in the Southern Ocean and had to be hauled to safety by the RAF, the story made the newspaper headlines. Caesar and Xoë were on the front page of the *Daily Mail*, and various other tabloids devoted two-page spreads to the event. As Canadian cruiser and father of four Carl Mailhot explains, 'If something happens to a child at sea it is far more dramatic. If there had been any negligence on the part of the parents they would be condemned far more categorically than if something happened in the backyard of their home.'

A capsize, or a collision with a sleeping whale or a container, *will* make the news, particularly if there are children aboard, but in reality these things are just the marine equivalent of a house fire or a car crash. They are a conceivable risk, but not one that you need to lie awake and worry about.

What about pirates?

Unfortunately, piracy is on the increase, but I have yet to hear of a family who have been attacked, and I believe that the presence of young children sometimes shields us from harm. While sailing off the coast of West Africa we often drew the attention of fishing boats. The smaller boats would come alongside, uninvited, and we were once circled in a rather menacing way by a big steel trawler. On each occasion I stood the children on deck and told them to smile and wave. Nobody ever waved back, but they did go away almost at once. Other cruising yotties claim that their safe transit of no-go areas in certain Venezuelan and Panamanian cities was due to the presence of their children.

Their children's health is another concern for would-be world travellers. Taken by and large, the cruising life is a healthy one. I cannot recall the last time any of us had a cold. The lack of fresh food and vegetables in our offshore diet has not caused us to suffer from scurvy, and thus far we have managed to avoid being bitten by sharks or contracting malaria. Stomach bugs are an occasional problem. They can be caused by drinking contaminated water, or eating unwashed food in countries where hygiene standards are poor.

A cruising yacht should carry a comprehensive medical kit containing antibiotics, anti-emetics, rehydration salts and painkillers, together with bandages, sutures, burn dressings and so forth. This is something that should be discussed with a GP. He or she will be able to supply a wad of prescriptions with which your needs can be met. You should also carry a good, up-to-date, medical handbook. We use *Where There is No Doctor*, by David Werner, and *The Ship's Captain's Medical Handbook*, which is an HMSO publication.

The biggest worry for most cruising families is appendicitis. If the problem is identified in sufficient time, infection and inflammation of the appendix can be treated with antibiotics, but if the appendix ruptures an operation is the only hope. What can I say? One either accepts the risk or stays at home.

Money matters

'How do you afford it?' This is the question to which everybody wants an answer, whether or not they are planning to cruise.

It is one thing for a couple to head off into the unknown – a couple of adults will always get by somehow – but getting by with the burden of two or three kids on your back is much harder. Most of the people who would like to cruise but who have not yet left cite finance as the obstacle. 'We wouldn't be able to afford it,' they tell us. Meanwhile we can afford to cruise, but cannot afford to live in Britain anymore.

Do you own a house? If you do, you are considerably richer, in financial terms, than Nick or I have ever been. Neither of us has ever earned enough money even to rent a house.

'What about mooring fees? What about insurance?' Leave England in your wake and there are no mooring fees to be paid. In 14 years of cruising we have used marinas just four times; twice because we needed to work on the boat, and twice because we wanted somewhere safe to leave her while we travelled overland. England is the only place we know of where you have to pay even to anchor. Hence we can afford to live almost anywhere else, but not there.

As for insurance, very few world-cruising yotties have insurance of any kind. Third party insurance for the boat is a requirement if you want to use marinas in the Mediterranean. World-cruising insurance is unaffordable.

If you are DIY minded, the maintenance of the boat is not a financial drain. Since we yotties travel with the wind we also have no fuel bills to pay. That just leaves our feeding, and since we have five mouths to feed, it is a major expense. How do we cover it?

One thing that you should *not* be thinking of to fund your life of leisure is Child Benefit. Child Benefit is only available to residents of the UK, and to claim it while you are overseas is illegal. In spite of this, some people do. One family of our acquaintance financed 18 years of travel with four children by claiming Child Benefit. They are now back home in England and live in fear of being found out. Over the years they have helped themselves to somewhere around £25,000, and repaying it would be beyond their means.

Cruising folk earn their bread and butter by many different means. Some manage to find a sponsor: either a commercial backer or a generous relative. Not a few take on paying crew. In fact, this is particularly popular with family cruisers. With paying crew you kill two birds with one stone; you finance your voyage with guests who also share the watch-keeping. This can work very well.

Some of us finance our travels by writing about them. It does not pay the whole bill, but every little helps. Many people trade in a small way, carrying African souvenirs to Europe, for example, or whisky to Brazil. Quite a number are craftsmen, who make jewellery or paint pictures and sell them along the way. Some friends of ours paid for their boat by selling knotboards which the family made as a team.

Arts and crafts can help to foot the bill, but most yotties earn their way around the world by stopping to work. A year or two of well paid employment in a country where the cost of living is high will pay for two or three years of travel in lands where the living is almost free. The French are particularly good at this; they spend two years working as teachers in New Caledonia, and then go off and live on fish and coconuts for five more. Nick spent two years working as a mechanic in Antigua, and this financed our travels in West Africa. As I write this closing chapter we are in Spain, where he is looking for a job which will pay for a journey around South America.

Most people do not like living hand to mouth, and it is true that the existence can be precarious.

Sea school

Their children's education is the really big issue for most parents, and it is a subject that also arouses the interest of everyone we meet along the way.

It would never have occurred to me to home-school my children had we been living in the UK. Indeed I was not even aware that you could, legally, take a child out of school and teach him yourself. Most people, I find, are equally in the dark. At best, they believe that in order to teach a person must have a degree of some sort. This is not the case. The law in England states that, 'It is the responsibility of the parent to see that the child is educated, in school or otherwise.' There is no law about who may teach, and nor is education defined.

Now that I have experienced home-schooling, I would never dream of sending a child to school – certainly not an under-11, at any rate. The subject of teaching teenagers is a thorny one, but only on account of the twin problems of the child's social needs and the potential employer's demand for qualifications. From a purely educational point of view, home-schooling still wins hands down.

Parents are generally very concerned about their child's schooling, but did you ever stop to ask yourself about the purpose of the exercise? What do you actually expect your child to gain from school? In short, for what purpose is he being educated?

The way in which you tackle the business of home-schooling will depend on how you answer this question. If your primary aim is to equip your child with qualifications of the sort which can lead onto university and a Good Career, then you probably need to be looking at an approved curriculum or course, but if you have opted out of the mainstream, feeding your kids a conventional school syllabus might seem to be something of a contradiction. On the one hand you are teaching him to view consumerism and the rat race system of jobs and mortgages in a negative light, but on the other you are implicitly preparing him for immersion in that world.

What is the purpose of education? Answer: a worthwhile education must fit the child for the life that he is going to lead. The world is changing so rapidly that we can hardly begin to imagine what opportunities lie ahead for our children, but there is one thing of which we can be sure: there will always be a place for a person who is numerate, literate, computer literate, well-read, quick to learn, open-minded, adaptable and resourceful. If you can see to it that your child acquires the first four qualifications, life on the ocean will take care of the others.

Options

Distrustful of their teaching abilities and fearful of failing their children, most cruising parents opt to make use of some kind of correspondence school.

Formal correspondence schooling is available, free of charge, for nationals of Australia, New Zealand, Canada and France. Homespun education is illegal in France and the curriculum followed by the schools is very rigid, with all children of a given age studying the same aspect of the same subject at the same time. Completion of the syllabus and achievement of 'the Bac' is absolutely crucial – or so one gathers, for all but the most bohemian of French cruisers puts his children through the mill. Happily we Brits do not have to go through this kind of thing; our education system is much more flexible. Unhappily, this also means that there is no free correspondence school for would-be followers of the UK National Curriculum. Nor does such a course exist for American children. Perhaps this is why so few British or American families cruise.

British sailors who are making a short-term voyage with kids of primary school age are usually able to persuade their children's teachers to provide an outline of the work to be carried out over the next year. Those intending to stay out for rather longer must fall back on their own resources but need not head out on their own. Adherence to the National Curriculum is perfectly possible for anyone who so wishes, and copies are freely available. The easiest way for a blue-water cruiser to access the curriculum is in stages, as the need arises, via the internet. The full curriculum is given on www.nc.uk.net.

I have to say that on first acquaintance the National Curriculum is like pesto spaghetti – a tangle of mumbo-jumbo decorated with jargon and lacking meat. The programme of study for the English language course for Key Stage 2, for example, tells us that 'Pupils should be taught how to use vocabulary and syntax that enable them to communicate more complex meanings', but it does not tell us how to go about achieving this aim. On its own the curriculum is little better than useless.

The associated website, www.curriculumonline.gov.uk, is much more helpful as it gives specific details, for every subject, of everything that should be studied. It also contains a comprehensive list of approved CD-ROMs which are pertinent to those subjects.

English and American cruisers who baulk at the idea of DIY education usually resort to using a correspondence course, the favourite one being the Calvert.

Besides being expensive, the use of a correspondence course entails practical problems, the main one being the difficulty of getting the child's work reviewed and returned. New material must also be received through the post, with the result that followers of correspondence courses frequently spend quite a bit of their time holed up in harbour waiting for mail.

The greatest drawback of any curriculum-based system of education is the irrelevance of its content to your child's life. What point is there in learning about the American Civil War or, for that matter, the Roman invasion of Britain, while you are cruising in the Caribbean? When in Rome, learn of the Romans. When in the Caribbean, learn of the Caribs.

Learning all the time

There are two extremes to home-based education. On the far right we have the classroom system of timetabled lessons, and on the far left, the School of Life. Most blue-water cruisers are followers of the first system; at nine o'clock each morning they sit their children down and attend to their intellectual nourishment. As you will probably have guessed, this is not the method of schooling which we use aboard *Mollymawk,* but nor are we so gung-ho as to believe that life alone is a sufficient teacher. The cruising life teaches many useful things, but it does not teach reading, writing and 'rithmetic.

Our teaching philosophy was inspired by John Holt, author of *Learning All the Time*, and consists, essentially, of grabbing every chance to teach the child about the things which interest him. We rarely give the children formal, sit-down lessons. Most of their learning is acquired 'on the go'. Children who have not been forced to learn actually like doing so. More, if their natural appetite has not been damaged by force feeding, they actually *crave* learning. When they are small, children learn by asking questions. A toddler will drive his parents mad with his curiosity, 'Why? Why? Why?', he asks all day. Once the child can read, the window of the world is thrown wide open and so early reading is an essential key to the learning-all-the-time approach to education. My children get a good deal of their learning from books.

Writing is another matter. Xoë and Roxanne love writing and write all the time, but Caesar does not. Since writing is a vital skill he has to be told to write, but we can make the matter a lot more palatable for him by getting him to write about things which interest him and are relevant to his life.

Teaching mathematics by our method is not easy, but nor is it impossible. There is plenty of maths involved in astro-navigation, which is Caesar's latest interest. Currency conversion and shopping also offer opportunities for learning, but I must confess that we also find it necessary to sit the children down and force feed them mathematics. Perhaps this is why the older two have learnt to dislike it. They find it a great deal more palatable when it is presented in the form of a computer game, and so we have begun to use CD-ROMs for this aspect of their education.

Left to their own devices, my children can find plenty to do and much of what they do is creative or educational, or both. Left to himself, Caesar spends long hours on the computer, writing programs or setting out his biannual newsletter. He also likes reading, and he likes fiddling about with electronic bits and bobs. He

● A maths lesson.

enjoys learning new fancy knots, making rope mats and weaving. (He has a small loom.) He is also an enthusiastic cook.

Xoë, when her time is not being directed by outsiders, spends the day reading or writing. Xoë has been reading fluently since she was two and a half (at which age, you may be interested to learn, she did not know her alphabet. Nor had she been taught phonetics, and she could not 'sequence', although this is said to be an essential prerequisite to reading.) Since she reads widely, Xoë's writing is also of a high standard. An English teacher, on reading a play which Xoë had written, was so impressed that she took it along to show her class of 15-year-olds. 'Why can't *you* do this?' she asked them. Answer: because they have had reading and writing rammed down their throats. Xoë, on the other hand, has never had a single formal English lesson.

Project work

Left to their own devices, the children would each grow up with a very lopsided education. Caesar would never write, and Xoë would still be innumerate. In order to balance the scales, I set them projects which promote a whole range of skills, including book reference, practical research, written and pictorial presentation of facts and ideas, use of grammar, composition, and (occasionally) use of the computer. The list varies according to the project and can be expanded to include art and design.

Education is a subject very close to my heart and I wish I had the space to say more – about the beautifully simple way in which children can learn to read, *if* they are given the opportunity; about teaching by the use of stories; about the ways in which infants learn to write and spell – but this is not the place for such things. Nor is it appropriate that I go into the details of the many projects which my children have done, but for interest's sake I will mention a few ideas that are applicable to the cruising lifestyle.

Sealife projects In its simplest form, a sealife project might consist of a request for two or three pages of writing about dolphins, or some other specific creature. The work could be illustrated and presented in a dolphin-shaped book.

For older children the project could be a more extended in-depth study of all marine forms: everything from seals and cetaceans down to squidgy blobs such as coelenterates and plankton.

To set them off in the right direction, ask your children questions. For instance, you might start the ball rolling by asking

them, 'What is a mollusc?' 'We don't know,' they say – and they don't care either. But when, given the appropriate book, they discover that whelks (for example) are molluscs, they begin to show a little more enthusiasm. Whelks are interesting. The children have surely met them on the beach and probably think of them as mundane things, but they will be amazed by what they read of the creatures' complicated private lives.

Remember that the object of the exercise is not so much to cram their heads full of knowledge – although one hopes that some of it will stick. The chief aim is to teach the children how to learn, and how to present facts in a coherent form. Or, to put it another way, 'how to use vocabulary and syntax that enable them to communicate more complex meanings'.

Map an island (or a marina, village, etc) using a hand-bearing compass.

History projects We always study the history of every place where we stop. If there are museums or archaeological sites to be visited, be sure to give your children some background information before you go, but keep pre-visit writing to a minimum. The writing should come afterwards.

Astronomy and astrology Boys like facts: how far away is Alpha Centauri? How big is the universe? Girls prefer to hear stories, and there are stories galore in the sky; every constellation has its own tale to tell. Offshore travellers have a heaven-sent(!) opportunity to study the night sky. Teach your children to recognise the shape of Ursa Major or Scorpio, for instance, and then in the evening let them find the constellation for themselves. If they are old enough or sufficiently good at maths, you can even throw in some astro-nav.

Discovery of the New World This can be broken down into several projects. On a crossing to the Caribbean, study Columbus; coming up from the Cape of Good Hope, study Bartholomew Dias, Vasco da Gama and the establishment of the route to the Indies by the Portuguese.

One project often leads into another. For example, consideration of the difficulties Columbus faced in identifying the New World for what it was can provoke an interest in geography or navigation. The main thing to remember is that the interest must come from the child. You can sow the seed, but unless it takes root there is no point in piling on the fertiliser/knowledge. We learn best when we learn what we want to learn.

Back to school on land

'This is all very well,' you say, 'All very nice, but what happens when the kids need to slot back into the system? What happens when they need to get a job? How will they get their GCSEs?'

I am firmly convinced that for children under 12, the learning-all-the-time approach to schooling is the very best. Children taught by this method do not have any problem slotting into a conventional school – or rather, if they have a problem, it is one of over-intelligence and over-eagerness. Caesar and Xoë were 11 and nine and had never sat in a classroom when, by way of an experiment, we packed them off to school in the English-speaking island of St Helena. Despite her lack of 'proper schooling', Xoë found herself at the top of her class in every subject except maths (for which she was in the top five) and IT, about which she knew absolutely nothing. She was very popular with the students and the teachers alike, although her habit of correcting her form teacher on her knowledge of history must have jeopardised that particular relationship!

Caesar, on his first day at school, got nonchalantly aboard a school bus and disappeared off towards a huge secondary school. The fact that he knew nobody in this strange new world caused him no anxiety. (I mention this fact because it is typical of the breed; sea-children are generally very self-reliant and self-confident.) Caesar, like Xoë, found his lessons pathetically easy. Socially he fared less well – the fact that he had never in his life kicked a football weighed heavily against him.

Other folk report similar experiences of slotting their pre-teens into school. Some cruising kids are put into school whenever the opportunity arises, and if it arises when they are in foreign parts, they learn a new lingo at the same time.

So much for children of primary school age. Inserting a teenager back into the mainstream of life can be much harder, and home-schooling a teenager afloat can be a difficult task, particularly if one is determined to put him through the GCSE mill, and at the age usual for these examinations. If this is the objective, then keeping to the National Curriculum would appear to be essential. In order to do this you would need to acquire a full set of course books or CD-ROMs, or else invest in a long-distance learning course. These courses seem to cost around £200 per GCSE subject.

If, on the other hand, you can bear the idea of letting the matter of qualifications slide, the education of your teenager might proceed as it has done over the last few years, with the child following his own interests. Burning bridges? No, we are not burning bridges for our children. When, and if, they need to acquire qualifications, our children will be able to do so by taking evening classes or attending college. Provided that they are, by then, over 16 this will cost only the usual, minimal adult rate. (Under-16s pay more: up to £3,000 for a year's evening tuition in a full range of GCSE subjects.)

For more information on long-distance learning courses and for all sorts of good advice about home schooling in general, contact Education Otherwise (www.education-otherwise.org). This British NGO is a support group run, on a voluntary basis, by parents whose children are not attending school.

Slotting back into the system is harder for teenagers than for younger children. The teenage years are years of conformity, and when suddenly immersed in a conformist world, your Boating Baby may become ashamed of his unorthodox lifestyle. I have yet to experience this phenomenon, but have witnessed it in other seafaring children; it can be a big problem. The most obvious solution, as I see it, would be *not* to toss the child back into the sea of mediocrity; instead, let him continue to be different and special, in the

company of the increasing number of shore-based, home-schooled kids. Ashore, home-schooling need not be a lonely, unsociable business

In view of my wholesome experience of home-schooling, I would certainly continue in this way even if we lived on terra firma. Mahatma Gandhi once said that 'the good home is the ideal place for education'. Live-aboard Carl Mailhot, who sailed around the world with four children aged from five to 16, called the adventure 'the best school a parent can offer'. I would go so far as to suggest that, within the next ten or 20 years, home-schooling is likely to become the fashionable option, and something of a status symbol. Doing it under sail, with the world as your textbook, is just going one better!

● Her first ocean passage was great fun, and she loves the cruising lifestyle, but will this soon-to-be teenager still be content to share a cabin with her brother after six months, or a year, of such living?

Shall we go?

Cruising is a fantastic lifestyle for kids; I can think of none to rival it. Cruising kids have the benefit of growing up with both parents always on hand and are witness to the ways in which we cope with whatever life may lob in our direction, whether it be fixing the engine, salting a glut of fish, appeasing customs officials, or riding out a storm. The cruising lifestyle demands an independent attitude and it is presumably for this reason that cruising kids grow up to be free-thinking, self-confident creatures.

From a purely practical point of view, sailing is the only sane way to travel with kids. Wherever they go, they are always at home; Teddy and their toys are always on hand, and they sleep every night in their own, familiar bed. The next best thing would be a camper van – but think of the fuel bills, and of the inconvenience of finding somewhere safe to park each night.

The best time to take your children cruising is while they are aged between three and 13. Under-threes are hard work, and teenagers – well, afloat as ashore, they can be quite a handful.

Children of primary school age are able to look after themselves to a large extent, and generally thrive in the midst of a close-knit family. Although they enjoy the company of other children, they are not critically minded and will accept the friendship of any other small person, regardless of age, nationality or sex. It is true that they do not much like being torn away from these friends; Xoë cried every day for a month after we sailed from St Helena, and all on account of a certain small boy. However, when we reached our destination she quickly forgot him and made new friends.

On the other hand, you need not delude yourself that your under-tens will gain hugely from travel as such. 'Where have you come from?' I asked a bright nine-year-old live-aboard. 'Oh! I don't know,' he answered. And neither did he know nor care whither he was bound. Nevertheless, although they may have only scant recollection of the places they visit, their experiences do foster in young children an appreciation for different cultures and different environments.

As they grow older, well-travelled cruising kids become very knowledgeable about geography, the wonders of the marine world, and suchlike. In the course of the last two years my children have sailed among seals and with whales and dolphins of several different species. They have climbed some of the world's tallest dunes in the world's oldest desert, seen lions stalking zebra, sailed in fogs and in sunshine, over oceans and around islands, and made friends with people of half a dozen nationalities. In the course of their travels, in these past two years, they have picked their way among penguins on a rocky islet, and scrambled down scree-covered slopes to look at ancient forts. They have navigated, cooked, learnt a little bit of Spanish and a lot of Spanish history, written and published their own newsletter, helped to record a series of radio shows … and much, much more. Compared with all this, what does school have to offer them?

A teenager will gain even more from the cruising experience. Not only will his travels broaden his mind, but the lifestyle also presents plenty of opportunities for personal growth and can therefore provide a great deal of satisfaction. However, on the debit side it has to be admitted that, even if one adopts a flexible approach, the education of a teenager is a fairly daunting commitment. Teenagers also take up more room – they each need their own cabin – and whereas the under-tens are happy to be around adults, children of 12 or 14 years and over have a powerful need to be with their peers. Raised in isolation they tend to go through a period of insecurity and it seems that 13 to 15 is the very worst age for a child to be hauled off to sea.

Friends who gave up cruising because their three teenage kids wanted to stop told us that their decision was based on a recent experience: they had been called to assist a couple whose son, when told that the cruising life was the only one for him, took an overdose. At the other extreme, I also know of families whose travels did not begin until the kids were aged 16 or 17 and who have nevertheless fared very happily. Presumably these children had already found their feet and their identity.

I have also come across second-generation cruisers; men in their early 20s who lived aboard and sailed throughout their teenage years but who eventually flew the family nest and bought their own boat. I have even heard tell of a second-generation cruising couple, a man and woman both of whom were raised afloat. Could it be that we are breeding a new race of Sea People?

What more can I say? A very great deal, but space does not permit. Should you go? Yes, go if you want to. If you feel the urge, why not go? 'Like the wild geese that migrate south, we answered a call,' says Carl Mailhot. 'We didn't know what lay ahead of us... We had to go, that's all. Henceforth we would be a family roaming at sea.'

Index